PRE-SEMINARY EDUCATION

Report of the Lilly Endowment Study

PRE-SEMINARY EDUCATION

by
KEITH R. BRIDSTON
and
DWIGHT W. CULVER

Augsburg Publishing House · Minneapolis

PRE-SEMINARY EDUCATION:
Report of the Lilly Endowment Study

Copyright © 1965 Augsburg Publishing House

Library of Congress Catalog Card No. 65-12141

*Acknowledgments of permission to quote from copyrighted works
are indicated in the footnotes.*

MANUFACTURED IN THE UNITED STATES OF AMERICA

CONTENTS

LILLY ENDOWMENT STUDY OF PRE-SEMINARY EDUCATION

BOARD OF ADVISORS

Introduction

"A threefold cord is not quickly broken."

Ecclesiastes 4:12

The Preacher says that "for everything there is a season, and a time for every matter under heaven. . . . I have seen the business that God has given to the sons of men to be busy with. He has made everything beautiful in its time, also he has put eternity into man's mind." It is dangerous to think about eternity without thinking about time. Man's busy-ness does indeed have to do with eternity. But it is "beautiful" only when it is appropriate to the times and the seasons. For every matter that man is busy with there is a fitting time.

This is an important educational principle, not least in ministerial training. "Pre-seminary education," the rubric of this Lilly Endowment Study, suggests the significance of the chronological factor in theological education. For one thing, time passes and therefore it cannot be ignored—or is ignored at one's own peril. The term also suggests that there is a given educational structure whose sequence is bound up with this chronological progression. This Study has taken the factor of time seriously, while not, it is hoped, forgetting eternity.

In that sense the Report is conservative. A basic presupposition behind it is that the sequence of pre-seminary, seminary, and post-seminary periods in the training of ministers—the standard

vii

chronological pattern in North America—is not to be accepted simply because that is what exists but because if properly employed it may offer the strands out of which the "threefold cord" is twined. The basic criticisms of the Report are directed, therefore, not against the institutional structure of American higher education but against the ineffective use of the educational progression which it potentially embodies. Unless that structure and progression are accepted and effectively used in the education of ministers the cord all too easily becomes raveled and knotted. When it is put to the test in a time of stress its tensile strength is diminished.

The basic question which the Report sets is: What are the essential educational requirements for effective ministry and how can the total educational resources available be used together to meet those needs? In the following pages no panaceas are offered. The functional rationalization of the whole process of ministerial training involves so many variables and is beset with so many complexities that simple solutions are out of question. A main contribution of this Report may be to point out these complexities and thus to inaugurate a widespread discussion of the basic issues of theological education today. As James Conant has said of his study on teacher education: "The most important objective in my book would be to have a vigorous national debate among educators and laymen on the question of how to educate the teachers of American youth."

Specific suggestions and recommendations are made in light of the findings of the Study. However, the nearest the Report comes to proposing a comprehensive "solution" for the outstanding problems now confronting American theological educators is found in the over-all outline of the Report—a pattern also evident in divisions of the Table of Contents in the symposium volume, *The Making of Ministers,* which preceded it. That is, applying a functional criterion to the question of what educational "equipment" the minister needs in his practice, three elements are proposed: secular cultivation, professional competence, and vocational integration. This is the "threefold cord" which if well plied "is not quickly broken."

It is in this context that "pre-seminary education" is considered. One plait in the strand cannot be disengaged from the others with which it is interwoven without seriously weakening it. The making of a cord is something different from putting interchangeable blocks on top of one another. The "pre-seminary" period of a minister's education might be thought of as just the four-year undergraduate segment of a uniform educational continuum, in which the curricular elements—the "blocks"—could be shifted from one to the other of the segments freely without essentially altering the basic structure. If ministerial education is thought of as an organic process, however, and not simply as institutional progression from "pre-seminary" to seminary levels, then what is appropriate for one "time" is not necessarily most fitting for another. "For everything there is a season," as the Preacher says.

Timing, therefore, is crucial in ministerial education: this may be close to the "thesis" of the Report. In describing Bell Telephone's experiment in providing liberal education for its executives, E. Digby Baltzell writes: "In Utopia, perhaps, men will be 'trained' in their teens and 'educated' in their thirties. While twenty may be the best age for learning mathematics, chemistry or engineering, maybe *Hamlet* and *Faust* are better understood in maturity. . . . A real education is an emotional as well as an intellectual experience."* To apply this to theological education, the question of the right relation between "pre-seminary" and seminary education is not one which can be resolved only in terms of the organizational relations or the curricular connections between undergraduate schools and graduate theological institutions. The gradual, and often mysterious, development of man into maturity is also a decisive factor in determining what is to be taught to the ministerial candidate—and where and when. The "seasoning" of the student as he grows to full manhood should be in part the result of the educational process; but, in turn, the logic of that process must be determined by this timing of personal development and not only by institutional rationality.

This more organic approach to ministerial education, as well as

*Toward the Liberally Educated Executive, ed. R. A. Goldwin and C. A. Nelson (New York: Mentor, 1960), p. 19.

the application of the functional criterion to its goals, also illustrates the conservative spirit of the Report. There has been much
discussion, often heated, in recent years on the ministry of the
laity in the church. John Robinson, Bishop of Woolwich, writes:
"I would put the question in all seriousness whether, with the
final disintegration of medieval Christendom, the distinction between *clergy and laity,* in contrast with the proper distinction between the various orders of the Body, should have any further
validity . . . the distinction between clergy and laity should
legally be abolished."* The World Council of Churches in its
Assembly at Evanston in 1954 affirmed: "Clergy and laity belong
together in the Church; if the Church is to perform her mission
in the world they need each other. . . . The word 'laity' must not
be understood in merely a negative way as meaning those Church
members who are not clergy. . . . The phrase 'the ministry of the
laity' expresses the privilege of the whole Church to share in
Christ's ministry to the world."

If these ecclesiological principles are put into effect, it is obvious that the traditional functions of the ordained "set-apart"
clergy will be modified. As one has put it, this means that the
minister in a congregation will be seen more as a "coach" training the team rather than being a "one-man gang" himself. But
whatever changes come, the functional criterion is still appropriate in ministerial education. The minister is to be trained to
fulfill the functions that he must assume in practice. If, therefore,
the Report concentrates on the principles behind curricular for-
mation or reformation rather than upon curricular content itself,
this should not be considered an evasive action but an honest
recognition that the most urgent dilemma facing theological educators today is the need for finding a criterion through which, in
the face of proliferating course offerings, decisions can be reached
on what should be, what might be, and what need not be taught
to ministerial students to prepare them for effective service.

Finally, it should be noted that the Report combines, in perhaps unique fashion for this genre, a theological and sociological

---

New Ways with the Ministry, ed. John Morris (London: Faith Press,
1960), p. 14.

approach to the issues of ministerial education. Dr. Bridston is largely responsible for the writing of the first section and Dr. Culver for the second. However, the Report—and the Study as a whole—is the joint product of both men's endeavors. It represents their common mind on the subject. Those who first projected the Study, and those on the Advisory Committee who supervised it, as well as the Lilly Endowment, Inc., whose generous grant made it possible, gave the directors complete freedom both in conducting the survey and in writing their conclusions. It is hoped that, whatever other limitations the Report may have or however much it may provoke dissent, it can at least be considered a modest contribution to the clarification of the questions at issue in this field and an encouragement for a deeper and more comprehensive discussion of them.

KEITH R. BRIDSTON
Director

DWIGHT W. CULVER
Associate Director

Part One

Report
of
Findings

CHAPTER ONE

CULTIVATION
AND INTEGRATION

"Every scribe who has been trained for the kingdom of heaven is like a householder who brings out of his treasure what is new and what is old."

Matthew 13:52

The period between Jesus' appearance in the Temple at Jerusalem, when he was twelve years old, and his entrance into a public ministry, when he was near thirty, has been called "the silent years" because nothing has been recorded about them. Yet, little as we know about that time, we recognize its importance, for those were the years of his ministerial training. We do know that "Jesus increased in wisdom and in stature, and in favor with God and man" in those eighteen years. They were, in short, "the preparatory years," "the maturing years," "the growing years."

Perhaps in that tantalizingly brief account we have a significant clue to the meaning of "pre-ministerial training" for today. The child grows in mind and body into the adult—the whole person. The growth takes place in relation to God and man—the whole of existence. The development is integrated so that this person both God and man find "in favor." There is not an imbalance between the growth into the "religious man" and into the "secular man": he is simply man. He is then prepared to minister. This favorable growth into mature wholeness, God-ward and man-ward, is the criterion for ministry, then and now.

It is, of course, the criterion for all Christian life; as the Apostle Paul wrote to the Ephesians: "We are to grow up *in every way* into him who is the head, into Christ." This gradual growth into mature wholeness, into full manhood, is complicated rather than fostered by training for "professional" religious service, however. The "scribe who has been trained" may by that very training grow into a "religious man," a "theological man," an "ecclesiastical man," and thus less than a whole man grown up "in every way."

This is the crux of the problem of training for the professional ministry. How is particular, specialized "religious" education for professional church service as a minister to be achieved without compromising the slow human growth into mature manhood? Presumably both are required for effective ministry—human maturity and professional technique—both are necessary for the "scribe," the minister, in his service. The professional technical training may stunt or distort the human development. A "deformation professionelle" may take place, endangering the process of mature human integration. Professional competence may be achieved at the expense of mature humanity: "The scribes and the Pharisees sit on Moses' seat; so practice and observe whatever they tell you, but not what they do; for they preach, but do not practice." This is the perennial warning against the dehumanizing potentialities of religious professionalism, personal disintegration, and human stultification.

Nevertheless, were this type of human degeneration inevitable in religious professions, there would be no point in criticism. Criticism implies responsibility and the possibility of change. It suggests things could be otherwise and is therefore in the last analysis hopeful. Yet this generation of ministers, and particularly of theological students, seems increasingly skeptical of the possibility of surviving the corrosive dehumanizing influence of professional religious training. The question is being raised: "What value is there in becoming a minister and losing one's own soul?" Paul, of course, faced the same problem in his suggestion that there was the possibility "after preaching to others I myself should be disqualified," but he considered this to be a matter of self-discipline and not intrinsic in his profession as such, for he affirms "the Lord commanded that those who proclaim the gospel should get their living by the gospel" even though he also says that he "made no use of any of these rights."

Perhaps the very fact that Paul renounced these security "rights" of the religious professional enabled him to accept them as a matter of principle. Today the form of the ministry and its relation to the religious institutions means that these rights are almost impossible to renounce in practice, whatever the theory. There does not seem to be the freedom in relation to them in which Paul rejoiced as one "free from all men," and therefore freely able to make himself "a slave to all." Paul can confidently ask the rhetorical question: "Am I not free?" The modern minister and theological student hardly dares pose that question to himself, much less to the institutionalized Christian community.

Many reasons for this current skepticism about the religious potentialities of religious professionalism can be cited. Kierkegaard, responsible for so many of the main currents in the religious stream of today, said that "to be a Professor of Theology is to crucify Christ." His artful but savage attacks against "Christendom"—the institutional forms, the doctrinal codifications, the official embodiments of "Christianity" (used in a derogatory sense)—have echoed and re-echoed down the ecclesiastical corridors since his time and have received an especially congenial hearing in theological student circles in the last twenty years. This radical iconoclasm against the traditional religious establishments—organizational, theological, ideological—has been accentuated and systematized by Barth, Tillich, the Niebuhrs, Bultmann, and the other dominant Christian thinkers of this period. The coincidence of theological iconoclasm and political cataclysm is epitomized in Bonhoeffer, who in his last letters from prison reveals an increasing remoteness from traditional "church" and an increasing identification with the "secular." Probably no writer is more sympathetically read among modern American seminary students.

From another side, the Ecumenical Movement has in both a positive and a negative way revealed the ambiguities of the major ecclesiastical consolidations inherited from the Reformation and helped to expose the decisive "nontheological factors" which have given institutional shape to modern Christianity. It is within these "denominational" enclaves, often with anachronistic dogmatic facades, that the ministry is institutionally isolated from the secular world. Ministry is seen as the functional service necessary to maintain outmoded ecclesiastical systems rather than the free service of Word and Sacraments to the world.

From yet another side, the sham, hypocrisy, and pretension of professional religiosity have been laid bare by modern novelists and playwrights in a way unprecedented since the time of the Roman satirists. And in a more scientific way the historians, sociologists, and other social scientists have been equally devastating in their critiques and analyses of ecclesiastical structures and church personalities. Horton Davies, in *A Mirror of the Ministry in Modern Novels,* illustrates the first.[1] Peter Berger's *The Noise of Solemn Assemblies* is a vivid example of the second.[2]

One might point out that these trends have not gone unmarked in previous decades of this century, or even of the last. At the same time, the conjunction of theological, cultural, political, and ideological factors leading to a searching scrutiny of the structure and forms of Christianity is unprecedented in modern times. Those in, those preparing for, or those contemplating full-time professional religious service can hardly be unaware, even if subconsciously, of the spiritual ambiguities and ambivalences in religious vocations as a result of the combined force of these various impacts on the secular and ecclesiastical *status quo.*

Earlier studies of theological education have noted these changes and have suggested what their ramifications might be for the Christian ministry and its training. William Adams Brown, in *The Education of American Ministers,* says: " . . . problems thus forced upon the minister, as he tries to meet the needs of persons who have been uprooted from their old associations and are trying to adjust themselves to new conditions, are intensified when he considers the wider forces that are operating in national and international life . . . all these place upon the modern minister a responsibility with which it requires exceptional wisdom and knowledge to deal."[3] The Niebuhr-Williams-Gustafson study, *The Advancement of Theological Education,* spells out the further complexities derived from the special ecclesiastical and educational revolutions on the American scene in the nineteenth and twentieth centuries in which, for example, the accidents of history have resulted in the fact that "the Protestant seminaries of today like the denominations have their roots in two related but differing conceptions of Protestant faith"—classical Reformation theology and frontier pietism and revivalism.[4] Tension results.

To say that this is a period of "revolution" is, to be sure, a commonplace. Nevertheless, the difficulty the churches evidence in coming to terms with its many manifestations indicates that it would be a mistake to underestimate its magnitude and significance. The "revolution" has been more felt than understood; more reacted against than responded to. Alec R. Vidler concludes his survey:

Christopher Dawson once observed that "men today are divided between those who have kept their spiritual roots and lost their contact with the existing order of society, and those who have preserved their social contacts and lost their spiritual roots." To survey the history of the Church since the French revolution is to be made aware of this schism in the soul of modern man and in the souls of many Christian men. It does not enable one to say with confidence whether or not the schism can be healed.[5]

Part of the frustration of present-day theological students arises from the recognition that the forms of the ministry for which they are preparing are in many cases irrelevant and obsolescent. Dean Walter G. Muelder of Boston University School of Theology in an address to the A.A.T.S. meeting at Toronto in June, 1962, asserted that rapid social changes brought about by an expanding industrial society have made perhaps 80 percent of present seminary curricula obsolescent. James H. Nichols has called the present pattern of seminary education "sensationally inadequate" in the face of the emergence of the "Great City." And

Franklin H. Littell has commented: "In the present seminary, the young minister is trained in the skills of being a community leader in a geographical community which existed fifty years ago."[6]

Previous generations and other professions have probably felt that their professional training was in certain aspects anachronistic. But the present generation of seminarians may be reflecting a deeper *malaise:* the feeling that not only is the training obsolescent but that the clerical profession itself is increasingly irrelevant. And beyond that the unsettling suspicion lurks that the main body of church life and thought are out of touch with the world. As Martin E. Marty observed of a recent ecumenical conference:

It is not the flight of theologians but the plight of theology in the world that is the problem. It is not only the "outside world" but the members of the churches who are seldom being confronted with the kind of word of God that issues from reflection about his purpose for man in the world. Not many are trained to be serious about theology, even in its simplest forms. . . . About the time Faith and Order was getting under way Walter Lippmann wrote that Christianity and the churches no longer incarnate human desires. And about the same time Alfred North Whitehead casually noted that Christian doctrines no longer inspire men. The world closes itself off without relating human desires to Christian doctrines.[7]

It is the unprecedented combination of these forces that makes the problem of reconciling spiritual integrity and religious vocation such an acute personal one for this generation. Can they be harmonized? Can they be related? Or are they basically antithetical? These are very much open questions among younger ministers and seminarians today. Walter D. Wagoner's *Bachelor of Divinity: Uncertain Servants in Seminary and Ministry* reflects the traumatic vocational quandary that many find themselves in as a result of this situation.[8] The Seminarian Questionnaire prepared for this Study attempted to take into account the depth of the vocational crisis felt by many men now preparing for the ministry. Even so, one student put it: "I hope this messes up your neat categories a little. I am a person, and all your neat categories fail to find that person. You will now say that I am hostile. No, I am lonely, tired, and angry." A Chicago seminarian, a Harvard graduate, wrote: "I hope you are aware that, for me and for a number of my peers in seminary, your categories are too restrictive to represent the very real confusion and uncertainty which is my lot at present. I hope you look beyond the poor examples, i.e. me, to the institution which has spawned these results: the church itself. I feel a very strong need to see in the church a hope and a promise and a real proclamation—things I do not see now. And, I am trying; what of those who don't even look?" A fifth-year seminary student writing of his vocational plans says: "I shall have no connection with the ministry or any organized leadership in the church" and describes himself as "one who defines himself *against* not only the church and the ministry *but* against Christianity." To underline the contradictions that this traumatic vocational crisis provokes, the same student after describing his theological position as "uncertain, but definitely non-Christian" goes on to say: "It should be clear that I am not interested in the institutional forms of the church but that I consider teaching in a seminary, department of religion, or Liberal Arts college a Christian vocation."

Such reactions may be dismissed as atypical and abnormal. Nevertheless, in view of similar comments by other seminary students on questionnaires, in letters, and in personal conversations there is reason to take them seriously as symptomatic of the disorienting effect of what Wagoner calls "sociological thunder and cultural lightning" on many students now preparing for the ministry. The theological shaking of the foundations adds to the general demoralizing and disintegrative effect, and reinforces this basic vocational uncertainty.

"The Search for Integration in a Schismatic Age" might be an appropriate title for a phenomenological study of the present seminary and pre-seminary student generation. Every era has its own peculiar problems of integration, and it is difficult to say in retrospect that one has been more or less difficult than another. Few, however, have faced as formidable a task of integration as is faced today. In part this is due, as has been suggested, to the multiplicity of integrative tasks now confronting the church and the individual Christians within it, and particularly that facing its professional leadership. For there are at least three major problems of integration that are only beginning to be dealt with, much less solved. They are: cultural integration, professional integration, and vocational integration. There are, admittedly, historical precedents in undertaking these integrative tasks; yet anyone who is presumably trained to meet them must bring "out of his treasure what is new and what is old" in order to attack them effectively, for both old and new insights are required to cope with this challenge.

Cultural integration can take place only when there is awareness of the culture, immersion in it, identification with it. In this sense, the first step in the educational integration of the future minister is secularization. The relation between the "religious" and the "secular" may be dialectic, but not contradictory, in theological training. The minister must be "in the world" in order to be a minister at all. For effective ministry the requirement is not "one foot in heaven," but both feet firmly on earth. The process of intelligent and coherent "secularization" is the fundamental educational basis for ministerial training. As Paul Tillich has written:

> The reason for the irrelevance of the Christian ministry in our time is that it has not learned to speak to the people of a largely secularized world in such a way that they feel: this message concerns us ultimately . . . . together with the less outstanding members of their group, they suffer from serious and almost insoluble conflicts which are produced by their encounter with a secularized world, outside and inside the churches. . . . The most conspicuous expression of our contemporary situation is not the quest for the conquest of finitude or guilt, but for the conquest of meaninglessness. This is an immediate consequence of secularism in the stage of emptiness. It is this situation which puts the ministry to its main test; here the decision is being made about its relevance or irrelevance for our time. But here history also has provided support by making the most sensitive minds of our time aware of the predicament of present society. Existentialist art, literature and philosophy are witness to it. A ministry which remains a stranger to such witness condemns itself to irrelevance; a ministry which uses these expressions of our predicament and shows their relation to the Bibli-

cal literature and the Christian message can become immensely relevant to our time.[9]

After World War II there was a searching discussion in the Studentengemeinden in the German universities about the "ghetto-existenz" of theological students, whereby both through the attitude of others and through their own they were cut off and isolated from the ordinary secular student life. Already as preministerial candidates they were anticipating the "ghetto" posture and mentality of their future profession and withdrawing from the everyday world of their fellows. They were the "religious" and therefore by popular consent (including their own) not "worldly" or "secular." In the student mind they had begun to fit the caricature of the minister as a "demi-angel in a black suit."[10]

This identification of the ministry with the "religious" is being profoundly shaken by the new positive attitude taken toward the "secular" in contemporary theology. Bonhoeffer's influence is decisive here and J. A. T. Robinson's popularization of Bonhoeffer's views in *Honest to God,* especially in his chapter on "Worldly Holiness," with its widespread impact on the Christian public, may mean that the old rigid separation between "religious" and "secular" has finally begun to be broken down in the popular religious imagination.[11] In his critical pamphlet commenting on Robinson's book, the Archbishop of Canterbury, Michael Ramsey, says:

Religion . . . can mean a set of pious attitudes and practices within which we look for God, forgetting that God may *sometimes* be found less amongst them than amongst the things we call non-religious or secular. Today, various trends show that attempts are being made to find God not in the realm of religion alone but in the secular; not on the fringe but right in the midst of the secular age. For instance, Edward Wickham, now Bishop of Middleton, in his book *Church and People in an Industrial City,* argued that the new scientific and technological organization of society was not to be seen as something apart from God but as something through which God himself is at work challenging us. But others have gone further than this. There are Christian thinkers who have gone right out into the secular world and have said in effect: "Do not look for God in religion *at all* as you have understood it in the past. Look for it in the midst of the human relationships of everyday life in our secular existence."[12]

An older view might be cited from an essay in a book on the ministry from England, *The Congregational Ministry in the Modern World:* "The New Testament is the minister's home. It is the place where he lives, the spring of his security and comfort, the creative source of his most intimate experience, the centre from which he goes out and to which he always returns."[13] The biblical-theological orientation of the minister's life, important as it may be, can become religiously one-sided unless even the Bible itself is seen as a secular book—a mirror of the world and a realistic portrayal of human existence in all its earthly dimensions. As Bonhoeffer puts it:

. . . the Bible does not recognise our distinction of outer and inner. And why should it? It is always concerned with *anthropos teleios,* the *whole* man. . . . The "heart" in the biblical sense is not the inward life, but the whole man in relation to God. The view that man lives just as much from outwards to inwards as from inwards to outwards is poles apart from the view that his essential nature is to be understood from his intimate background.[14]

Bonhoeffer's concern "to work out a non-religious interpretation of biblical terminology" is based on his conviction that theology was only beginning to participate in "*one* great development which leads to the idea of autonomy of the world," which has already been seen historically in morals, politics, or science through such diverse intellectual pioneers as Montaigne, Machiavelli, Grotius, Descartes, Spinoza, Kant, Fichte, Hegel, Nicolas of Cusa, and Giordano Bruno. History shows, says Bonhoeffer, that there is "no longer any need for God as a working hypothesis" and through this he sees that "God is teaching us that we must live as men who can get along very well without him." In the face of the recognition of "the autonomy of man and the world" some seek a way out by the way of "heteronomy in the form of clericalism." As he says:

At this point nervous souls start asking what room there is left for God now. And being ignorant of the answer they condemn the whole development which has brought them to this pass. As I said in an earlier letter, various emergency exits have been devised to deal with this situation. To them must be added the *salto mortale* back to the Middle Ages, the fundamental principle of which, however, is heteronomy in the form of clericalism. But that is a counsel of despair, which can be purchased only at the cost of intellectual sincerity. It reminds one of the song:

> It's a long way back to the land of childhood,
> But if only I knew the way!

There isn't any such way, at any rate not at the cost of deliberately abandoning our intellectual sincerity. The only way is that of Matthew 18:3, i.e., through repentance, through *ultimate* honesty. And the only way to be honest is to recognise that we have to live in the world *etsi deus non daretur.*[15]

These remarks are particularly pertinent to a study of theological training, for they suggest that certain forms of the ministry—"religious" clericalism, for example—are not simply anachronisms and in this sense irrelevant in the modern world but that these forms actually incorporate and embody a false conception of the nature of the world, of man, of Christianity, and of God himself. By refusing to recognize a world which has "come of age"—i.e. autonomous—a man debars himself from participation in the world and the only exit is into a special, closed "religious" world. Needless to say, the training of a ministry for one way will be radically different, or should be, than that for the other. If a Christian, and a minister, is, as Bonhoeffer believes, to "plunge himself into the life of a godless world" and is not to attempt to gloss over its true character with "a veneer of religion" or to try to transfigure it, he

must live a "worldly" life and so participate in the suffering of God. He *may* live a worldly life as one emancipated from all false religions and obligations. To be a Christian does not mean to be religious in a particular way, to cultivate some particular form of asceticism (as a sinner, a penitent or a saint), but to be a man. It is not some religious act which makes a Christian what he is, but participation in the suffering of God in the life of the world.[16]

When one considers education the question always raises itself as to what can actually be taught and learned through formal academic channels and instruments. To this question there are, of course, no clear-cut answers. Against the background of the traditional distinction of "religious" and "secular," theological education has been identified with the former. That is, "theological" is thought of as a discipline related to the religious sphere and theological training is considered to be primarily "religious" indoctrination. The distinction between pre-seminary and seminary education also tends to be interpreted in these same categories; thus pre-seminary education is thought of as nontheological and not an integral part of the whole process of ministerial education. It is simply something that comes before sequentially.

If, however, "secularization" is an essential part, an indispensable foundation element, of the education of a relevant ministry for the modern world, then theological (as distinct from "religious") education is as much related to pre-seminary education as seminary training. Leonard Hodgson begins his book *The Bible and the Training of the Clergy:* "Once upon a time there was no problem of the training of the clergy. Not because there were no clergy, but because there was no training."[17] Because we have submitted the education of ministers to the prevailing educational system, we must ask: Does that system lend itself to this kind of positive "secularization"? Can students be *educationally* secularized? Or must this ultimately be left to chance and natural development?

This might be the answer except that certain characteristics of American clerical education militate against natural secularity. The Seminarian Questionnaire of this Study reveals that large numbers of American seminary students come out of "religious" homes (in many cases, ministers' homes), have been raised in small "religious" communities in which the church is still a dominant institution in the social establishment, have attended church-related colleges, and have gone to their denominational seminaries. They are products and representatives of the world of the church; they are a part of a special "religious" culture, which in America has always been, despite the varying influence of the churches on society in different historical periods, a subculture. In short, the prevailing pattern of ministerial education actually militates against the "secularization" of which we have been speaking. However its effectiveness may be judged, part of its apparent "success" may be ascribed to the fact that it is a subculture education for a subculture community: it is "ghetto" training for the "ghetto." And one of the special problems of all ghettos is that the "secular" within it can never be easily identified, or the legitimate autonomy of the "secular" readily accepted, when all of the subculture is thought of as "religious" as distinct from the "world" outside. All this may be rationalized in terms of the ministry of the church being by definition the ministry *to* the world; but the fact is that they tend to be *two* different worlds.

Educational "secularization" therefore presents a peculiar problem in American theological training. Recognizing the sequential segments of ministerial education, the issue presents itself: Can pre-seminary education play a unique role in the total process of ministerial education by providing for and facilitating integral secularization of preministerial students (identifiable as such at that stage or not)? If so, what are the means, what are the marks, of the educational process of secularization at the pre-seminary level?

The most coherent recommendation for pre-seminary education so far offered is outlined in the "Statement on Pre-Seminary Studies" adopted by the American Association of Theological Schools at its Biennial Meeting at Berkeley, California, in June 1956. In essence it is simply affirming that the seminary student should be educated *before* he comes to seminary. It defines education in the first place in the familiar categories of intellectual and technical competence: "The college work of the pre-seminary student should result in the ability to use certain tools of the educated man: (a) The ability to write and speak English clearly and correctly. . . . (b) The ability to think clearly." Equal to the "intellectual," however, the "cultural . . . foundations essential to an effective theological education" are stressed: "The college work of a pre-seminary student should result in increased understanding of the world in which he lives:

(a) The world of men and ideas. . . . (b) The world of nature.
. . . (c) The world of human affairs." In general, "the emphasis
is on a 'liberal arts' program because, in the judgment of the Association, the essential foundations for a minister's later professional studies lie in a broad and comprehensive college education."

Some of the more specific criticisms which have been made of
the curricular suggestions and recommendations regarding college fields of concentration, particularly by various spokesmen
of the National Association of Biblical Instructors (now the American Academy of Religion) which aroused the debate out of which
this Study developed, will be discussed later. At this stage the
reasons why the present Statement does not seem to provide an
adequate *rationale* for pre-seminary studies may be mentioned.

In a certain sense, the A.A.T.S. Statement is simply an injunc-
tion to the colleges by the seminaries that they should do a good
job in educating their students. The Statement recalls the colleges to the educational goals which they themselves have set
up. Its general thesis and its tenor remind one of the description
of the marks of the educated man in the Harvard Report on
General Education in a Free Society:

> to think effectively,
> to communicate thought,
> to make relevant judgments,
> to discriminate among values.[18]

Its concept of a liberal education is similar to that given in a 1958
report of the Commission on Higher Education of the National
Council of Churches:

A liberal arts education is a search for the values and principles
which undergird civilized life. As such it seeks to orient students towards the great ends for which human life is organized. . . . It is
further to be seen as cultural rather than technological and vocational.
. . . From the above it must follow that a liberal arts education tries
deliberately to discover those values which inform civilized life, to dis-
criminate among values as to their relative significance, and to bring
about a steadfast commitment to them.[19]

Though the briefness of the A.A.T.S. Statement no doubt precludes it, the fact remains that it does not offer any clues as to why liberal studies are *theologically* important for a pre-seminary student. Nor does it suggest why they are *vocationally* essential for the future minister, not just for his seminary studies but for his profession. Furthermore, it does not set the pre-seminary studies in the context of a comprehensive philosophy of theological education in which pre-seminary, seminary, and post-seminary are all integral elements in the whole process of ministerial training.

If it could be said that to be educated is to become cultured, the theological significance of pre-seminary education may more easily be understood. And it may also be seen why, in terms of the tension between "religious" and "secular" already referred to, this creates special problems for the pre-seminary student. For if to be "cultured" means being "secularized," this runs against the grain of the prevalent theological tradition in the American churches and is contrary to the ethos of American Christianity. Only if "secularization" is theologically reappraised in a positive way can it be seen as an essential element in ministerial education, and this theological revolution has only begun to take place.

Set in these terms, the relation between "liberal education" and "seminary education" is far more dialectical than the A.A.T.S. Statement would suggest. The A.A.T.S. recommendations do not hint that seminary training itself might have to be radically re-examined if pre-seminary education produced the kind of educated, cultured (i.e. secularized) men that the seminaries are asking for. There is evidence that even on the purely academic level superior students from first-rank colleges often find the seminary course of study an intellectual disappointment. At one of the regional consultations sponsored by this Study, with representatives from both colleges and seminaries, a university dean said: "When we really do give a man a good college preparation, he often finds that the seminary does not live up to his expectations as a graduate level institution." A professor of history at an independent New England university queried on this point said that this disparity in academic standards might be true of more graduate schools than generally thought, citing as examples his own disappointment with graduate study in history and that of two recent graduates of his institution who had dropped out of a famous medical school because it was "kindergarten work."

The significant number of seminarians who have indicated in the Seminarian Questionnaire that they feel their college courses were on a superior academic level and intellectually more demanding in comparison with seminary work is a warning to the seminaries that they themselves may not be prepared to do academic justice to the kind of students who have met the standards which the A.A.T.S. Statement sets up.

Another reason why the seminaries must be equally self-critical as the colleges in examining themselves in the light of the Statement's recommendations is the possible discrepancy between the cultural ethos of seminaries and that of the colleges and universities. As has been pointed out, a great number of seminary students have remained within one relatively homogeneous cultural ethos from their childhood through college into seminary. And, as so prevalent in the American denominational system, when such students come out of their church-related colleges into their church seminaries (analogous to the "farm system" in baseball) the cultural clash is less likely to occur. The well-educated student may appear "cultured" but in effect cultured in the religious subculture and therefore not truly "secularized" in the sense used previously. "The world of men and ideas" to which he has been introduced is a relatively limited and circumscribed world, and may in many cases be almost exclusively a religious world. This is, of course, the grave danger of deliberately orienting the whole college life around some supposed "theological" or "biblical" idea to make an educational institution "religious": Such integrating ideological principles are often sectarian and to that extent less than fully Christian theologically and catholic culturally. In the eyes of the seminary its "best students" may seem to come out of this culturally contiguous educational milieu; but are they "best" because of their cultural affinity with the ethos of the seminary? Are they therefore easier to teach in the seminary and do they find the seminary more congenial intellectually than do their fellow-students from a more "secular" educational background? Are they best because they "fit" culturally? And do they "fit" because they are "religious" rather than "secular" types?

The point is that pre-seminary education must not simply be considered a means of making good seminary students but of making good ministers. The criterion of "good" cannot be only what appears good for the seminary, or even for the churches, but what is genuinely good for the world in which the man must minister. When, therefore, the seminaries set up a recommendation that "The college work of a pre-seminary student should result in increased understanding of the world in which he lives," they themselves must be prepared to be judged on that same basis by such students. A real understanding of the secular world may make the religious seminary a very difficult place to understand and an even more difficult world in which to live—unless, of course, the seminary itself also understands the world and is itself an authentic microcosm of it, even if devoted to particular professional theological pursuits. There is a difference between a theological school and a religious ghetto, and a student who has been cultured by his education, that is, secularized in the right sense, soon detects it even if the seminary does not.

There is little doubt that part of the uneasiness and discontent of many seminary students, and the source of at least some of their vocational tentativeness, arises from the tension between secularized student and religious school. There is statistical evidence which might suggest reasons for the widespread character of this phenomenon noted by many veteran theological educators in recent years. That is, whereas seminaries—almost by definition—are, if not church-supported or church-related, at least church-oriented, the students who attend them come out of all the variety of educational institutions in North America (not counting those abroad), ranging from Bible colleges to military academies. And very large numbers of them come out of independent or state-supported schools, which by legal restriction, intentional policy, or otherwise are definitely secular. Without making any value judgments, the student who is educated in such institutions is likely to be cultured in a different way from the student in an institution which deliberately attempts to be "religious" in its educational program.

The analysis of the baccalaureate origins of seminarians made in this Study indicating the wide variety of academic backgrounds of seminary students (not to speak of the multifarious fields of study pursued in them—"what does one do with a major in poultry marketing?" a seminary professor plaintively asked in one of the Study's regional consultations!) and the large number of graduates of "secular" institutions in comparison with products of the classic church college-church seminary progression on which most denominations lay such stress and place such value, would seem to argue that the seminaries should examine themselves to see if their academic program, their community life, their spiritual discipline, is adequate to deal with this—perhaps increasing—cultural diversity of their students. In particular, is their theological approach of a sort which can come to terms effectively with radical secularity—that is, the world outside— and provide a theological integration of sufficient weight and inner vitality to balance the secularized cultural integration achieved by the well-educated man?

The dialectical relation of the "religious" and the "secular" is only one reason why the relation between pre-seminary and seminary education cannot be viewed as a straight continuum. If the term "pre-seminary education" is implicitly, if unintentionally, condescending in regard to the importance and integrity of undergraduate college and university education in realizing cultural integration and intellectual competence, neither can seminary education from the other side be considered simply as an extension of university education in the religious field, nor an extension of liberal arts studies on a higher level in the area of theology. An examination of the course offerings in seminary catalogs is disconcerting in this respect, because they clearly reveal the lack of a coherent philosophy of ministerial education. And they do not, in most cases, seem to evidence any integral conception of theological education in the narrower professional sense. Some seminaries are, of course, more academically oriented than others, particularly those which are in essence graduate schools of religion attached to universities. Others are definitely committed by policy and program to prepare ministers —especially as "preachers"—for local congregational service. But nearly all seem to mix, in varying proportions or disproportions, elements of classic theological disciplines, liberal arts subjects, and practical courses in ecclesiastical techniques and methods.

H. Richard Niebuhr, in the first part of the report of the Study of Theological Education in the United States and Canada, recorded similar impressions of "Seminaries in Quandary":

> The theological schools of the churches in America share all the perplexities of the contemporary Protestant community and its ministry. Though they also participate in the movements toward clarification and reconstruction apparent in the latter the first impression they give is like the one produced by the pluralistic churches and a harried ministry: an impression of uncertainty of purpose. We have, indeed, found in the schools evidence of that pluralism and harassment; for they reflect in the multiplicity of their numbers, the variety of their statements of purpose and the conglomerate character of their courses of study the lack of unity symptomatic of their social context.
>
> Perhaps it is a mistake to say that the first impression given by the theological schools is one of multiplicity and indefiniteness of purpose. The first impression many observers receive is one of inertia and conservatism. . . . Yet the apparent conservatism is indicative of perplexity. For in the case of the schools as of the ministers, doing the traditional things does not mean doing them for a traditional reason; nor does it mean that these acts are internally integrated. . . . So considered the conservatism of the theological schools does betray a certain repetitiveness of individual actions and lack of great unifying conceptions . . . the loss of a controlling idea in theological education. . . . What has always been taught is now being taught so far as the elements are concerned; but one thing previously implicit in all that was taught is not now being transmitted: the unifying idea. Thus the apparent conservatism of the schools is really indicative of uncertainty of aim.[20]

Little needs to be added to this sharp critique of the "lack of unity," "lack of a sense of direction," "conventionality, which is sometimes downright antiquarian," not to speak of "self-satisfied provincialism, inert traditionalism and specious modernization" in American and Canadian seminaries. The main focus of this Study is, in any case, on pre-seminary education. If anything could be added it would be to note that the "Signs of New Vitality" also mentioned in the Niebuhr Study are perhaps more evident now than then. And if the generous participation of the A.A.T.S. seminaries in and their encouragement of this Study are any indication, the critical comments made above have been taken to heart and the seminaries are very much involved in stringent and honest self-criticism and fundamental reexamination of their purposes and aims at the present time.

It might also be considered presumptuous to propose definitive answers to the Niebuhr Study's observation that "no clear-cut idea of the theological school or of theology as a whole is as yet in prospect."[21] On the other hand, the view has been taken in this Study that ministerial education must be seen as a whole in which the pre-seminary, seminary, and post-seminary periods all have their distinctive but interrelated roles and functions in the educating and equipping of the "complete minister." As Alfred North Whitehead once wrote: "You may not divide the seamless coat of learning." The seminaries do not alone and by themselves educate men for the ministry. Congregations educate ministers after they leave seminary.

More than one minister will testify to the invaluable education—sometimes painful and not always welcome—which he received in the first years of his ministry and still receives from wise and candid laymen and women in his parish, and not infrequently outside his church. The minister also continues to be educated through his fellow ministers. And if "pre-seminary" were to be taken quite literally, who knows what he did not learn *before* he came to seminary?

Failure adequately to recognize this indivisible wholeness of ministerial education may be the reason for some of the quandaries of the seminaries about their aims and purposes. The scant attention paid to pre-seminary education in the Niebuhr Study may be indicative of this inclination toward academic introversion in the seminary world. As H. Richard Niebuhr, one of the first persons interviewed by the directors of this Study, pointed out in *The Purpose of the Church and Its Ministry* and reemphasized in personal conversation: "A theological education which does not lead young men and women to embark on a continuous, ever-incomplete but ever-sustained effort to study and to understand the meanings of their work and of the situations in which they labor is neither theological nor education."[22] If a minister continues his education after seminary, he has certainly already begun it before coming to seminary. The seminary is educationally "open-ended" on both sides, in relation to both the before and the after.

This is one reason why the term "pre-seminary" may be as misleading as "pre-theological" in referring to the undergraduate college years of a ministerial student. The view is widely held that the seminary *is* the church, educationally speaking; this reflects a seminary-centric idea of ministerial training. "Pre-seminary," when thus applied to undergraduate university studies, is valid if used pragmatically and not ideologically. For though the college "preparation" does lay certain scholastic foundations for later seminary studies, which as the A.A.T.S. Statement indicates the seminaries feel they have a right to expect, that educational period has an integrity of its own in providing the opportunity for the cultural integration already mentioned. Such integration is an essential element in ministerial preparation, but it cannot be totally explicated or comprehended if it is understood exclusively as "*pre*-seminary."

In other words, the relation between seminary and "pre-seminary" education is not one in which the chronological continuity strictly mirrors the educational process. The relation may be, to use Mortimer Adler's terms to describe the connection between the order of teaching and the order of discovery, one which is not "deductive and scientific" but "inductive and dialectical." Or to put it another way, both cultural integration and theological integration are needed in the making of the "complete minister" and, though they are interrelated and interdependent, they are distinguishable and separable. Indeed, unless the dialectic relation between the two is maintained, the final stage of integration—vocational synthesis—is not likely to be satisfactorily achieved.

In this context the role of the seminary in theological education may be more precisely defined. If theological understanding has a place in both the pre-seminary cultural integration and in the post-seminary vocational integration, the seminary has a peculiar responsibility for professional-theological integration itself— theology being used here in a narrower and more specialized sense as a scientific discipline. There is always some uneasiness about defining theology in this more circumscribed way as a "pure science," just as there is about calling a theological seminary "the intellectual center of the Church's life" (Niebuhr). Yet, however distinctive theology may be as an intellectual enterprise and however inadequate analogies of other scientific disciplines to it may be because of "the extraordinary status of the 'matter' with which it is concerned" (Walter Künneth), it is and has been a true science. If it is "incomparable" it is primarily because of its subject of recognition and not because of its intellectual method and its rational approach, which it shares with other sciences.

Theology may be treated in this scientific way, unashamedly and without apology, if the diversity of the life of the church in all of the forms of service are seen as a part of its wholeness and unity. Recognition of the diversity of gifts and operations is a liberating limitation for all of them. In the same way, the theological seminary as the organ in the ecclesiastical body primarily responsible for the intellectual pursuit of theology as a science is likewise liberated by the recognition of its specialized limitations in relation to other diversified organs in the corporate whole. The seminary is, of course, constituted of the same "tissue" as other organs, the same spiritual flesh and blood make it up and nourish it. But it has a specific function which, unless it is fulfilled, will result in suffering both for itself and other organs, and a malfunctioning of the whole.

Acceptance of such functional and organic diversity and mutuality as applied both to theology and to the theological seminary as an institution has definite organizational implications.

From the curricular standpoint, for example, the increasing number of liberal arts courses in the seminary curricula must be critically reappraised. Introductory surveys in philosophy, history, sociology, literature, may make the seminary curriculum appear "modern" and "relevant." But is this the task of the seminary? It may be argued that such subjects are a remedial necessity, either because of the variety of fields of undergraduate study of seminarians or because of the inadequacy of the college courses actually taken. However, the fact is that the average seminary cannot do everything. If too much energy is expended in remedial work, little will be left for its own distinctive educational tasks. R. H. Tawney, in *The Acquisitive Society,* says that "A profession may be defined most simply as a trade which is organized, incompletely, no doubt, but genuinely, for the performance of function."[23] In comparison with other professions, the functional training of the minister cannot be as easily circumscribed nor as simply reduced to "practical" competencies to be acquired through the professional school set up for that purpose. As Willard L. Sperry, former dean of the Harvard Divinity School, once wrote: "He ventures by those intuitions which we call faith, into realms of which we have no certain knowledge, and yet which concern us quite as truly as the colonies of the human mind conquered and administered by scientific certainty."[24]

Even so, there are wide areas of ministerial responsibility which require exact professional skill. Both technical competency and intuitive faith are necessary parts of full ministerial equipment for service, and professional training for a *function* is the peculiar *raison d'être* of the seminary. Remedies are never fully curative—at least of serious ailments—and remedial cultural education in seminary cannot finally heal the ills of uncorrelated and unintegrated pre-seminary and seminary education. More radical treatment is required for this type of malfunctioning.

The need for this awareness of educational mutuality in the training of ministers between colleges and seminaries was evidenced by the decision to set up a study of pre-seminary education under the sponsorship of two bodies—the N.A.B.I. (A.A.R.) and the A.A.T.S.—representing through their constituencies both the colleges and the seminaries. And the series of regional consultations initiated by the Study substantiated the wisdom and strategic value of this bipartisan approach. In the consultations, when seminary and college representatives met one another face to face, some of the mutual suspicions between the groups which had been aired in a series of articles before the Study was begun, did indeed come out. As one college dean at the Atlanta Consultation said: "I have wondered among other things about the exact motives, open or concealed, of the seminary people and the people in the departments of religion who urge that we guide these students to major in religion." But in each meeting, as the discussion progressed and the barriers of vested interest lowered, a considerable degree of consensus was achieved.

For one thing, both seminary and college men were concerned at the low level of religious literacy among students today. They agreed that no person, including one who entered seminary, could be considered truly "educated" who was almost totally ignorant of the content of the Bible or of the historical religious heritages. One seminary dean at the Dallas Consultation said that the results of a Bible content examination given to graduating seminary seniors had been a "humiliating experience." In view of this situation, the college and seminary forces have a common cause.

For another thing, it became clear that men from college religion departments were not, as a whole, advocating a religion major for pre-seminarians as a way of anticipating their professional studies in seminary in a specialized, technical sense. As Professor Jack Boozer of Emory University at the Atlanta Consultation said in a paper: "The college department must resist pre-professionalism in this field as well as in all others in the interest of liberal arts," and he went on to argue: "The flight from the college toward graduate and professional school status has accelerated the erosion of the liberal arts and sciences ideal in the college. This trend is not equally present in all institutions, but all institutions operate in an atmosphere influenced by the trend. Thus, within the conditions that prevail today, the ideal of breadth and relatedness may well be more nearly achieved by a college major in religion than by a major in Philosophy, History, or English. For example, it would never happen that a major in religion would have all his courses in a given quarter in a given subject field. But apparently this is possible in other major fields." In view of this, Professor Boozer says, "The exclusion of religion from the list of fields recommended as desirable areas of major study in college is out of date."

It would appear that a religion major is generally less demanding in terms of course hours required than other fields and does, in this sense, offer the possibility of a broad liberal arts coverage in other fields for the student which may be excluded by majoring in one of the classical humanities subjects. However, as Dr. Charles M. Cooper, president of Pacific Lutheran Theological Seminary, said at the Claremont Consultation, real college education implies "mastery of a subject in depth" and such a major may not meet that criterion. If it does, then it may tend to be preprofessional. The alternative to this is to see a college major "in depth" as one which provides educational breadth for a student *providing* it is in another field than that of his professional studies. And in a number of cases, at Yale for example, religion "majors" have included a majority who are going on into other professional and graduate studies than theology, such as law and medicine.

As has been indicated, the consultations revealed that the college and seminary representatives had the same long-range interests at heart and the chief problem they met was in agreeing on the best means of realizing them. All of them were disturbed by the discrepancies between stated principles and operating realities at both the seminary and college levels. Seminary representatives admitted that they were inclined to be too rigid by not recognizing work done in college and setting up only one curriculum for all entering students. And college representatives confessed that, despite the lip-service paid to the liberal arts principle, many "religion" courses were actually concentrated on practical professional training. As one said at the Dallas Consultation: "I think no one has said it here, but I think everyone is aware of the fact that—whether we like it or not—many of our pretheological students are now engaged in the ministry. I would like to take them out of Podunk Hollow and back into college classrooms without that, but at the moment it doesn't seem to work." As a result, a religion department may be forced in the direction of not only being preprofessional, but actually a professional school substitute for the seminary. As another said: "I think we should note that the Bible Colleges forthrightly claim that this is an alternative to seminaries: in four years they say they can prepare a man for the ministry. I think we need to take a pretty hard look at whether this is what we are really trying to do: to run competition with a Bible College at a four-year level."

In brief, in an atmosphere which had been cleared of competitive jealousies, where failings were frankly admitted on all sides, and, above all, one in which the common concern to find the best possible way to utilize all the available resources in training good and effective ministers was obviously shared, the institutional and curricular problems were seen in a new perspective. As Dean Joseph Quillian at the Dallas Consultation said: "We may say that we are talking about two stages of one rocket. We all know the big secret of how much pay-load you can get into the air is how effective the first stage of a rocket is. It is really too simple to think of college and seminary as one seven-year continuum, all completely of one piece, with no movement, or change in focus, or differentiation in essential context. The colleges have got to get things off the ground and well on up into the stratosphere if the second stage of the rocket is going to get anywhere. Perhaps where we come nearest to being all of a part is in our awareness of the total oneness of objective. We are looking at what kind of student we set out walking from seminary graduation; whatever assuredness and effectiveness and firmness there is in his step as he graduates will have been tremendously influenced and determined by what happened to him in college."

Once the special functional contributions of the various educational segments of ministerial training to ministerial practice can be determined, *then* the relationship *between* the segments can

begin to be rationalized. If this approach is not followed, the
danger is that the chronological progression is taken too seriously
and its natural rigidity resists attempts to rationalize it functionally. Introducing the criteria based on the functional necessities
of education for ministerial service helps to prevent the relationship between pre-seminary and seminary education from being
treated in purely academic terms and categories, and exclusively
determined by the ethos of the *academe*.

What are the major functional requirements of the ministry
which educational training can meet, or help to meet?

In the first place, *religious faith*. From every quarter—seminarians, college and seminary teachers, laymen, ministers—the
fundamental importance of a deep and living faith, a profound
religious conviction, a transparent sensitivity to "things not seen,"
an evident awareness of the presence of God, is considered to be
a *sine qua non* of the effective minister. If one divests the term of
its usual sentimental and moralistic connotations, the general
consensus is that a minister, whatever his other limitations,
should be a man of piety. It is difficult, of course, to pin down
"spiritual" attributes and it is even more difficult to determine
what, if any, educational means foster them. Again divesting the
term of its romantic overtones, the minister must be a "man of
God," conscious of being called by him and under his authority
—this is generally agreed, but has education anything to do
with it?

"Without controversy, great is the mystery of godliness." So
wrote an old apostle to a young pastor. Mysterious as it is, however, it has always been considered within the Judaic-Christian
tradition as something which is amenable to being strengthened
and nurtured by education: "Bring up a child in the way . . . and
he will not depart from it." Even the Pioneer of the Faith is
considered to have "grown in wisdom" and "learned" obedience
under human and divine parental discipline and chastening. Thus,
though such exceptions as the late convert must be kept in mind,
the classical view is that the primary educational instrument for
this ministerial "function" is the parental home. Or, to translate
it into the contemporary educational categories appropriate for

the Study, this particular aspect of "pre-seminary" education has been largely completed by the time of entrance into college or university.

In the second place, *secular cultivation*. Both classical religious experience and contemporary psychology testify to the importance of this first educational stage in providing a mind set or spiritual orientation which remains relatively unchanged for the rest of life. What follows educationally builds upon it and develops it, but the basic religious "structure" or "gestalt" is given. In American society the break with the home "nest" and the beginning of independent, adult life in the world is most clearly marked by the entrance into college. But because it is a transitional break and entrance, it is educational. Again looking at its peculiar functional significance in the educational process, the undergraduate college has a unique role in *secularizing* its students. It is not primarily concerned with perpetuating the religious nurture of the home, nor in preserving the intimate "family" ethos in other respects. Its task is to introduce its students to the world. Furthermore, this does not—as in high school, for example—mean a largely theoretical introduction, but because of the age of the students at the beginnings of maturity, it is, as Alfred North Whitehead put it, not only a "preparation for life, it is life itself."

For the future minister this secularization is peculiarly essential. As Daniel Jenkins has written: "He is the one man among all men who cannot be permitted the luxury of a sheltered life. . . . Like Lear, he must experience humiliation and agony and the storm before he is ready to be one of God's spies and seek out the mysteries of things."[25]

In the third place, *professional competence*. There are certain functions which the minister must perform in his service which require special, technical skills. The exact type of his service, the special characteristics of the place where he is, the nature of the particular institution in which he works, and his own natural gifts are factors which help to determine precisely which skills he will need and what demands will be placed upon his technical competence. In the parish ministry, for example, his teaching responsibilities will require special mastery of biblical literature, preferably including competence in the original scriptural languages, as well as knowledge of teaching methods; his role as congregational leader will require administrative and financial know-how; his preaching responsibilities will demand literary and speaking skills; as the director of worship he will have to have liturgical training; as a pastoral advisor he will need some basic psychological and counseling equipment.

His fundamental religious temper, his awareness of the world, and his theological outlook will penetrate his whole ministry and give it its quality. But without the technical skills which his institutional functions demand these other less tangible attributes become dissipated and wasted. "Professional" inevitably implies and involves *techne*. Technical skills are the gear-wheels necessary for the primal spiritual powers to be applied effectively in actual ministry.

In the fourth place, *vocational integration.* The term "success," as usually understood, has little relevance for the ministry. Even the usual criteria for judging professional competency in other fields have to be carefully scrutinized before applying them to ministerial service; ultimately they are to be held accountable as "ministers of Christ, and stewards of the mysteries of God. Moreover, it is required in stewards, that a man be found faithful. But with me it is a very small thing that I should be judged of you, or of man's judgment: yea I judge not mine own self."

The fact that a minister has to render only one vocational account and that this will not be settled until the Lord himself judges it at the last day, gives the minister unbounded professional freedom. Even his own anxieties about his service are to be set aside, not to speak of others' judgmental opinions about it. The one continuing requirement is that he be found "faithful." Or, as the original Greek suggests, he should be integrated. In other words, he is to serve as a whole being—his created powers, his natural talents, his acquired skills are all to be employed in coherent effectiveness. Having been freed from "childish things," the mature man applies all that he is, all that he has learned, to his work. He has realized his personal identity. He is functionally integrated. He is a professional. So he works.

The "making of ministers," as the symposium volume arising out of this Study spells out, is a mysterious process. As in all creative activities, the interplay and mutual stimulation between the constitutive elements are not entirely understandable, nor can the educational process itself entirely explain them. But it seems evident that the cultivation and integration which are essential to creativity are fostered and sustained and promoted by the mutual cohesiveness of all the parts involved, and the common recognition of the need of the one for the other.

In view of the functional requirements for the ministry just described and considering the pedagogical sequence provided by the American institutional pattern of education, the problem presents itself: Does this "given" pattern lend itself to meeting the functional requirements? Do the natural educational segments coincide sufficiently with the functional needs so that they can lead to the final vocational integration demanded for effective work in the ministry? Does the acquirement of the functional necessities follow the same logical progression that the present educational structure dictates?

It is in answer to this problem and these questions that the following chapters are offered.

FOOTNOTES

1. New York: Oxford, 1959.

2. New York: Doubleday, 1961.

3. Vol. I, "Ministerial Education in America: Summary and Interpretation" (New York: Institute of Social and Religious Research, 1934), p. 8.

4. H. Richard Niebuhr *et al.*, eds., *The Advancement of Theological Education* (New York: Harper and Brothers, 1957), p. 4.

5. Alec R. Vidler, *The Church in an Age of Revolution: 1798 to the Present Day* (London: Penguin, 1961), p. 273.

6. *The Interseminarian*, 2: 1, May 1963.

7. "Reflections on Montreal," *Christian Century*, 80, August 14, 1963, p. 999. (By permission of the *Christian Century*.)

8. New York: Association Press, 1963.

9. In *Making the Ministry Relevant*, edited by Hans Hoffman (New York: Scribner, 1960), pp. 23, 33.

10. Keith R. Bridston, *Theological Training in the Modern World* (Geneva, 1954), p. 28.

11. Philadelphia: Westminster Press, 1963.

12. *Image Old and New* (London: S.P.C.K., 1963), pp. 3 f. (American Edition: Forward Movement Publications, Cincinnati, Ohio.)

13. H. Cunliffe Jones, editor (London: Independent Press, Ltd., 1955), p. 52.

14. *Letters and Papers from Prison* (London: Fontana, 1959), p. 118.

15. *Ibid.*, p. 121.

16. *Ibid.*, pp. 122 f.

17. *The Bible and the Training of the Clergy* (London: Darton, Longman and Todd, 1963), p. 1.

18. Paul H. Buck and others (Cambridge, Mass.: Harvard University Press, 1945), p. 65.

19. *What Is a Christian College?* (New York: 1958), p. 17.

20. *The Purpose of the Church and Its Ministry* (New York: Harper and Brothers, 1956), pp. 95 ff.

21. *Ibid.*, p. 102.

22. *Ibid.*, p. 134.

23. R. H. Tawney, *The Acquisitive Society* (New York: Harcourt, Brace and World, Inc., 1920), p. 92.

24. "The Call to the Ministry," *Harvard Theological Review*, July 1922 reprint, pp. 3 f.

25. *The Protestant Ministry* (Garden City, N.Y.: Doubleday, 1958), pp. 126 ff.

CHAPTER TWO

PORTRAIT OF
THE PRE-SEMINARIAN

A study of pre-seminary education has to take into consideration the contemporary theological situation as well as the given educational structure in which ministerial training takes place. The background which has been presented, as well as some of the live issues under debate regarding recommended pre-seminary studies, provides the contextual setting in which this Study began.

In order, however, that the approach should also be empirical the Study was focused on, among other things, the student himself. In the maze of recommendations, suggestions, proposed and actual curricula, what *in fact* was the pre-seminary education which students had before they came to seminary? What courses were they taking? What were their major fields of study? Where had they gone to college? Did their college background, or their area of academic specialization as undergraduates, really make any difference to them or to the seminaries in which they enrolled? Finally, what type of person was the pre-seminarian? What did he look like?

To obtain this information was not as easy as it might first appear. One student queried said that such questions were "none of your business." A seminary faculty—but only one—refused to have their students approached for the purpose of getting information on the factor of upward social mobility in the decision to enter the ministry because "there are some questions students should not be asked." Research in religious matters is often difficult because people feel that this is too "personal" and "private" an area for such scientific analysis.

The problems of making an empirical approach in this Study were complicated by other less emotional factors. For example, it became evident that it is impossible to identify pre-seminarians with certainty while they are still pre-seminarians. Many pre-seminary students identify themselves as such while they are undergraduates, or even before. Through registration or other official college records, through membership in pre-seminary campus clubs, through affiliation with denominational vocational supervisory committees, undergraduates may indicate that they *intend* to go on to seminary for professional theological training. This is only their intention, however, and there is no guarantee that they will in fact eventually enroll in a graduate theological institution. The undergraduate years are a period of career decision, and this often means a change in future professional plans. An adequate study of preministerial "dropouts" has not been made, but if it were it would obviously throw a good deal of light on the factors leading to this revision of career plans. There is no reason to suppose, from what is now known, that the attrition rate among pre-seminarians is different from that of other pre-professional students. Nor should the mere fact of vocational revision while in college be a particular cause of concern. Indeed, this type of vocational "shakedown" probably should be especially welcomed in relation to a profession in which the motivational factors are possibly more mixed and psychologically "supercharged" than in any other. One of the greatest disservices to the students involved, as well as to the profession in which they are to serve, may be to seek artificially to inhibit or control this natural vocational selection during the undergraduate period of education simply in the interest of quantitative recruitment of seminary and ministerial candidates. To place an onus on those pre-seminarians who decide to go into another vocational field while they are undergraduates, or even to put psychological pressure on them to hold to their original vocational plans, is to fail to recognize how important it is that the ministerial calling and vocational choice should be based on the firmest foundations possible—personal maturity, intellectual conviction, and spiritual insight. Full exposure to a free academic market may be one of the best ways to test this.

A good "pre-seminary" education may mean for the identifiable "pre-seminarian" either a confirmation of his original vocational plans or a change of them. At the least, the pre-seminary undergraduate years ought to encourage a thorough re-examination and re-evaluation of such vocational intentions. One could think of few more crucial criteria for judging what good pre-seminary education should be.

For the same reasons, numbers of college students are not certainly identifiable as pre-seminarians while they are in college. They may have decided but do not wish to identify themselves or to be identified as "pre-seminary," or they may not actually have decided. A substantial number of students (30%) decide to enter seminary while they are in college. Obviously a considerable number of these are themselves "dropouts" from other pre-professional categories. The undergraduate years, in short, lose some pre-seminarians and gain others. Until a study is made of this phenomenon of vocational shifting in college, one can only surmise that it is to the advantage of everyone concerned that it actually does take place. As has been suggested, it would probably be a serious mistake to try to control it too carefully, especially if such controls were initiated by professional vested interests.

At any rate, for the purposes of this Study it was decided that the only person who was definitely a "pre-seminarian" was one who actually enrolled in and attended a seminary. By definition, a seminarian is one who as an undergraduate was a pre-seminarian. His undergraduate education was, by definition, pre-seminary education. Accordingly, a major research instrument of this Study has been a Seminarian Questionnaire. Through it both the general contours of pre-seminary education and the general profile of the pre-seminarian emerge. The picture that begins to take shape may be neither what many have supposed it to be nor what others may wish it to be. It simply is, phenomenologically, a description of what exists. That fundamental empirical evidence needs to be registered as a basis for further study and discussion, having the intention of improvement and reform. Without such a hard core of empirical data, such considerations all too easily become abstract and disembodied speculation and theorizing with little chance of actualization.

The following portrait is based as largely as possible on the *median* response to each item of the Seminarian Questionnaire —the one appearing at the middle of each graded series of answers. Thus, for questions dealing with age, the hypothetical seminarian described here has an equal number on each side of him in the age distribution of all seminarians. On other variables which are not ordered in this way, the measure of central tendency used is the *mode*—the response which appears with greatest frequency. For example, the portrait describes a seminarian who majored in religion in college—the largest response —although it was given by only 15.4% of the total.

What, then, have contemporary seminarians revealed about themselves as pre-seminarians and about their pre-seminary education through their answers to the Seminarian Questionnaire?

The Protestant seminarian is 25½ years old. He is male and white. He is married. The ministry is regarded by him as having a social standing higher than the occupation of his father, a skilled worker. His paternal grandfather was a farmer. He is an older child in a family of three children. The education of his parents is less than his own, and his mother had a higher educational attainment than his father. The family income was just over $6,000 annually. The community in which he grew up is described as "farm or open country."

As to his religious background, the approximate size of the church he attended during his last year in high school was between 300 and 400 members. He is a member of the Southern Baptist Convention and his parents attended a church of that denomination. He was encouraged to attend Sunday school and church services. In his family, grace was said before meals. There was at least one religious periodical regularly in the home. He can remember ministers and/or missionaries being entertained in his home. On the whole, however, he would not regard his parents "as deeply religious persons." He became a full member of his church before he was 15 years of age but he "never had a feeling of *not* belonging to the church."

Though there may be some uncertainty in his mind, the vocational area in which he expects to serve immediately after leaving seminary is the parish ministry. Eventually, however, he expects to leave it; if he does, he thinks of going into college or seminary teaching.

His pastor encouraged him most in his decision to enter the ministry, and his mother was next most encouraging, followed by his father. However, the person most likely to discourage him was his father. The commitment to enter a church-related vocation was made at no definite time or place that he can remember, but over a long period of time. Still, he remembers making the decision about the vocational area in which he might serve sometime during his college years. In considering factors which most strongly influenced his choice of a church vocation, the most significant external factor was the "influence of other people." The chief internal factor was an interest in "study and the intellectual opportunities of the ministry." His decision to enter the ministry was based on "an intellectual conviction which developed gradually," rather than through "a vivid religious experience at a certain time and place."

He has this to say about the ministerial calling: "In deciding whether to accept a candidate for the ministry, a seminary should be more concerned about whether he has a genuine call of God than about his abilities and qualifications. When I decided to enter seminary, I felt that the professional ordained ministry is in no sense superior to other forms of work rather than in some way a superior form of Christian service. It seems to me that a person who is ordained without a distinct certainty of being called by God to the ministry may commit a serious error—even a sin in some cases—but is more likely simply being honest with himself and can still be a good minister. I think that a person should enter the ministry if he is a sincere Christian, and thinks the ministry is where he can contribute and not only if he is certain it is God's will. It is my belief that God's call to the ministry quite often extends to persons of extremely modest ability through whom he can show his power and definitely should not be understood to more or less imply that a person have the necessary intellectual qualifications."

In considering the activities of ministers, he has this to say about the adequacy of the minister in his home church, before he went to college: "My minister was quite adequate in officiating at worship, in private devotions, prayer and Bible study, in preaching the Word, and in studying and preparing sermons—in that order. He was fairly inadequate in community leadership, in pastoral counseling, in visiting church members, and in teaching—in that order. In the work of *any* minister I would consider studying and preparing sermons, preaching the Word, pastoral counseling and private devotions, prayer, and Bible study to be relatively most important—in that order—and denominational and committee work relatively the least important, followed by community leadership, administration, and direction of program —in that order. In my own ministry I would expect preaching the Word, teaching, private devotions, prayer, and Bible study to be equally enjoyable, and denominational and committee work to be the least enjoyable, followed by administration and direction of program and community leadership—in that order."

In other words, both through his observation of ministerial practice and in terms of his general standards for superior ministerial performance he is inclined to rate the private and the "impersonal" official liturgical functions of the ministry higher than those involving direct person-to-person relations or those having to do with administrative and organizational aspects of parish life. Or, to put it in another way, he apparently expects to perpetuate this pattern in his own ministry by indicating that he anticipates that he will most enjoy those aspects of the ministry which will least involve him directly with other people or those in which his official status as religious and liturgical leader most separates him from other church members and in which his authority is most bolstered by traditional religious and theological sanctions and least challenged through direct interpersonal relations or through new, more "democratic," organizational and administrative forms. In belief, he sees a traditional ministerial prototype, he largely approves of it, and he expects to conform to it in his own ministry. But, paradoxically, he expects to leave it, hopefully—as was indicated earlier—to be a college or seminary teacher.

This potential dropout from the parish ministry is, as a theological student, well on his way to full ministerial status, with the rights and privileges thereof. He has served in a local church in a ministerial capacity. In evaluating his experience he affirms that his pastoral work has been valuable and he does not regret having begun it when he did. He does not think he started it too early and he says it has not raised serious doubts in his mind about continuing in the ministry. He definitely thinks that his pastoral work has helped to make his studies meaningful and he would recommend that pastoral work begin before seminary graduation. Yet, this pastoral experience has not actually reduced the likelihood that he will sometime leave the parish ministry. Indeed, this possibility has been increased by his years of premature professional practice as a pastor.

As to his educational background, he is a graduate of a denominational, regionally accredited college. Considering five basic fields of study in college—social sciences, physical sciences, English, religion and Bible, philosophy—he found the physical science courses most dull, followed by philosophy; and the social science courses most interesting, followed by religion and Bible. He thinks the academic standards were highest in English and lowest in the social sciences. Teachers in religion and Bible most urged him to continue in the field and those in the physical sciences the least. He tended to admire the teachers in religion and Bible, as persons and not just as professors, but did not have the same feeling toward those in the physical sciences. By and large, he finds more teachers in the physical sciences to be "*not* the kind of person I'd like to be" than he does in any other field, and the fewest of such persons are in religion and Bible.

Not unexpectedly, he was a major in religion with a minor in English or history. Among his undergraduate courses he found those in language and mathematics most difficult, and they were the ones he liked least, followed by those in the biological sciences, economics, and education. The courses which were most helpful in preparing him for seminary were, in his opinion, those in religion and Bible, philosophy, and English. The most significant course he took (not necessarily as preparation for seminary) was in philosophy, followed by those in religion and Bible, English, history, psychology, and sociology.

Among his fellow seminarians who did *not* major in religion or Bible in college, he finds that they do not feel, as a group, there were significant pressures to abandon a church vocation in the department in which they majored. Insofar as there were influences which could channel ministerial students away from the ministry in other departments than religion and Bible, they list the following, as most important: opportunities in other vocations, and intellectual excitement in other fields.

As a religion major he took more courses in religion in college than in any other field. Among his fellow seminarians who took *any* courses in religion in college, the average number of courses taken was between five and six. If he had to do it over again, he would take the same number of courses in Bible and religion, or possibly more. In his judgment, his college teachers of Bible and religion were "equal in training and ability to teachers in other departments" and in general were more likely to be superior than inferior to teachers in other departments; he shares these views with those seminarians who did not major in religion. Along with a majority of religion majors in seminary, he believes that he received "as broad a background as other majors" through his chosen area of concentration.

In his college religious activities, he was a member of a denominational student group; among his fellow seminarians the other two most popular forms of religious activity were participation in a religious "cell-group" or small discussion group and a preministerial club. He finds that their religious activities were more likely to have been in connection with a denominationallyrelated organization than with interdenominational groups such as a campus "Y," an SCM, or IVCF.

In his secular activities, he was a member of a special interest group in music. The next most common type of secular activity among his fellow seminarians was through a fraternity (or its equivalent). But about one-fifth of his fellow students apparently took no part in any organized secular activities, just as one-sixth of them also seemed to have participated in no organized religious activities while in college. In evaluating his extracurricular activities in terms of their value for him as preparation for seminary he believes religious activities were more important to him than secular activities (one-third of his fellow seminarians would disagree) and he definitely feels (along with most of his colleagues) that his academic work was more valuable to him than these extracurricular activities.

His college academic record was not outstanding. He received no special honors. Among his fellow students he finds that only 3% are members of Phi Beta Kappa and only 13% graduated from college with honors (cum, magna, or summa). His over-all grade average was B-minus. He estimates that his class standing in his college senior year was "average" or slightly above and that it may have been slightly lower the first year in seminary, but tended to improve.

When he entered seminary he was fully accepted for a degree program. He is completing his second year in seminary and is working toward a B.D. degree, which is the highest degree he expects to attain.

His training in languages includes a modern language—German—and a classical language—Greek. The fact that, though seminarians consider languages the most "difficult" (along with mathematics) field of study in college, almost two-thirds of them have at least one year of Greek may suggest the effectiveness of seminary *requirements* over against recommendations in determining the pre-seminary curriculum for a seminarian: Greek is the one subject most widely required either on entrance or before graduation in North American seminaries.

In reviewing his undergraduate and seminary studies he feels that there has been, in some sense, a duplication of courses. This has been, on the whole, a "helpful duplication." He finds this to be true particularly of Old Testament and New Testament courses.

Comparing seminary and college courses in other respects, he finds higher standards of work and a higher level of difficulty in seminary. He believes that the seminary teachers are more competent, but he finds little difference in methods of teaching or size of classes. To the extent that teaching methods do vary, there was probably more lecture in college and more discussion in seminary. He has more individual contact with the professors in seminary than he had with professors in college.

In considering factors determining who will become effective ministers, he lists (in order of significance) as "very important": having a definite call to the ministry, having a broad academic background, possessing public speaking ability. Those which he thinks are "relatively unimportant" are: being a minister's son, majoring in religion in college, having a scientific background, and attending a denominational college. Those which he thinks "somewhat important": having a work experience before seminary, specializing in some academic discipline, and having mother and father interested in the church.

Reviewing his own study of theology, he is inclined to think he was not ready for courses in theology before he was permitted to take them, primarily because "I needed preparation in other fields before taking theology courses." Among his fellow seminarians, he finds about one-half of them disagree with him, believing they were ready for theology courses before they actually took them, but they are equally divided between those who think they would have benefited by taking courses in theology earlier in their academic career and those who feel that there would have been no advantage in doing so.

In face of proposals for abbreviating the period of college-seminary study by consolidating them, or by other means, he believes that the present pattern is preferable and thinks it essential that seminary study for the parish ministry should assume a preparation in a four-year undergraduate college program. He, with a majority of his fellow students, holds that, assuming seminaries require a bachelor's degree for admission to the professional course of ministerial training, a master's degree should be granted for the completion of the three-year seminary course. A slightly smaller group of students feels that the B.D. (or S.T.B.) is an appropriate professional degree for the course. Less than one-tenth of his fellow seminarians believe a doctor's degree should be granted.

When asked about terms used to describe full-time, professional, religious leaders he said that "minister" was the term he most frequently heard used, followed by "reverend," "pastor," and "brother." The term "pastoral-director," suggested by the Niebuhr-Williams-Gustafson Study, was the one least frequently used. For himself he definitely preferred the term "pastor" followed by "minister"; and least preferred "prophet," "pastoral-director," and "parson." He most disliked to have applied to himself the term "reverend," followed by "prophet," "priest," and "brother."

Analyzing ministers he has known he rated their greatest deficiencies in the following order:

> Overconcern with denominational promotion and statistics.
> Inability to communicate.
> Tendency to be autocratic.
> Insensitivity in interpersonal relations.
> Lack of social and political awareness.
> Limited intellectual ability.
> Lack of a clear doctrinal position.
> Lack of courage before church officials or laymen.
> Ineptness in organizational matters.

He thinks that these deficiencies can best be overcome in the future by "emphasis in seminary on devotional and spiritual life," "individual study," and "internship training under direct guidance of a competent minister." He has least confidence in "post-seminary training," "emphasis in seminary on organizational problems of the church," and "courses at the pre-seminary level" for providing effective correctives for these deficiencies. In other words, he places more faith in personal means than institutional and curricular ones for improving the ministry and correcting its weaknesses.

Looking back on his own career, he thinks of the times when he seriously hesitated about going to seminary and feels that the major reasons were: "feeling of personal inadequacy or lack of talent for the ministry," "financial expense of seminary," and "interest in another profession or field of study." In his case, the "advice of professors," the "social disapproval of other students," and "parental dissuasion" were relatively unimportant as causes of hesitation on his part.

Re-examining his theological position, he would describe himself on entering college as "conservative" and considers himself to be the same—perhaps slightly more liberal—today. He has changed less in theological position during that period than any other theological group with the exception of those who call themselves "liberal." Those who have changed most are those who considered themselves to be "fundamental" on entering college. Among his fellow seminarians he finds that the positions which have gained most new adherents, proportionately, are "neo-orthodox" and "ecumenical." On the whole, his student generation has moved in a more liberal direction since beginning college, though the term "conservative" is still by a considerable margin the one most used by present-day seminarians to define their theological stance.

❂ ❂ ❂ ❂

Such are the main lines sketching the profile of the average Protestant seminarian of today. It is a rough outline and it is not sufficiently filled in to make positive identification possible at this time. Nor can it be said that this profile describes the "typical" seminarian. By running the I.B.M. cards of the 17,565 seminary students who answered the Seminarian Questionnaire through the machines it would be possible to find the one seminarian who most nearly approximated the picture that has been projected. Presumably, he would be the "typical" seminarian; he would be "Mr. Seminarian." But by that very fact he would be not "typical" but "exceptional." In other words, the analysis of the empirical data from the questionnaires, while it forms a useful basis for generalizations, does not lend itself easily to more refined identifications or depictions. Indeed, perhaps the most striking fact that emerges from the analysis of these returns is the amount of deviation from the "average" profile and the variations of it. This is particularly evident in the more detailed and cross-correlated analysis of the data.

Insofar as this data may be used as a basis for generalizations, certain facts seem to be undeniable. The chief of these is the complexity of background of seminary students. A comparative study of other professional schools would probably indicate the extent to which theological seminaries are faced with a peculiar problem in this respect. Until such a study is made (one of this Study's recommendations is that it should be) to confirm or contradict this, it would appear that seminaries have a greater problem in this respect than other professional institutions, and by a wide margin.

For example, an analysis of the baccalaureate origins of seminarians shows that over 700 colleges and universities had students in A.A.T.S. seminaries in the period of 1961-62. A study of this list, particularly the top of the list of big "producers," shows —as might be expected—that church-related schools occupy the top of the list. This is even more evident when the index figures based on student population are examined. Nevertheless, the number of seminarians who are graduates of state-supported or independent schools is significantly large, and this may be surprising to those who have assumed that church college graduates form the vast majority of seminary students and that the others are only an insignificant minority which can be largely ignored either in planning recruiting programs or in forming seminary educational policy and curricula.

Furthermore, it is self-evident that even when the seminary student population can be categorized as graduates of various "types" of undergraduate schools, the schools differ so much among themselves within the same "type" that very little can be taken for granted in dealing with specific students on the basis of their baccalaureate origins. This is true even when students have taken the same kind of courses in the same "type" of institutions. The courses may have the same names, but even a casual scrutiny of the catalog descriptions of these courses (not to speak of the different teachers that give them and the variance between the actual content of the courses and their catalog descriptions!) instantly reveals the variety between them.

All this has to be added to the manifest complexity of backgrounds in major fields of study in college, whatever their "type." What are the implications of this fact? A seminary dean and a professor reflect on this in relation to their own institution, but what they say might be applied to many others, probably most:

Theological students now come from a very wide variety of backgrounds. Boston University School of Theology draws heavily from every section of the United States and from more than two hundred educational institutions. These students come with extremely divergent preparation, academically, religiously, and in church work experience. To provide for every one what that one needs in order to become an effective minister of Jesus Christ is an herculean task. This problem is in the background of every discussion of curriculum and often comes to the fore.

Should we lay down definite requirements concerning specific courses which must have been taken in college? This would undoubtedly help, but it would also turn from our doors many fine candidates. Moreover, it would help less than might at first appear. Courses by similar titles have such different content and spirit, as taught in different colleges, that the results would be far from uniform. Would they be good enough to be worth the heavy price? Probably not. Yet to take into the School graduates of engineering institutes, business colleges, teachers colleges and colleges of liberal arts, however good, and seek to start them all in one curriculum leading to adequate preparation for the ministry seems more than should be expected. No final solution is in sight.[1]

If present trends continue, it may be supposed that this complexity is likely to become greater in the future. In face of this, what ought to be done? One obvious solution—admittedly partial —is to change seminary recommendations for pre-seminary preparation into formal requirements. It would obviously take a great deal of discussion and deliberation within the A.A.T.S. to get a consensus on what exactly such requirements might be. There is little evidence in the reports of seminary faculty consultations on pre-seminary education for this Study to indicate support for the proposal of a required pre-seminary major in religion. Nevertheless, it does not seem impossible that a short list of pre-seminary required subjects might be drawn up which would gain general approval and might form the basis of an agreed admissions policy on the part of A.A.T.S. institutions.

One way in which this could be put into practice would be through an A.A.T.S. entrance examination, analogous to the College Board or the Graduate Record examinations, insofar as the latter are not adequate for this purpose. Depending on their severity and specificity, such examinations might mean that certain students would have to take an additional remedial year of study after college graduation to prepare for them and successfully pass them. It would also mean, as another chapter will indicate, that the seminaries would have to be more clear and specific about their educational goals and clearer about their peculiar role in the total educational process of ministerial education; only when that clarification takes place can preparatory requirements be formally established.

Another way to view this evident complexity of collegiate background of seminary students is to see it as a welcome realization of A.A.T.S. policy as expressed in the Statement on Pre-Seminary Studies advocating a "broad" educational preparation. This breadth is exhibited, not necessarily in each student but in the seminary student body *as a whole*. Since students also educate each other in the course of their study, it might be supposed that this varied student group in seminary would within itself exert a widening and deepening liberal influence among its members. This increasing variety of undergraduate background, despite the complexity it poses for the seminary curriculum, may perhaps be something to be welcomed rather than deplored by seminary representatives. And if entrance requirements were set up, their purpose would not be to reduce this "liberal" variety, but to seek through it to establish a minimal base of technical competencies indispensable for the seminaries to pursue their own educational goals efficiently. Demonstrated mastery of elementary Greek, basic English, history of philosophy, are examples of such basic educational competency which seminaries might reasonably expect of entering students, whatever their pre-seminary education might have provided otherwise. As has been said, this can be effected only if there are requirements and these requirements are given the teeth of entrance examinations.

This more positive approach to the varied pre-seminary backgrounds of seminarians can be bolstered by the other main impression which is conveyed by a study of the results of the Seminarian Questionnaire. Though their academic work reflects a bewildering variety of college preparation, the seminarians tend to come out of a relatively homogeneous family ethos and cultural environment. This sociological homogeneity can be interpreted as a counterbalance to the academic variety. It forms an invisible base—also academically—for the theological enterprise of the seminary. It probably explains why, despite the variety of formal educational preparation of their students, the seminaries are able to operate as successfully as they do and are not totally incapacitated in their educational work by the complexity of the college pre-seminary training of their students. They are, in brief, religiously cultured.

Whether this cultural homogeneity of seminarians is to be welcomed for other reasons is another matter. When seminary students, irrespective of their college background or major field of undergraduate study, are seen to be those who have been baptized before they were 16 (86%) and considered themselves to have had full church membership before they were 21 (89%), we realize they represent a segment of the general population which is strikingly atypical in its religious orientation. This means that not only are most seminarians much more "religiously" cultured than the general run of society, they also come out of homes of regularly attending church members (73%) and so out of an even more exclusive ethos—an ecclesiastical culture. They have been trained from childhood to look with favor on the church as a religious institution and to take an active part in its organized life and program: 83% say that they were "encouraged to attend Sunday school" and 77% that they were "encouraged to attend church services," for example. A glance at recent sociological studies such as Gerhard Lenski's *The Religious Factor* indicates how unusual this background is.[2]

It is not surprising that a large majority of ministerial candidates are recruited out of this religious-ecclesiastical ethos. Nor is it unexpected that seminarians should reflect the attitudes toward religion and organized religious institutions characteristic of this culture. This identification may be so strong, and the ethos itself so exclusive and self-contained, as to justify the previous assertion in certain cases that they are products of a "ghetto." Certainly in general it can be said that the "typical" seminarian described in the profile outlined at the beginning of this chapter is a product of and represents a religious-ecclesiastical subculture. Such subcultures are usually defined in terms of definite ethnic, racial, and socio-economic differentia; but religious homogeneity is also an important factor in defining such subcultural groupings and not infrequently provides the decisive cohesive "glue" for them. The central finding of Lenski's study was that "religion in various ways is constantly influencing the daily lives of the masses of men and women in the modern American metropolis. More than that: through its impact on individuals, religion makes an impact on all the other institutional systems of the community in which these individuals participate. Hence the influence of religion operates at the social level as well as at the personal level."[3]

In this sense, the Protestant seminarian is *church-bound*, and doubly so. He is vocationally bound *for* a church occupation and sociologically bound *by* a religious and ecclesiastical ethos. That the "typical" seminarian, after leaving his family home, is likely to have attended a church-related college and gone on to a denominational seminary—both within the same religious ethos—leading to a position within a clerical caste which is the "hard-core" of the religious-ecclesiastical subculture, would suggest that his educational progression is one which involves an increasing cultural narrowing and an increasing identification with that subculture to the exclusion of other cultural exposure. It is against this background that the term "ghetto" seems to be less inappropriate than it might at first appear. As has been said, fellow students accused their theological colleagues in German universities of leading a "*ghetto-existenz.*" If this is possible in secular state universities, where most theological institutions are located in Europe, it is evident that in the American situation with both undergraduate colleges supported and controlled by churches and denominational seminaries closely connected with ecclesiastical bodies and generally independent of state-supported and private secular universities, the chance of theological students' growing up and being largely educated in this kind of ghetto-like isolation is even greater.

The strictly pre-*seminary* education of seminarians, then, has to be seen as something which may have been to a large extent completed *before* college. The subculture's indoctrination, especially through the family, is what "prepares" a man for seminary, and his college career then becomes either a general confirmation of this preparation or a temporary excursion around it. This might be the explanation for the difficulty seminary faculties find in deciding what college course best prepares men for seminary and why they have never found it necessary to set up formal entrance requirements based on undergraduate curricular studies. Presumably such requirements would have been established if the seminaries could not effectively operate without them. Their absence argues for the relative unimportance of college training as essential pre-seminary education. The demand for a bachelor's degree for entrance may be nothing more than the expression of the necessity to keep professional status in comparison with other kinds of professional training.

To be less cynical about it, however, the bachelor's degree entrance requirement may reflect the experience of the seminaries that a four-year interval between leaving the family ethos and beginning formal theological training provides the seminarian an essential means for breaking away from the narrow boundaries of the religious subculture of the parental home and neighborhood. Here again the exact curricular content of those undergraduate years is less important than the fact that they take place.

This in turn suggests that the chief function of college preparation as pre-seminary education is its *secularizing* influence. Both socially and curricularly the student finds the parochial horizons of his religious ghetto background opened and widened. Even in a church-connected institution and in curricular and extra-curricular religious activities the familial subcultural patterns are stretched and not infrequently broken. This educational "secularization" may mean for some a change in vocational goals—deciding to leave the ministry for some other profession, or to leave some other field and go into the ministry; for others a clearer idea of which ministerial specialization they would prefer —deciding for teaching rather than the parish ministry, or vice versa; and for still others a reconfirmation of their original vocational intentions, strengthened and deepened by the cultural and educational exposure of college life.

This "secularization" through college training may make the educational task of the seminaries more difficult. This is not only because of the complexity of college fields of study in which seminarians have done their work, but perhaps even more because, having to a lesser or greater extent moved out of the narrow subculture ethos of their "religious" home environment, they return once again to the more "religious" parochialism of the seminary, now aware of its nature and limitations and not infrequently critical of it—some might feel overly critical. In some ways, then, the religious-ecclesiastical subcultural continuity between home and seminary is disrupted by the period of college "pre-seminary" education. And, one might say, the more effective that college education is, the more difficult it makes the task of the seminary in digesting its products—that is, if the seminary has uncritically accepted a position as the citadel of the religious "ghetto" and the chief indoctrination center for the central leadership of it, which often appears to be the case.

This should make it evident that though every part of a minister's education presumably trains him for his occupation, the relation between the different educational segments is not continuous but dialectical. That is, though college education and seminary training are contiguous chronologically, they are not so simply related pedagogically. In order for this to be demonstrated, it is necessary to approach the problem from the other direction in terms of this question: What do the various segments of a minister's education contribute *functionally* to his actual ministerial service?

Viewed from this functional perspective, it can be seen that college education cannot be judged solely in terms of its relation to and "effectiveness" for seminary education. It is, indeed, "pre-seminary" education, but it is also "preministerial," and it may be that the latter category is the more important *functionally* in determining the special and peculiar contribution of college education to the total education of the minister. Thus college preparation has a dual goal: preparation for graduate professional *studies* and preparation for postprofessional school *practice*.

The priorities which are established depend in part on the actual requirements which the professional schools set for their students. As will be pointed out, the colleges must depend on the professional schools themselves to decide what these academic proficiencies should, or must, be. But in the second place, in view of their eventual professional practice and what is required for it, priorities are determined by an evaluation of what the student himself *is*. That is the significance of the empirically-based seminarian profile which has been presented. If it could be assumed that the pre-seminarian was adequately cultured, or "secularized"—assuming this to be essential for his ministerial effectiveness—then a greater degree of specialization in the field of religion might be justified during college. However, the profile projected shows that this "secularization" cannot be assumed, and therefore the college course has to be structured accordingly, to meet the real professional needs of the future minister and not just his needs as a professional school student.

It is against this background that the first educational stage of integration for the minister, the undergraduate college years, must be considered.

FOOTNOTES

1. Walter G. Muelder and L. Harold DeWolf, "Philosophy of the Curriculum," *Nexus*, 1, February 1958, p. 63.

2. Garden City, N.Y.: Doubleday, 1961. The percentages of white Protestant respondents in Lenski's Detroit Area Study who were "doctrinally orthodox" or "active devotionally" ranged, for different subgroups, from 22 to 34 (p. 362). Lenski cites a six-year study by H. L. Orbach, who found that "roughly one third of the white Protestants in Detroit attend worship services every Sunday. Slightly more than 20 per cent attend from one to three times a month, and 14 per cent never attend. The remaining third attend occasionally" (p. 35).

3. *Ibid.*, p. 289.

CHAPTER THREE

SECULAR
CULTIVATION

One of the major thrusts leading to the inauguration of this Study arose out of the dissatisfaction of college teachers of religion with the Statement on Pre-Seminary Studies adopted by the American Association of Theological Schools in 1956. They objected particularly to: (1) the exclusion of religion from the list of recommended undergraduate majors; (2) the recommendation of only three courses in religion during the four college years. The criticisms were expressed especially through a series of articles in the *Journal of Bible and Religion* by J. Allen Easley, Ernest C. Colwell, Walter G. Williams, and J. Arthur Baird— the latter's article in October 1959 based in part on a study of seminary students who had graduated from the College of Wooster.

A main concern, expressed by Colwell, has been: "Theological faculties have made almost no effort to articulate the theological curriculum with the curriculum of the college." Hopes were expressed, particularly through the National Association of Biblical Instructors (now the American Academy of Religion) that seminaries would recognize the religion courses in college by granting students who had taken such courses advanced standing in seminary.

But of even greater concern to the college religion teachers was the presupposition, as they saw it, behind the A.A.T.S. Statement that concentration in religion is necessarily "narrowing" academically or that it does not provide the best base for a liberal arts education for pre-seminary students. Professor Easley of Wake Forest College argued: "Nothing could offer a better integrating center for a student than religion. . . . No discipline in the college curriculum can surpass it as a natural center of educational interest. . . . A major in religion need not be narrowly projected."[1]

The editor of the *Journal of Bible and Religion*, reflecting the general consensus of the constituency of the N.A.B.I., wrote in the April 1959 number:

Departments of religion ought to assume responsibility for a guided pre-theological program which seeks to integrate, as perhaps no other program can, the whole of liberal learning. . . . Here we have the only real justification for the view that a department of religion may serve as a focus and guidance center for the education of the pre-theological student. . . . Where proper facilities are available and high academic standards are observed, a major in religion can readily achieve, or in some situations even exceed, the breadth and comprehensiveness found in majors within comparable disciplines.

Reference is made to Baird's study of Wooster graduates which reported: "Every one of the former Religion majors who answered this question indicated that their major in Religion enabled them to get as wide and varied a background in college as they would have gotten in some other field."[2] Baird later observes: "the Wooster Survey printed in the *Journal* for October 1959 strongly suggests that no one major field per se insures breadth, but rather that the tendency of the whole major system is in the opposite direction."[3]

In other words, the publication of the A.A.T.S. Statement provoked a discussion on the question of closer articulation of the college and seminary curricula. This in turn led to a consideration of the preferred college course for pre-seminary students. Finally, the more comprehensive problem of the place of religion, and of a department of religion in particular, in college education was raised.

Consideration of the place of religion in the college undergraduate curriculum has two main dimensions to be dealt with: in the first place, the institutional, and in the second, the personal. The institutional dimension has to do with the relation of religion to higher education in general and its relevance to liberal arts training in particular. The personal dimension has to do with the place of religion in the education of a student in general and with the professional preparation of a pre-seminary student in particular.

The essays of Robert Michaelsen, John Hutchison, William Nicholls, and others in *The Making of Ministers* indicate the history as well as the present state of the debate over the place of religion as a college field of curricular study. Those essays, as well as a large number of other books and reports on the field of religion in higher education available, make an extended discussion of the institutional problem unnecessary at this point. However, it might be well to underline a simple fact which underlies all of these investigations: The pluralistic American religious and educational environment makes generalizations about educational policy in this area highly suspect. Not only is it difficult to generalize about the actual situation today in this field, but it is literally impossible to project a general institutional policy for the future which would have any substantial content. All that probably can be said at this juncture is that the American educational environment is more open to the teaching of religion as a recognized academic discipline than it has been in many years. Even in avowedly "secular" institutions or in state-supported schools where there are actually legal restrictions defining how religion may or may not be taught on the campus (curricularly and extra-curricularly) religion has gained footholds in the curriculum. These are sometimes precarious toe-holds under various guises of other more "respectable" subjects such as philosophy, history, literature, sociology, or anthropology: for either psychological or legal reasons the term "religion" is often rigorously avoided. But the fact remains that a great amount of religion is actually being taught in American universities and colleges under other rubrics through other departments.

This surreptitious invasion by religion of the secular academic citadels has been deplored by some and hailed by others. There are, of course, some obvious limitations to any system which attempts to deal with a subject under false pretenses, whatever that subject may happen to be. Legal prohibitions, for instance, may exclude the possibility of courses in religion as such in certain institutions. The avoidance of these technical prohibitions by the surreptitious approach may be the only way in which religion may be dealt with under these circumstances. But what legal necessity requires may be interpreted as ideological reality: that is, that religion is not intellectually respectable and is not, ideologically speaking, worthy of academic recognition in an institution of higher learning. Taken as a whole, American higher education may be casting this unfortunate aspersion on religion by omission rather than commission. By its exclusion from the academic world as a subject in its own right, the impression is given, inadvertently or not, that religion does not belong at the highest levels of intellectual endeavor: it belongs, presumably, to the young, the innocent, the pious, the uneducated, the old—in short, to the religious world and its peculiar denizens. It is then quite appropriate—from the academic viewpoint—to approach religion as an interesting historical, sociological, psychological phenomenon. It may be objectively analyzed or dissected, more as an autopsy than a diagnosis however. So regarded, it is not *itself* a living enterprise or an intelligible, rational, academic discipline.

In brief, the omission of religion as a field of study and intellectual exercise in the college and university *in its own right* is the institutional assertion that religion is academically marginal, even expendable. It is further the assertion that the well-educated man can be well educated without knowing anything about religion, or at least knowing anything about religion on an intellectual and academic level that is comparable to his knowledge of his own or other related fields that he has received in his university training as a whole.

Historians, philosophers, sociologists, psychologists, and anthropologists, whatever their own religious views, must admit the simple existence of the fact of religion. Thus, no self-respecting educational system can exclude the study of religion if it wishes to be true to its own standards of intellectual integrity. This phenomenological approach has its validity, and even in institutions which are religiously oriented or ecclesiastically related this objective, scientific, analytic approach to religion has a place—perhaps even more important than in the secular institution, for it provides a useful corrective to emotional and/or ideological religious bias and extremes.

The question remains, nevertheless, whether religion has relevance to the academic enterprise at the college and university level other than purely historically or phenomenologically. Professional religionists and theologians have become increasingly aware of their intellectual responsibility to the academic world and have become increasingly articulate in arguing the right of religion to be granted academic recognition as a college and university discipline. They are not willing to give up their field of study to the amateur efforts of specialists from other fields, whether these amateurs are sympathetic or hostile to religion. In some ways the sympathetic academic dabbler in religion is the most subversive to the cause of religion in higher education as long as religion is not granted full academic recognition in the university curriculum; the hostile critic is likely to arouse religious interest and theological curiosity as a reaction to his views, whereas the amateur dabbler may inadvertently create the impression that religion can gain entrance to the academic groves only by patronizing sufferance and not through the intrinsic intellectual claims it may have for recognition by the scholarly community. Opposition, in short, is more complimentary than condescension, and in the long run it may be less dangerous too.

In any case, the movement seems to be in the direction of a full academic recognition for religion. Manning M. Pattillo, formerly Director for Education of the Lilly Endowment, Inc., in writing on "Directions of Liberal Arts College Development,"[4] suggests that one of the most significant trends in liberal education today and particularly evident since World War II, is the new intellectual interest in religion. A number of colleges have established or strengthened departments of religion which operate in the same way as any other department of instruction. Even colleges of arts and sciences in public universities, where the problem of teaching in this field of knowledge has been thought to be more difficult than in the private institutions, have been experimenting with ways of giving their students an understanding of religion. . . . The present interest in religion is in sharp contrast to that of the earlier decades of the 20th century when most students were apathetic to religion, and too often college teachers were actually antagonistic. . . . In institutions having no formal department of religion and lacking a teaching staff of competent scholars in religion the student frequently gained his sketchy impressions of religion from faculty members in other departments, who, though competent in their own fields, were scarcely any better informed in religion than the students themselves. Progress is now being made and in dozens of colleges and universities we find able students and faculty members taking religion seriously as a basic field in liberal education.

The question now seems to be not *whether* religion ought to have a recognized place in higher education, but *how*. As will be indicated later in this chapter, even for so-called "church-related" institutions, where religion has generally had an important place in the curriculum (not infrequently through compulsion), the question of *how* is not an easy one to answer. But it is in independent and state-supported colleges and universities, especially the latter, that some of the most interesting discussions and experiments are now going on regarding the place of religion in the curriculum. Two examples may be cited: Iowa and Princeton.

The first is the School of Religion at the University of Iowa. Its rationale is, in the words of a former Director of the School, that: "Religion, theoretically and practically, is inseparable from education; hence it should be taught, even in a tax-supported university, not indirectly or surreptitiously, but unapologetically, comprehensively, and in line with the best educational procedures." Dr. Robert Michaelsen, the present Director, has outlined the educational philosophy and the actual program of the School in a number of papers including the C. W. Hall Lectures on Biblical Studies in Higher Education (1961) wherein he states its intention: "Religion should be approached, in other words, as the full-bodied phenomenon which it is, in its institutional, historical and theological aspects, in terms of belief, worship, practice and sacred literature." He argues against the idea that religion should be taught *within* the existing departmental structure of the university on the basis that for "theoretical and practical reasons . . . a separate departmental or administrative structure is necessary. This happens to be the way in which a university is organized to engage in systematic study."[5] He holds, as does William Nicholls in the Canadian scene, that though some believe legal restrictions exclude the teaching of religion in many state-supported institutions, "so long as the purpose and procedure are educationally sound, the legal question need not be a barrier."

The main point here may well be the question of "educationally sound." The hostility and suspicions that many academic teachers and administrators have about introducing religion into the curriculum of higher education are frequently well grounded and based on previous bad experience in which courses in religion have tended to become instruments of sectarian indoctrination, catechetical rather than educational in orientation. This dogmatism, "bootlegged into the curriculum for both positive and negative reasons," as Michaelsen has put it, has set the guardians of the intellectual integrity of the university on guard against anything that calls itself "religion." And rightly so. As William Nicholls writes in *The Making of Ministers*:

Indeed, the case for the establishment of departments of religion in this type of university, which seems to me to be overwhelming, has nothing to do with the contest between "religionists" and "secularists" as such. The question is about the proper role of the university. A university that omits to study anything so important to mankind and its history as religion is clearly shirking parts of its own role and risking the justified charge that it is content to be less than a true university.[6]

The history of the teaching of religion at Princeton University is one of the best examples of the changing *raison d'être* for religion in higher education, from a confessional to a scientific, from a dogmatic to an academic approach. Up to 1900, courses in

Bible were required for freshmen and sophomores, and the college president gave instruction in philosophy and ethics which was "essentially religious in content and outlook."[7] By 1920-21, however, only two courses in religion appeared in the catalog and it was not until a special faculty committee, through a report submitted in 1935, started steps leading toward a department in religion with a major in 1946 and eventually a graduate program leading to the Ph.D. degree in 1955 that the full circle had been completed. Religion was then academically re-established but on a different basis than originally: namely, on a firmly critical approach using the historical method. As Paul Ramsey, Chairman of the Department of Religion, pointed out in an article in *The Journal of Bible and Religion* describing the new graduate program, the structural relation between the undergraduate and graduate studies is parallel to that of other fields of study at Princeton and the whole study of religion with an "independent place in the curriculum" (as the 1935 report put it) is pursued "as an element of liberal culture and as one of the humanities."[8]

Professor Clyde A. Holbrook, whose study *Religion, a Humanistic Field* was partially prepared during a sabbatical year at Princeton, takes much the same line, quoting with approval A. D. Nock's contention that "the serious study of religion is a part of humanistic study in general, and for its well-being needs to be conducted in a community where history, language, and philosophy receive the full service of scholars who have integrity, competence, and zeal."[9]

It is one of the striking signs of the educational times that it is on this "educationally sound" basis that religion in fact is being introduced and reintroduced to an increasingly large number of institutions of higher learning in North America. Dr. Seymour Smith, formerly of Yale and now president of Stevens College, made a study in 1958 including seventy larger state universities and colleges and reported that "over ninety-five percent of the major state universities, by one device or another, do make provision for courses in religion," and a sampling of state colleges "did not reveal an appreciably different over-all picture."[10]

An analysis of catalogs from colleges and universities which had graduates studying in A.A.T.S. seminaries in 1961-62 indicates the same general situation, although twelve (17.1%) of the 70 sample schools given special attention still do not show in their catalogs any provision for courses in religion. The catalogs and letters from presidents and other officials of institutions who responded personally to requests made for information by this Study also indicate that the curricular patterns through which religion is offered follow the main types described by Robert Michaelsen in his C. W. Hall Lecture in 1961 (with percentages of each type among the 70 sample schools of the Pre-Seminary Study indicated in parentheses):

1. courses listed in other departments or divisions of the college or university but not specified under the heading of religion (18.6%).
2. an interdepartmental program in religion with a coordinated curriculum administered by a committee (1.4%).
3. a department of religion (or Bible, or Religious Education) (47.1%).
4. a combined department of philosophy and religion (18.6%).
5. a department of philosophy with courses in religion offered (2.9%).
6. a school or institute of religion, supported by religious agencies but officially recognized by the college or university.
7. denominational courses offered by religious foundations, sometimes under the title of "Bible Chairs," and given academic credit.[11]

Some of these programs are advertised as "pre-seminary" and take cognizance of the A.A.T.S. or particular seminaries' recommendations for pre-seminary work. However, the University of Minnesota catalog suggests that its own heading, "Preparation for Theological Training," is "accurate in fact but misleading in emphasis." It explains:

That the studies taken in a liberal arts college actually precede seminary training is obvious enough. That their main function should be to prepare the student for seminary work is dubious. An even more important task is getting the student ready for his total responsibility as a minister and as a citizen—most particularly in those areas where the liberal arts college can do the job more efficiently than a specialized seminary program conceivably can.

The student should, of course, learn as early as possible what seminary he plans to attend and what prerequisites it demands. But he should study its catalogue just as much to learn those areas in which it does *not* offer training as to ascertain those in which it does. For he should plan his program with a clear sense of his mission as a minister and of the part that the liberal arts can play in fulfilling that mission.

As Robert Michaelsen says: "For the most part the courses in religion offered in the publicly supported institutions are of a liberal arts nature and are not designed specifically to prepare the student for any type of professional service. While many public institutions offer a major in the field of religion or a program designed for pre-ministerial students, the majority of students who take courses in religion are non-majors or nonspecialists."[12]

Even in institutions where the "pre-seminary" purposes of the program are emphasized, this is often apparently done for public relations reasons, having to do with recruitment of students and to create a favorable impression on the governing bodies and general constituency.

It is in comparing the programs in religion in state-supported public institutions and church-related colleges that this difference in educational philosophy becomes most apparent. A. R. Sharp's doctoral dissertation for Duke University (1963), *A Study of Protestant Undergraduate Pre-Theological Education in the United States,* is based on a questionnaire sent to all of the accredited, Protestant, church-related colleges and universities in the United States, with a 68.9% return representing 84.1% of the 44 denominations with which institutions of higher learning are affiliated. He found that an undergraduate major in religion is offered in 86.7% of the institutions responding to the questionnaire. This figure would probably be only slightly reduced by the nonrespondents and so represents roughly the general picture in this type of institution.

There are several interesting facts which emerge from Sharp's study. In the first place is "the obvious lack of popularity of religion as a major" among pre-seminary students. One of his tables shows that in more than half of the institutions reporting, fewer than 20% of pre-seminary students major in religion. The most popular majors are, in order: social studies, philosophy, English, education.

Sharp's two explanations for this are: (1) "It must be concluded that the small number of ministerial students majoring in religion is due in part to the influence of the A.A.T.S."; (2) "second, the apparent lack of interest in a religion major may be the result of proselyting on the part of faculty members in other disciplines." It is possible that other factors contribute to the result reported by Sharp. "In spite of the fact that the National Association of Biblical Instructors has gone on record favoring the undergraduate religion major, 61 per cent of the schools responding to this study indicated that they encouraged students to major in religion either 'seldom' or 'never.'"

In brief, the reasons for the lack of "popularity" for religion as an undergraduate pre-seminary major are unclear. But the fact remains that the pre-seminary students themselves, for whatever reasons, tend to choose other majors.

The explanation for this ambiguous situation may be found in another finding of Sharp's study: Of the 202 institutions responding to the question of the "personnel responsible for guiding church-vocations students" only five, or 2.5%, reported that "persons outside the Religion Department have the responsibility for program direction." In 128 schools it was the chairman of the department of religion, in 24 the college chaplain, and in 19 a member of the religion department faculty. In other words, the departments of religion are clearly looked to as the main arm of the church-related college and university for supervising church-vocations students. In many cases this also involves supervision of "field work" for students used to supply churches in the vicinity: 64.7% of the institutions reporting to Sharp indicated that their students were involved in such "field work experience."

The image of the church-related college department of religion that emerges is one that appears to have little similarity, at least formally, to the role of the department of religion that is projected by those who are concerned to have the teaching of religion in higher education primarily reflect its "liberal arts nature" in the academic context and its humanistic and cultural orientation. The religion department in church-related institutions seems to be expected to provide the essential religious education for the whole student body—guaranteed in most cases by provisions demanding credits in religion for graduation. The fact that 34.8% of directors of pretheological programs are "directly responsible to the president" of the institution, as compared to 24.7% responsible to the academic dean and 14.1% to the department of religion chairman, would seem to indicate that both the department of religion's academic work and its supervisory task for pre-seminarians are seen as an integral part of the administrative and public relations policy of church-related institutions. This is also borne out by the extent to which in brochures and catalogs church-related schools stress their importance for the work of their churches in recruiting students for church vocations, especially the ministry.

Under these circumstances it might be suspected that students in church-related institutions get an impression of religion as an academic discipline which is something less than one which can hold its own with other subjects in free intellectual competition. It appears, and apparently is seen by the students, as a part of the necessary program of a "religious" institution but not something which is intellectually challenging or academically distinguished as a field in its own right. If religion is so lacking in attraction as a major field of study for those whose future professional plans are so closely related to its subject matter, its appeal as a major for other students must be even more limited.

This conclusion is underlined by the significant number of students in seminary who majored in religion as undergraduates coming from non-church-related institutions, where presumably the academic resources in this field were more limited and where little, if any, encouragement was given by the administration to the religion department as a preprofessional training center.

Thus one may feel that a department of religion which projects an image of its subject as one which is necessary for the policy and public relations of an institution rather than as one which is fundamental to the academic integrity of the institution engaged in liberal arts education, or projects an image of itself as the recruiting, training, and supervising arm of the institution for future ministers rather than the group of scholarly experts

who through teaching and research are contributing in the field
of religion to the intellectual wholeness of the college and university as academic institutions, has abdicated its possibilities
of projecting the true character of religion to the academic community, among both teachers and students.

This tendency of the church-related schools to project the institutional and professional aspects of religion through its religion
departments rather than the academic and humanistic-cultural
orientation prescribed for "secular" college and university departments by Michaelsen, Nicholls, Nash, and others in *The
Making of Ministers* may illuminate a basic divergence of philosophy among those who have engaged in the debate on pre-seminary education up to now. The issue is really whether undergraduate education's chief rationale is professional. And at stake
is the whole future of the liberal arts tradition in American higher
education.

The importance of the departmental pattern of religious education set by the church-related institutions is twofold. In the
first place, it provides a kind of institutional and organizational
prototype for the academic structuring of the teaching of religion
in higher educational institutions which have previously not been
engaged in this field of study. Being first in the field, the church-
related institutional pattern tends to define what in fact a "department of religion" is and does for those who are new in the field. In
the second place, this pre-eminence established by seniority has
certain disadvantages for the whole cause of religion in higher
education because the peculiar function of religion in a church-
related institution makes the institutional prototype it projects in
certain respects inappropriate for "secular" colleges and universities. At the least the applicability of the prototype to other situations and other institutions has to be carefully examined. And it
may be that the traditional pattern of departments of religion in
church-related institutions may be not only inappropriate for
public tax-supported schools and independent institutions of
higher learning but may also have become anachronistic in the
church-related schools themselves.

This Study suggests that broader educational issues are in-

volved in the question of the nature and function of a department
of religion than the category "pre-seminary" allows. To be specific: It would appear that the role of a department of religion
in either a church-related or non-church-related institution has
ultimately to be defined in terms of the *raison d'être* of liberal arts
education as such and not in terms of its providing professional
studies for ministerial students. The latter is a problem, but it is
not *the* problem. In fact, the whole discussion of the role of departments of religion, particularly as that discussion has progressed over the years in the circle of the N.A.B.I., may have
been vitiated by being considered so exclusively under the "pre-
seminary" rubric. In so doing, the extent to which *the* problem
has been obscured is difficult to estimate. For it may be primarily
and fundamentally the disquiet which representatives of departments of religion, particularly in church-related schools, have
felt is only symptomatic of a general malaise in American higher
education: that is, increasing professionalization in all fields
moulding and forming the entire system of higher education into
a new and unprecedented pattern. That new pattern is one in
which the demands of postgraduate and professional training are
more and more determining the form and content of undergraduate academic work. Humphrey Doermann, Director of
Admissions at Harvard, has described this change:

With an abler student body planning increasingly on graduate study,
the quality of scholarship in the college has certainly risen. Unfortunately the pressure to get good grades for their own sake has risen also.
. . . Among those who continue their education after college, a growing number of Harvard graduates—about three out of ten—will work
towards the Ph.D. Fifteen years ago the law and medical schools attracted the largest number of students with the best academic records.
Now the largest number of top scholars point towards the graduate
schools of arts and sciences.

This change in turn often generates pressure towards earlier undergraduate specialization. The Harvard graduate schools of law, business, and medicine (with the exception of four required science
courses) have not suggested prerequisite undergraduate study programs. Their admission practice does not give any hint of preference
for undergraduate specialization. It is the quality of the work, not the
specific subject, which matters. But a man generally obtains a Ph.D.

in the field he concentrated in as an undergraduate, and the incentive to earn good grades, early and in the field of eventual specialization, often seems greater to this undergraduate than to the man with other career plans. The penalties for not doing so also seem greater. While Harvard and Radcliffe students now may choose from over seven hundred different courses—more than twice as many as were available thirty years ago—the new pressure to specialize may restrict the actual pattern of choice.[13]

In the present situation in higher education, therefore, every department, including the department of religion, feels increasingly under the necessity of justifying its existence, both for students and faculty, in terms of its relation to later graduate or professional study. The danger is that for the department of religion this rationalization may come more easily than it should and for the simple reason that it has *already* been "professionalized," not only in orientation but also in practice. This is particularly true of the church-related college department of religion. It has, as has been pointed out, the function of serving the "religious education" needs of the whole church-related institution. But it is also given in many cases the specific professional task of recruiting, supervising, and teaching future ministers. This is revealed by the extent to which church-related college departments of religion have become engaged in pulpit supply and "field work" supervision in many places. A. R. Sharp, reflecting a pattern more characteristic of the South but not exclusively found there, says in his study: "Religion has more demands made upon it than most other academic areas. Most church colleges are obliged to train the ministry and to serve the church constituency while doing so. Many Protestant religious bodies have numerous small churches in the area surrounding the church colleges which lack sufficient funds to maintain a resident ministry. Those churches turn to the church colleges for ministerial students to supply the churches."

The curricula of such church-related institutions reveal functional courses such as "Sermon Preparation and Delivery," "Town and Country Church," in the religion department which indicate this professional orientation. Indeed, as representatives from such colleges reported to the Dallas Consultation arranged

by this Study, for many of their students the undergraduate
degree was terminal and this meant, in effect, that the department of religion was for them their seminary training. This was
not necessarily the policy of the college, nor was it put forward
by those who presented it as the ideal pattern, but it was simply
described as the actual situation. In such institutions, the preparation of men for seminary, professionally oriented as that may be,
is a venture in liberal education when compared to serving as a
substitute for seminary.

Considering, then, the emerging pattern of increased specialization and professionalization in undergraduate education, of
which Harvard is probably symptomatic rather than exceptional,
and the background of professional orientation in many church-
related religion departments, it is evident why the term "pre-
seminary," with its professional connotation and overtones, has
exerted an almost magnetic attraction and become the polar focus
for discussions of the place of departments of religion in higher
education.[14] And though a number of N.A.B.I. spokesmen have
emphasized the value of a major in religion as providing a superior base for a full and well-rounded liberal arts education, this
has often been done against the background of the seminaries'
preference, as embodied in the A.A.T.S. Statement, for a liberal
arts background for their entering students. Liberal arts itself,
then, becomes professionally rationalized, and is justified in terms
of its professional function in graduate study. As Martin Marty
indicates in *The Making of Ministers*, liberal arts education does
have a practical, functional significance in equipping a minister
for his service; but that value is ultimately negotiable in his
eventual pastoral activity and not to be judged purely in terms
of its immediate value in making him a good theological student
in seminary: "good pre-theological humane learning for the sake
of post-theological fruitfulness," is how Marty puts it.[15]

An interesting example of how professionalization has subtly
infected the thinking in this area may be cited. In describing
Princeton University's graduate program in religion, Paul Ramsey states that this program "was shaped in accordance with the
features, philosophy and goals of the Department as set forth

originally in a *Report of the Special Committee of the Faculty on Religious Education (1935)*. . . . Accordingly, a summary of the principles on which our graduate program is based can be derived through selected quotations from that document. An 'independent place in the curriculum' is insured for religion only by clearly distinguishing 'between the study of religion and the practice of it.' Thus, the study of religion is pursued 'as an element of liberal culture and as one of the humanities.'" Ramsey goes on to argue: "In music, poetry, drama, and religion are exhibited actual modes of man's inner life. . . . In this sense, just as the study of music ought to involve learning what music is about and not simply learning *about* music, so the study of religion at Princeton is not the study of the literature or history of religion only, but the study of *what religion is about.*"[16]

It is understandable that since Ramsey is writing about the graduate Ph.D. program he is thinking about the value of that program in the professional preparation of teachers of religion. However, he argues the case *for* a graduate department largely on the grounds that it is a necessary aid to the *professors* of religion in maintaining high scholarly and academic levels in *their* work:

> . . . when in 1955 the Faculty of Princeton University moved to establish in its Department of Religion a program of graduate study leading to the Ph.D. degree the question to be decided was not whether the undergraduate department should now be allowed to admit and teach graduate students but whether we should be permitted to continue to teach religion to undergraduates unless we also engaged in graduate instruction like our colleagues in all other departments with the stimulus this gives to any teacher to keep alive his scholarly interests.[17]

There is a certain conflict of interests between the professional concerns of the teacher for his scholarly production and his status in the academic community, on the one hand, and the interests of the student to be given basic religious knowledge, on the other. It is not unknown for undergraduate levels in a university to be neglected because of the concentration of professors on graduate programs. In the past it was sometimes true that students would not get the "top" professors until they were upperclassmen; now it is true that they may not get them at all unless they go on to graduate school. And even there they may not have firsthand contact with them until they are engaged in a specific research project.

A college religion teacher says: "The first concern of the college teacher is with the college student, not specifically the pretheology student." On the other hand, Baird concludes: "If this modest survey has done anything, it has convinced the writer that depth of specialization must begin in college, even as breadth of coherent synthesis must continue in seminary."[18] It is apparent that the claim of the general student body for basic religious education and that of the preprofessional in the field for "depth" specialization are not easily harmonized, especially if the teacher is considered by the college to be largely responsible for the first task, whereas his own professional interests incline him toward the second. This may be particularly true in those institutions without graduate schools, in which a professor might find an outlet for his specialized scholarly concerns and an academic base for his "depth" research.

It might be hoped that the role of a religion department would not have to be decided between two mutually exclusive interests: that of the students for a sound but basic introduction into religion and that of the teachers for an institutional base in the academy for the pursuit of specialized theological learning. However, at the moment it does not seem to be clear what the major concern of the religion teacher is. As Clinton D. Morrison, a professor at McCormick Theological Seminary and a participant in the Chicago Consultation, wrote in a letter to the Study directors:

I was surprised by the turn of the discussion in the afternoon. Assuming that the college profs were interested in participating effectively in the total theological education enterprise, I hoped to make clear that at this particular time seminaries need something to build on, and because we have nothing, we have to provide remedial introductions to studies which should have been undertaken earlier. We want and need their help.

Far from showing any interest in Marty's beautiful and vigorous description of the scope of pre-seminary study, they seemed to fasten only upon the implication that their departments were not to be the bulk and center of it all. My call for their help was taken to be a sign of the seminary's weakness.

In short, those who came to fight for the "Religion Department" were soon well on their way to the conclusion that they could after all do a much better job than the seminaries at the job of theological education proper.

This is a distressing situation. . . . My own feeling is that the best hope for a sane discussion is with college deans, who can offer the full resources of their liberal arts curriculum and faculty without feeling that their professional competence and status are being threatened. The professors of religion show less interest in pre-seminary education than the status of the religion department. . . .

In any case, I should hope someone in the liberal arts would seriously consider the magnificent and urgent opportunity to share effectively in the preparation of men for the ministry, to participate in theological education by cooperation with the seminaries, each type of institution supplying what it is best equipped to offer at the best time.

Whether this critical evaluation is accepted or not, it should be no surprise that religion teachers and departments of religion are concerned for their academic status. Nor is it unexpected that in a time of increasing specialization in an academic situation that is largely structured around the "major system," each department is concerned to attract the students and to sign them up as "majors," for this is commonly assumed to legitimize their departmental existence in the eyes of their colleagues and the administration.

The question remains, however, Is this institutional necessity actually being rationalized as "pre-seminary education"? To put it in another way, is the supposed connection between the graduate, professional seminary and the undergraduate department of religion as "pre-seminary" the only, or even the best, way to justify the existence of a religion department in a college? Is there not a danger that this professional orientation may negate the prime concern of the religion teachers, as expressed through the policy of the N.A.B.I., to contribute to the total enterprise of liberal arts education?

There is clear evidence of this mixture of motives and confusion of goals which has come to light through this Study.

It is clear that departments of religion, insofar as they have "majors" and interpret their own *raison d'être*, generally relate this to the professional goals of students planning to enter seminary and eventually the ministry. Dr. J. Arthur Baird, chairman of the N.A.B.I. Subcommittee on Pre-Theological Studies, which laid the groundwork for this Study, reported: "There are many who have expressed concern to the N.A.B.I. study committee that pressures within various departments to go into professional work in other fields are having disastrous effects upon the erstwhile pre-theological plans of some of their finest students."[19] This concern was voiced many times to the directors of this Study in interviews with college religion teachers, and it was made plain that they considered themselves in a competitive situation with *other* preprofessional departments.

As is known, religion departments are often looked upon by the churches and by the colleges as ministerial recruiting agencies and as the institutional centers for supervision of pre-seminary students. It is also often assumed that these departments, and their teaching staff, have a special obligation to hold such students to their ministerial commitment. What is not often realized—or if recognized not appreciated—is that the better departments sometimes exercises a dissuasive influence on students planning to go to seminary, especially if that decision has been reached before coming to college. As Professor Jack Boozer said at the Atlanta Consultation: "If he made a decision to enter the ministry upon a cultural and not a biblical understanding of the Word of God, it is better that he learn this in college than in Theology School, and there reaffirm or disavow the previous decision. On the other hand, if another student decided against the ministry under the cultural illusion, he might well find himself again confronted with this option, and, in college, reaffirm or disavow his previous decision. The door is open both ways; and the careful, informed, competent study of religion in college is an asset to the pretheology student as well as to his nonpretheology colleague by exposing the religious question during the college years."

One of the problems of the religion major for pre-seminarians is that the college period is not just one of sharpening professional tools, or preparing for future professional study, but it is for many students a period of vocational transition and redirection. If a religion major involves either a premature professional narrowing of perspective, or an isolation from other fields of thought, this vocational re-examination may only be delayed until seminary —a phenomenon noted by numbers of seminary educators today. This happens in other professions as well. An applicant for a Rockefeller Brothers fellowship for a "trial year" in seminary writes of his long-time plan to be a doctor: "Consequently, it seemed to me at that time my dreams and goals were to be realized. They weren't. My interest wavered in medical school, not because of disinterest in medicine, but because my interests were finally branching out after years of a narrow-minded approach to my future; that is, no intellectual activity, except that which would pertain to my becoming a doctor, ever aroused any curiosity in my mind until my stay in medical school. At that time I started to read philosophy—which was a mistake. Medical school is a full-time job with no room for any other interests."

It may be, therefore, that not only a decision to enter the ministry "under the cultural illusion" needs to be corrected in college, but equally the decision to enter the ministry under a biblical, theological, or ecclesiastical illusion. And this is precisely the importance of the broad liberal arts exposure, including religion in *that* context, for the avowed pre-seminary student. If the department of religion can provide the integrating center—or perhaps disintegrating, in some cases!—for this vocational reappraisal, well and good. However, to do so effectively it must resist the academic pressures to produce more "majors," or the ecclesiastical pressures to produce more ministerial candidates.

If, on the other hand, a religion department must seek elsewhere for its *raison d'être,* where is it to find it? And who will recognize it? The dilemma of the religion department in this respect is symptomatic of a more general dilemma of higher education as a whole. As Baird has been quoted as saying, if one is concerned for educational breadth, it must be acknowledged "that the tendency of the whole major system is in the opposite direction." Or as a dean of a liberal arts college in California said in an interview: "Departments exist to solve problems which departments have created."

This departmental fragmentation, combined with increasing professionalization of the curriculum, threatens the whole liberal arts fabric of higher education. Who is being generally educated in the humanities today? Who, given the present academic structure, actually can be?

John Dewey, in an article on "The Problem of the Liberal Arts College," suggests that this development is a necessary adjustment to the fact of technological and social change in our society, and the colleges cannot ignore it. "The problem," he writes, "of securing to the liberal arts college its due function in a democratic society is that of seeing to it that the technical subjects which are now socially necessary acquire a humane direction."[20]

This counsel of expediency—almost of despair—may be the best that can be offered for a number of fields. But is it not possible that a department of religion can do something better? Is it right that religion should be considered, by others or by its teachers, as one of the "technical subjects" in this sense at all? As the N.A.B.I. statement already mentioned indicates, its "justification" is something entirely other than technical-professional training. The difficult problem, of course, is to get this recognized by the academic community as a whole, especially when the prevailing tendency within it is to confuse "technique" and "science" as well as "skill" and "learning."

There seem to be two main reasons why college teachers of religion tend to be "departmental" in their approach, and have therefore not been notable in their resistance to this fragmentation of college education which has made them, to use Clark Kerr's words, "multiversities."[21]

In the first place, because of their own professional background and their institutional connections with the ecclesiastical establishment (whether they are teaching in church-related colleges or not) they are inclined to see their own academic work in this context. This comes out vividly in the College Teachers Questionnaire. For example, in comparing the opinions of college teachers on the desirability of different professions (Table 2), the religion teachers' first preference by a wide margin was "clergyman" and they were 10 times more likely to recommend this to a student who came to them and asked their opinion than were other teachers. And, though both groups of teachers considered English, history, and philosophy as the fields of study at their schools as the ones in which a student is "most likely to obtain a broad liberal arts education," religion teachers rated religion far higher than their colleagues did in this respect—39.2% to 5% (Table 3). The religion teachers were also more likely to recommend an undergraduate major in religion to a student "who plans to go on to graduate theological study" by almost 3 to 1—29.7% to 11.7% (Table 5), and would be more inclined to recommend that "persons studying for a professional religious career" should take more "courses in religion and Bible than other students *while in college*," in comparison with their teaching colleagues in other fields (Table 6). Finally, they rated denominational colleges much higher than did other teachers as offering the "type of college-level training (which) provides the best preparation for theological studies"—36.1% to 13.6% (Table 7).

In brief, like the seminarians so many of them once were, college religion teachers also tend to be "church-bound" in their orientation, including in their academic work.

In the second place, it has been observed by many (including religion teachers themselves) that they have a certain sense of academic insecurity. This appears in the fact that on the College Teachers Questionnaire the smallest difference between the two groups of respondents—the religion teacher and others—is on their evaluation of the teaching skills of the faculty member in religion: This is the point at which the religion teacher is least confident and on which his colleague is most favorable (Table 9).

Several reasons might be given for this uncertainty of religion teachers about their academic status. In some cases, religion departments have a traditional, preferred position in a college because of the church affiliation of the institution; it may be felt that without this institutional guarantee the department of religion might not maintain its privileged, and sometimes dominating, academic role. In other cases, the teaching of religion is being introduced for the first time as an official academic offering, and this also may give rise to feelings of instability and insecurity. Also, the teaching of religion in the academic community often has the background of being taught by "superannuated retired clergymen" at a very superficial and unscholarly level. One teacher describes the "aims of college courses in religion" as follows: "In our college we make the Life and Teachings of Jesus the basic course . . . primarily it is the teaching of Jesus about which we are most concerned. . . . Courses in religion should first bring students into a vital spiritual experience, and then they should send those students out with the consciousness of a divine mission of service to mankind. We who teach these courses have a heavy responsibility."[22]

As the statements of the N.A.B.I. and the articles cited from the *Journal of Bible and Religion* make clear, this is no longer the prevailing attitude of religion teachers, nor does it represent the ethos of the best religion departments. Nevertheless, the tradition is one which sometimes vitiates the claims of religion teachers and departments for academic recognition.

As a result of these two factors, and others, religion is not yet "at home" in higher education, and its teachers do not yet feel fully at ease within the academic community. Thus, "departmentalized" religion may seem to offer a certain security over against this, and may appear—particularly by its preprofessional pretensions—to bolster its academic respectability.

Ironically, there appears to be little basis for these insecurities on the part of those concerned for the place of religion in higher education. Increasing numbers of independent and state-supported institutions are taking initiatives to establish religious studies—often, as in the case of the University of Minnesota for example, through the efforts of faculty members and administration without pressure from outside "religious" bodies or groups. Furthermore, the evidence gathered in this Study indicates a generally favorable attitude toward the place of religion in the college curriculum. The letters from university and college presidents were, on the whole, sympathetic to the idea that religion had a legitimate place in a total college education, and invited suggestions as to how this might best be accomplished. The Seminarian Questionnaire shows that students themselves are generally favorable in their judgment of the academic performance of religion teachers and departments of religion. Perhaps most telling is the favorable evaluation of college teachers, who are most likely to be critical on such matters. In the College Teachers Questionnaire, for example, 73.1% of teachers *not* teaching religion answered "yes" to the question: "Do you believe that formal courses in religion belong in all schools offering a liberal arts baccalaureate degree?" The percentage is not significantly smaller than the similar positive reply of religion teachers: 83.5% (Table 8).

A perplexing, and intriguing, question is why 14.6% of religion teachers answered "no" to the question. Half of those who answered "no" explained this on the basis that it would be "unconstitutional in state colleges and universities"—a common view, but never carried to a final legal decision in the highest courts—and half on the basis that it would be "educationally inappropriate in some schools." No doubt for some it might appear "inappropriate," but why to a college religion teacher? Is this another symptom of an academic inferiority complex?

It is particularly significant that the college teachers in other fields than religion are overwhelmingly of the opinion that religion has a place in a liberal arts education as a formal part of the curriculum because "the study of religion is concerned with a central aspect of human culture" (Table 8). This, together with the generally sympathetic attitude of university and college administrators, would argue that it is through the academic community itself, and in relation to its concern for the liberal arts tradition, that the place of religion in higher education is secured, and not through its connection with postgraduate professional studies. In fact, precisely this connection may endanger its academic position most in the long run.

Without implying any invidious judgments, it can be stated simply that the teaching of religion in college has a different orientation than the teaching of theology in seminary. In college or university, religion is a part of the curriculum (or should be) because religion is essential to culture and, in the West, the Christian religion is an integral factor, if not *the* integral factor, of Western civilization. This means that a true liberal education, whether offered in a church-related or secular institution, is neither liberal nor education if it does not provide for the teaching and learning of religion. And obviously this applies to all students, whatever their ultimate vocational intentions, for liberal education is no respecter of persons.

It is obvious that the teaching of theology in seminary has a different foundation. It is directly and indirectly related to the professional occupation-training of men for the ministry of the church. The difference is of sufficient magnitude to throw considerable doubt on the theories of those who posit an uninterrupted continuity between the theological teaching in college and that at seminary; it appears to betray a lack of understanding of the meaning of liberal education or theology, or perhaps of both.

In light of this, what are the implications for the understanding of the relation of pre-seminary education to theological training? The following provisional theses are proposed:

For the college and university, the purpose of teaching religion is to provide its students with a full education.
For the pre-seminary student, the reason for studying religion in college is to be fully educated and not to anticipate his theological study on the seminary level.
For the seminary, the purpose of pre-seminary education is to produce educated men—not little ministers.

Some consequences of these propositions should be explained. For one thing, the chronological continuity between the pre-seminary collegiate period and the seminary time should not be thought to be strictly mirrored in the relation between the liberal education provided in the one and the theological training provided in the other.

For another, undergraduate professional specialization and deliberate occupational anticipation in the choice of courses may be a handicap rather than a help in graduate study as well as a possible limitation in professional effectiveness in a career. In theology, as in other professional fields, there is the danger of an occupational indoctrination which leads to the "multiplication of highly trained specialists, who are, fundamentally, uneducated men," as President Stringfellow Barr of St. John's College put it.[23] Or as Jacques Maritain, in his Yale lectures on education, said: Liberal education was meant as a preparation "for human work and human leisure. But such education is killed by premature specialization."[24]

A recent book, *Toward the Liberally Educated Executive*, echoes this theme over and over again in reference to the world of business: "On one point all authorities have agreed, Narrow specialization is not enough. . . . Thus, there has been a growing call for 'breadth' in educational preparation for management, and a surprising degree of agreement on the need for more *liberal arts* in colleges. . . . "[25] Another striking confirmation of the same point comes from the former president of Carnegie Institute of Technology, Robert E. Doherty, in regard to engineering:

From personal experience, extending over a decade, in examining and following the professional progress of very large numbers of electrical and mechanical engineering graduates from over a hundred engineering colleges, it is my studied observation that they have acquired at college notable facility in certain routine engineering techniques; that they have in memory a large body of engineering information; that their long drill and experience in careful measurement and numerical calculation have engendered in them a quantitative sense, a profound respect for fact, and habits of thoroughness, orderliness, and accuracy, all of which are distinctive attributes of a scientific, professional mind. However, with all these recognized values, their college courses have left most of them at graduation mentally clumsy, relatively narrow in interest and perspective, and awkward in writing and speech. Their minds have not been sufficiently disciplined in straight thinking, and consequently they are lost when they encounter a problem which does not conform to certain special types. They are practically incapable of analyzing problems or situations in terms of general principles. They think narrowly in terms of special formulae and specific cases. Moreover, under the pressure of time they have not developed a real interest in other vital aspects of life. Without historical perspective, with little knowledge and almost no interest in the thoughts and lives of great thinking men in other fields, engineering graduates have tended to remain in the comparative isolation of technology. Now the sin of professional isolation is not confined to engineering; the same charge, it seems, might be leveled with justification at any of the other professions.[26]

Is this at all applicable to the college graduates who come to seminary for theological study? Recently, during an interview for a fellowship, a pre-seminary student, who according to his transcript had taken a course in art appreciation, was asked to give his reaction to a modern, abstract painting that happened to be hanging in the room. He said it meant nothing to him. "But," the interviewer said, "I thought you took an art course in college?" "I did," he replied, "but when we got up to 1850 we ran out of time." He apparently had no ability to translate the practical material into general principles and to apply these to new cases. He was, at least in this realm, uneducated, although he was intelligent, a college graduate, and planning for graduate study.

To put the point in its most bizarre form, a student may have graduated from college with a major in religion and appear on the front steps of the seminary as a basically uneducated person and therefore also basically unprepared for advanced theological study. As one seminary professor said of these types of "miniature theologians": "They know the answers—but they don't know the questions."

Saying this does not, it should be evident, prejudge the question of the function of a department of religion. It does suggest that such a department has its primary raison d'être in relation to the ultimate goals of liberal education rather than in producing prefabricated ministerial students for the seminaries. It is not inconceivable that a religion major may get a more comprehensive and well-integrated liberal education than one who majors in a more specialized and time-consuming liberal arts subject. However, assuming that a four-year liberal arts course cannot provide a full education to anyone, it is doubtful that a pre-seminary student would find such a major as broadening as it would be for the student who cannot look forward to additional theological study. In other words, a major in religion might be the core of a more truly liberal education for a future doctor or teacher, for example, than it would be for a future seminary student. Even if courses in religion taken by a pre-seminarian would anticipate what he might be expected to get in seminary, would these courses then be most relevant for the ordinary "lay" student going into another profession? The impression given by some courses in religion at the undergraduate level is that they are simply geared-down seminary offerings, a simplified rehash of courses the teacher himself may have taken in his seminary study. In brief, religion as taught at the collegiate stage should largely be determined in content and method by its liberal arts context.

The one irreplaceable, irreducible, essential quality of pre-seminary education is that it should be real education. One may define this in various ways. Robert Doherty, already quoted, has one list:

> What are the intellectual qualities to be cultivated in college? The first is the habit of scientific thought. This is ability to analyze a situation rationally and come to an intelligent, constructive, and trustworthy conclusion. . . . The second quality which should be aimed at is the ability to organize thoughts for clear, logical expression. This quality might have been defined more simply as the ability to write well. . . . The third essential quality is a *genuine grasp* of fundamental science. . . . The fourth is a historical perspective of social, economic, and institutional developments. . . . As a fifth quality I include cultural balance. . . . And finally I include the ability to cooperate in group activity.[27]

And Alfred North Whitehead has a very simple one-line definition: "Education is the acquisition of the art of the utilization of knowledge." But his book on *The Aims of Education* begins with another word, perhaps unexpected: "Culture," he says, "is activity of thought, and receptiveness to beauty and humane feeling. . . . What we should aim at producing is men who possess both culture and expert knowledge in some special direction."[28] This is reminiscent of Newman's words: "I say, a university, taken in its bare idea, and before we view it as an instrument of the Church, has this object and this mission; it contemplates neither moral impression nor mechanical production; it professes to exercise the mind neither in art nor in duty; its function is intellectual culture; here it may leave its scholars, and it has done its work when it has done as much as this."[29]

To sum up: *The task of pre-seminary education is cultivation and its purpose is to produce cultured men.*

The cultivated man is, in brief, one who has intellectual style. With the minimum of waste and the maximum of economy, and with what the Greek philosophers might call a "symphonic" comprehension of the reality of the world in which he lives and of which he is a part, the cultivated man uses the powers and talents which he has to their best advantage—that is, to the glory of God.

It may be felt that the intellectual aspects of pre-seminary education have been overstressed. But is not this stress a legitimate one in considering higher education? Worship, for example, may be tremendously fruitful as a "cultivator" of intellectual virtues, besides the more obvious and direct spiritual benefits which it confers. But as Leonard Hodgson once pointed out in a brilliant essay, prayer *may* become (and particularly in a Christian institution) "an evasive substitute for thinking."[30] *Corruptio optimi pessima.* We are called to worship the Lord our God with our minds, as well as with our hearts and souls—an institution of higher learning is the pre-eminent corporate embodiment of that obedience.

To put it in a paradoxical way, the task of undergraduate education during the pre-seminary period—the inadequacy of the term "pre-seminary education" should now be evident—is to make future ministers and theologians truly secular; it may be the last chance. They are, to be sure, not called to be *of* the world; but they are placed *in* it. To be "secular," then, is not to be less Christian but more; and the cultivated man, by recognizing the secular dust of which he is made and the secular culture of which he is a part, has a vision of the true nature of things which enables him to be in, but not of, this passing world. "The Word became flesh, and dwelt among us, full of grace and truth . . . for God so loved the world."

It is in that incarnational context that the task and function of the entire educational process is to be worked out. As John Henry Cardinal Newman wrote many years ago:

> For why do we educate, except to prepare for the world? Why do we cultivate the intellect of the many beyond the first elements of knowledge, except for this world? Will it much matter in the world to come whether our bodily health or whether our intellectual strength was more or less, except of course as this world is in all its circumstances a trial for the next? If then a university is a direct preparation for this world, let it be what it professes. It is not a convent, it is not a seminary; it is a place to fit men of the world for the world. We cannot possibly keep them from plunging into the world, with all its ways and principles and maxims, when their time comes; but we can prepare them against what is inevitable; and it is not the way to learn to swim in troubled waters never to have gone into them.[31]

It is this secular cultivation which is not only the best preparation of future students in the seminary, but even more important, the best background for the ministry in the world. When a student is thus secularized and thereby liberally educated—whether in a four-year college or not, or whatever his major might have been—he is ready for the professional training for the ministry he should expect to find in seminary.

FOOTNOTES

1. J. Allen Easley, "The 'Statement on Pre-Theological Studies,' " *Journal of Bible and Religion*, 25, July 1957, p. 212.

2. J. Arthur Baird, "Pre-Theological Training: An Empirical Study," *Journal of Bible and Religion*, 27, October 1959, p. 304.

3. J. Arthur Baird, "The Lilly Endowment Study of Pre-Seminary Education," *Journal of Bible and Religion*, 29, January 1961, p. 17.

4. *Cresset*, 25, May 1962, p. 9.

5. Milton D. McLean and H. H. Kimber, *The Teaching of Religion in State Universities: Descriptions of Programs in Twenty-five Institutions* (Office of Religious Affairs, University of Michigan, 1960).

6. *The Making of Ministers*, edited by Keith R. Bridston and Dwight W. Culver (Minneapolis: Augsburg Publishing House, 1964), p. 76.

7. *Ibid.*, p. 61.

8. "Princeton University's Graduate Program in Religion," *Journal of Bible and Religion*, 30, October 1962, pp. 291-8.

9. Clyde A. Holbrook, *Religion, a Humanistic Field* (Englewood Cliffs, N.J.; Prentice-Hall, Inc., 1963), p. 54. (By permission of Prentice-Hall, Inc.) It should be apparent that the conclusions of this Study are consistent with Holbrook's statement that "as religion needs constant confrontation with other humanistic studies, so they in turn require the challenge and supplementation which religion provides when it enters fully into the academic atmosphere of the college and university" (p. 54), but *not* with his recommendation that "the standard of admission to theological education should be a major or high degree of concentration in the field of religion" (p. 219).

10. Seymour Smith, "Religious Instruction in State Universities: A Report of Recent Trends," *Religious Education*, 53, May-June 1958, pp. 290-4.

11. A more detailed description of the various types of programs may be found in Milton D. McLean and H. H. Kimber, *op. cit.*, and in Robert Michaelsen's chapter, "Religious Education in Public Higher Education Institutions," in *Religious Education: A Comprehensive Survey*, Marvin J. Taylor, ed. (New York: Abingdon Press, 1960).

12. In his C. W. Hall Lectures, 1961.

13. "The Changing Face of Harvard College," *Saturday Review*, 46, October 19, 1963, pp. 62 f.

14. See Part Two, page 167 for the limits set by the term "pre-seminary education."

15. *The Making of Ministers*, p. 140.

16. Ramsey, *op. cit.*, pp. 295 f.

17. *The Making of Ministers*, pp. 100 f. (reprinted from *Theology Today*, January, 1961).

18. J. Arthur Baird, "Pre-Theological Training: An Empirical Study," *Journal of Bible and Religion*, 27, October 1959, p. 309.

19. J. Arthur Baird, "The Lilly Endowment Study of Pre-Seminary Education," *Journal of Bible and Religion*, 29, January 1961, p. 17.

20. *The American Scholar Reader*, copyright 1944, © 1960 by United Chapters of Phi Beta Kappa (New York: Atheneum Publishers, 1960), p. 123.

21. See "The Multiversity: Are Its Several Souls Worth Saving?" *Harpers Magazine*, 227, November 1963, p. 38.

22. *Christian Education*, 32, September 1949, pp. 226 ff.

23. *Report of the President*, July, 1942.

24. *Education at the Crossroads* (New Haven: Yale University Press, 1943), pp. 58 f.

25. Frederic E. Pamp, Jr., "Liberal Arts as Training for Executives," in *Toward the Liberally Educated Executive*, edited by Robert A. Goldwin and Charles A. Nelson (New York: Mentor, 1960), p. 54.

26. *Development of Professional Education* (Pittsburgh: Carnegie Press, 1950), pp. 5 f.

27. *Ibid.*, pp. 24 f.

28. Alfred North Whitehead, *The Aims of Education* (New York: Macmillan Company, 1949), p. 13. (By permission of Macmillan.)

29. *The Idea of a University* (New York: Doubleday Image, 1959), p. 149.

30. *Essays in Christian Philosophy* (London: Longmans, Green, 1930), p. 162.

31. *Ibid.*, p. 236.

CHAPTER FOUR

PROFESSIONAL TRAINING

In an interview the president of a distinguished seminary on the East Coast during the course of the Study suggested to the directors that the curricular revision and adjustment necessary to integrate pre-seminary and seminary education could be achieved through an intensive weekend conference between the proponents of the various institutional interests and educational policies involved. This sanguine appraisal of the scope and dimensions of the problem may be shared by some of the theological educators in the seminaries and colleges. But not by most. The symposium *The Making of Ministers,* published in connection with this Study, reveals the widely divergent educational philosophies current in present-day ministerial training. The viewpoints presented by the essayists in the volume are not likely to be reconciled easily or quickly; they differ not only on the solutions they offer to the problems presented in integrating pre-seminary and seminary education, but they disagree at many points on their analyses of what the problems are. Furthermore, their theological and educational presuppositions, on which these solutions and analyses are based, are also evidently contradictory. What is theology? What is the ministry? It is on such crucial fundamentals that there is widespread confusion and lack of consensus in the North American theological community. As long as that is so there seems little likelihood that a coherent and functional pattern of ministerial education can be developed. We are not sure whom we are training, or in what. Is it surprising we cannot agree on *how* it should be done?

H. Richard Niebuhr, in *The Purpose of the Church and Its Ministry*, used such sharp terms as "uncertainty of purpose," "pluralism and harassment," "lack of unity," "multiplicity and indefiniteness of purpose," "inertia and conservatism," "perplexity," "repetitiveness of individual actions and lack of great unifying conceptions," and "uncertainty of aim" to describe theological schools in America as he observed them in a lifetime of teaching and through his Carnegie Study.[1] Conrad Bergendoff, in his report *The Lutheran Church in America and Theological Education*, writes of finding "evidence of much uneasiness about the place of the seminary in America today."[2] Other observers echo similar criticisms.

Whether such critics are overly pessimistic is debatable. It is evident, however, that the seminaries as a whole find themselves in a transitional period in which their traditional role and function is being thoroughly re-examined. Changes in the place of the church in society, a new understanding of the nature of the ministry and particularly of the place of the laity within it, a fresh appreciation of the secular world as God's dominion, are only some of the factors challenging deeply traditional theological institutions. As Dr. Bergendoff puts it, "An atmosphere of unreality rests on much of theological education today, sensed by the student probably more than by the faculty member, but inspiring in both an apprehensiveness that robs the seminary of an authority it once possessed."[3]

One of the hopeful things uncovered in this Study is the fact that there is widespread concern among seminary educators over these issues. Every seminary visited, in all parts of the continent and representing a wide spectrum of ecclesiastical and theological orientations, gave evidence of struggling with their *raison d'être*, and in none was there unqualified complacency or self-satisfaction over what they are or what they are now doing.

But it is exactly this ferment, together with the self-scrutiny and experimentation in new methods and curricula arising from it among the seminaries, which makes definitions of "pre-seminary" training so difficult to pin down. The preparation for seminary cannot be discussed intelligibly if what comes after it is not taken into consideration. As long as the seminaries are in flux it is next to impossible to prescribe a rational educational preparation for them. It has long been obvious that a poor college preparation may undermine the educational standards of seminaries. What has not been so obvious is that, conversely, a poor seminary education may negate a good college preparation. A well-trained student from a first-rate college can find a second-rate seminary education a frustrating experience. And such students, if they suspect that seminary training represents an academic decline in comparison with their college work, are likely not to turn up in seminary at all. This may be borne out by a fact that emerges from the Seminarian Questionnaire: Seminarians tend to be very average college students (See Table 59). Superior students are not being attracted to the seminaries in significant numbers. This fact, combined with the realization that upward social mobility is an evident factor in drawing men to the ministry, means that seminary education may appear to some the only open door academically to "graduate" study and eventual professional status.[4] It suggests that the seminaries, and the ministry recruitment agencies of the churches, may have to take the index of academic accomplishment in college much more seriously in screening candidates than has been done in the past.

Dr. Bergendoff, in his report on Lutheran Church in America theological education, makes a point which on the basis of the findings of this Study would appear to have general applicability: "One of the most surprising results of the survey was the academic standing of the students revealed by the records. We have long lived under the impression that the ministry has attracted the best of our college graduates. It comes as a shock, therefore, to find that in all our seminaries there were in 1962-63 only 117 students with an average of A from their college. The college grades of all students were distributed thus:

A: 117 — 11%
B: 313 — 30%
C: 427 — 41%
C—: 183 — 18%

"Almost 60% were in a C classification, which means that this number would have difficulty in gaining admission to graduate schools in other fields."

Dr. Bergendoff anticipates the objections to taking college grade averages too seriously in recruiting and training pastors by arguing that if C students can make good pastors "are we to assume that A and B students will not make good, or even better pastors?" The fact that "the Lord can use men with limited intellectual endowments . . . does not excuse a church which cannot attract its most gifted men into this high calling." He fears the church may already have lost its leadership in current thinking because of its inability to compete with other professions and graduate fields of study in drawing superior students into the ministry.

He counters the argument that "college grades are not always the best measurement of a man's ability" by citing the experience of a large corporation, American Telephone and Telegraph, which on the basis of a survey of 17,000 college men in business found that "The single most reliable predictive indication of a college graduate's success in the Bell System is his rank in his graduating class." Here again it may be said that "success" in the ministry and in a large business corporation are not comparable. However, the particular form of the Protestant ministry does place great weight on intellectual ability. As a president of a small independent college, widely recognized for its high academic standards, said in an interview for this Study: "I can think of no other profession which places such great intellectual demands on its practitioners as the ministry—or where stupidity is more disastrous." He expressed distress at the small number of graduates from his institution who were going into the ministry, and even more at the apparent lack of initiative of the churches in competing with others recruiting students for advanced study in such "secular" but first-rate colleges.

Finally, Dr. Bergendoff is disturbed by the results on the academic level in seminaries of this low standard for entrance. It is not only demoralizing for the better students, but may well be decisive in determining which kind of men do and do not choose to enter seminary and go into the ministry. His solution is that the seminaries have "the right and the obligation" to ask that applicants prove themselves good students in college, and proposes that seminaries might follow the example of graduate schools in many universities by *requiring* a B average for entrance.

Raising the academic standards of seminaries is, of course, no cure-all for them, or for the church in raising up successive generations of effective ministers. It must also be admitted that providing adequate numbers of ministers for the churches is a legitimate concern, which an upgrading of academic entrance requirements for seminaries could militate against. However, this might only be a temporary effect; in the long run the higher standards may in themselves help to solve the problem of numbers of ministerial candidates. Quality attracts quantity. In any case, as St. Thomas Aquinas wrote: "Should it ever become impossible to maintain the present number, it is better to have a few good priests than a multitude of bad ones. . . . God never abandons His Church; and so the number of priests will be always sufficient for the needs of the faithful, provided the worthy are advanced and the unworthy sent away."[5]

This illustrates a basic conclusion of the Lilly Endowment Study of Pre-Seminary Education: The seminary is the fulcrum of theological education. In the last analysis, it is the seminaries which can provide the point of leverage for lifting the academic standards or altering the shape of ministerial education. The seminaries alone can determine which students should be admitted and what academic caliber they should be to pursue theological studies. If they wish to fill their classrooms with C students, this is their own business: the colleges cannot decide this for them. Nor is there any chance that a rational system of pre-seminary education is going to be provided if it is assumed that this will be achieved by unifying the multifarious character of American higher education. Again it is the seminaries which must decide what is a relevant and effective pre-seminary education and embody these principles in their entrance requirements. Only then can a student tailor his undergraduate course, whatever type of college he may be in, to meet these requirements; and only in this way can colleges seek to provide the necessary curricular offerings, insofar as it is within their capabilities to fit in with these demands.

This is one of the chief reasons why in a pre-seminary study it has been found necessary to focus attention on seminary education itself. One denominational seminary reports: "The majority of our students come from one institution." And in Canada the relatively smaller number of universities and their general homogeneous academic ethos make the integration of college and seminary education a less complex problem. But on the whole, even where the traditional pattern of church college—church seminary sequence remains the standard for the majority of students, a wide variety—probably increasing—of types of colleges and major fields of study is found represented in the student body. In this situation, the only effective controlling factor in providing efficient integration and continuity between undergraduate studies and seminary education is the policy of the seminary, both through its entrance requirements and its curricular structure.

This does not mean, however, that the seminaries are able to set this policy by themselves. The basic thesis of this Study is that the education of a relevant and competent ministry is a *totality,* an *integral process,* in which college education, seminary training, and professional experience all have their essential and distinctive functions. The colleges, the seminaries, the churches, all have their responsibilities for the whole process. If each is pursuing its concerns independently, without awareness of the other educational elements that are being provided in other ways and through other means, integration becomes impossible. Fragmentation results—mainly to the detriment of the student, who presumably is the crux of all these efforts. Therefore, though the seminary is the institutional fulcrum for changing the pattern and the only effective point in the educational sequence where a theological education policy can be injected to influence the whole pattern, the policy itself needs to be worked out with all the other parties involved in the enterprise—including, it should not be forgotten, the students themselves and the "ex-students"— the ministers, and, not least, the laity—who in the long run are most affected by the results.

The value of this comprehensive approach was indicated by the series of regional consultations sponsored by this Study in Minneapolis, Chicago, Atlanta, Claremont–Los Angeles, and Dallas. Representatives of colleges, seminaries, and church agencies found the meetings mutually stimulating and in several cases agreed to continue the discussions on a regular basis. But the participants admitted that they should have met before and the consultations revealed embarrassment at the discovery that relatively close academic and ecclesiastical "neighbors" had not met one another, even in cases where they had taught the same students and were actually members of the same denominational educational system. This substantiated the feelings of some college teachers of religion that theological education has tended to be segregated, with almost a caste line between college and seminary theologians. One of the contributions of this Study will have been in helping to break down these barriers and in establishing communications within the whole theological community. It may also have facilitated a frank and unprejudiced consideration of the legitimate differences between the approaches of those teaching theology in the seminary and those teaching theology in the "academy," as Paul Ramsey of Princeton has argued persuasively in The Christian Scholar, both of which are valid and both of which are fruitful contributions to theological science and are in an ultimate sense "church service."[6]

This may also help to clarify the distinction between two terms often used interchangeably: "pre-seminary" and "pre-theological." As the essays of Martin Marty and Arnold Nash in The Making of Ministers make clear, the term "pre-theological" is the much broader one, both in its academic and philosophic connotations. The term "pre-seminary" is more precise. It is, among other things, professionally oriented and, unlike "pre-theological," lends itself more easily to educational rationalization and curricular treatment. It is for this reason, and not simply because the Study is so named, that the focus in this report is on the pre-seminary and seminary relationship. At the same time, clarification of this segment of the problem may elucidate those more general aspects of theological education to which the term "pre-theological" is more appropriately applied. In this way again, the role and function of the seminary itself is the touchstone for the whole complex of issues now debated under the rubric of theological education.

The dangers of confusion at this point are illustrated by Paul Ramsey's essay in *The Making of Ministers* which makes what many have considered the best "case" for college departments of religion. He shows the inevitable complexities and ambiguities of integrating the theological resources of both colleges and seminaries in the theological enterprise. However, because he has touched on many of the deeper theological and institutional factors involved and has not simply concerned himself with superficial curricular manipulations, he has in certain respects raised more perplexing questions than he has answered.

This is said less in criticism than in appreciation of the breadth of his argument, which supports the conclusion of this Study that the relation between pre-seminary and seminary education cannot be adequately explicated in purely curricular terms. For example, he is particularly interested in finding a pattern which "keeps clear the distinction between elementary liberal arts education and graduate professional studies"; it is his thesis that only when the importance of religion in the college curriculum is recognized by the seminaries will they "stand for graduate theological work."

The main thrust of his essay is to rehabilitate the academic respectability of theology as one of the fundamental scientific disciplines of the university. A college which provides less scholarly resources for theological study than for other fields, such as literature, history, or the natural sciences, is providing less than a full liberal education for its students. He believes that even when seminaries are attached to universities as integral schools, this in no way removes "theological study from among the primary tasks of the college." Indeed, in his opinion, such cases afford "a special opportunity to demonstrate that they were meant, and mean, to build firmly and directly upon the foundation of a full course in the study of religion, theology, Bible, philosophy of religion, church history, biblical languages, etc., at the college 'level.'" He looks forward to that day "when graduates with majors in this (religion) department may be regarded as normative for admission to seminary, and the deficiency in the backgrounds of other admittees be measured accordingly."

There is reason to doubt—on the purely strategic level—whether the recognition by seminary of college departments of religion as their preparatory counterparts will necessarily commend theology as a respectable scientific discipline in the university community at large. In fact, there might be a suspicion among skeptics that this indicated the college theological forces were not confident of being able to stand on their own feet intellectually in their own academic community and were therefore turning to their seminary "older brothers" for institutional support.

There is also the question whether the understanding of seminaries as basically graduate schools of theology is not too limited and restrictive. Ramsey uses the phrase "graduate theological work" to describe the task of the seminaries. But if the analogy is drawn from other academic disciplines, such an undergraduate-graduate progression in theological study would logically lead to the doctorate, and also, presumably, toward a career in teaching. Is the minister pre-eminently a teacher? Should he be trained as such? This is precisely the criticism leveled at seminaries by C. Umhau Wolf in *The Making of Ministers:* he thinks they are too academically oriented already and not sufficiently related to parish life. Paul Holmer makes much the same critique in his introductory essay in his discussion of the difference between the language *of* faith and the language *about* faith and proposes as one corrective a more active role of the congregations themselves in the training of ministers.

Those who have been most critical of the lack of integration *between* undergraduate and seminary theological education seem to be relatively sanguine about the general form of seminary education itself. Their proposals in effect envisage the classical seminary curriculum projected backwards into the undergraduate level. But what of Dean Liston Pope's view expressed in an address to the A.A.T.S. meeting in 1950 that "despite the tampering that has occurred around the edges, the theological curriculum is still largely medieval in structure and purpose"? If this charge of anachronism is at all justified, seminaries need to take a long, hard look at whether such an education is giving future ministers adequate and relevant training.

Some college teachers of religion have protested that "the seminary is not the church," meaning by that the importance of the theological contribution of both college and seminary teachers to the life of the church. On the other hand, the college department of religion is not likely to prove the point by becoming a "little seminary." For if undergraduate departments of religion are not simply, or even primarily, preparing future ministers for seminary study, but providing theological education for the whole body of the church—future clergy and laity—there is reason for thinking that a "largely medieval" curriculum is even more inappropriate in the college department than it is in the theological seminary. Indeed, there is a real possibility that the experimentation of college religion departments in finding ways of presenting theology in the most appropriate and effective way to the general academic community may be showing the way for the seminaries in their theological work rather than vice versa.

If there are serious reservations about the relevance of the traditional forms of seminary training in preparing competent ministers, there must be considerable reservations about any new plans of pre-seminary education based on integration with these forms. Superficial curricular adjustment to make such an accommodation (which would mean, in the long run, only the extension of the present seminary form of theological education into the college world) is doomed to futility. For to seek ways in which undergraduate training, in theology or otherwise, can be related to and integrated with seminary training *as it now is* fails to take seriously the possibility that Richard Niebuhr and others have been right when they have found "participation of the schools in the confusion of churches and ministers" about the ultimate purpose of the church and the ministry.

This "confusion" is not likely to be dispersed easily, for the answers to some of the dilemmas rest in theological issues which are only beginning to be thoroughly examined. Nevertheless, the "uncertainty of aim" in seminary education appears to be closely related to some of the major concerns of this Study, which may be approached in a more pragmatic and empirical way within an educational context.

For example, one of the underlying sources of the confusion may be the blurred self-image of the seminaries. They cannot, as one observer has put it, "decide whether they are to be graduate schools to produce theologians or professional-trade schools to prepare parish pastors." This schizophrenic attitude almost inevitably means that neither is done well. The history of ministerial training in America throws some light on the reasons for this personality-split of the seminaries in which the striving to raise academic standards in theological education has always been in tension with the practical demands of expanding American churches for greater numbers of ministers. The anxiety so openly expressed by denominational officials and seminary administrators over the supposed decline of ministerial candidates recently is evidence of this "production" mentality in regard to seminaries.[7]

On the other side, the seminaries are caught in the high degree of competition between the professions both for talent and for status in which an occupation must be able to "document its high status . . . by being able to take its pick of the young people about to enter the labor market, and then to keep them in school a long time before admitting them to the charmed circle."[8] This requires, as Everett Hughes says, scholastic ability, ambition, and financial means—especially the latter—and can be realized only when "reinforced by the expectation of good income and high prestige." As he goes on to point out:

Not all occupations which aspire to professional standing can promise enough of either of these ingredients to get the most talented and then to keep them in school as long as do medicine, law and the sciences. Characteristically they seek to improve their position in both recruitment and the education system; in the earlier phases of their move toward professionalism, the people in an occupation may have to earn their way slowly and painfully to higher education, and the professional school may have difficulty in getting itself accepted in universities. It may take an operation bootstrap to get a corps of people in the occupation academically qualified to teach succeeding generations and grant them professional degrees. This competition for status is accompanied by a trend toward prolonging the professional training at both ends: at the beginning by multiplying prerequisites for entry to professional school, at the finish by prolonging the course and the various apprentice or internship programs.[9]

Furthermore, as Bernard Barber suggests in an article on "The Sociology of the Professions" in the same issue of the *Proceedings of the American Academy of Arts and Sciences:*

Nearly all the well-established professions are located in some measure in the university; the more professional ones, according to our definition, having the more university-connected schools. Within a given profession, the "better" or more professional schools are more likely to be in a university, and the very best ones are typically in the very best universities. Where a well-established profession is not, for some special reasons, located in the university, it has usually sought to construct an institution that approximates one. . . . As we shall also see, the emerging or marginal professions, when they are trying to raise standards for themselves, seek to locate themselves in universities. If they already have a marginal connection there, they seek to improve their position in the university.[10]

These analyses may help to explain why most seminaries, whether university-connected or not, are caught in this schizophrenic tension between their church-oriented role as a producer of ministers and their academically-oriented role as a graduate school in the status competition with other graduate university-type studies. This is accentuated in ministerial education more than in other occupations because of the institutional strength of the churches which provide an impressive counterbalance to the institutional strength of the universities, and which offer the promise of vocational security over against the less tangible inducements of status and prestige offered by the university alone.

In other words, the ministry has not needed to depend on the university connection of its schools of professional studies as much as some other professions to achieve or maintain its professional status in society. This situation may, however, be changing. And if there is a feeling that the ministry is losing status as a profession, the importance of recognizing the general status criteria for professional recognition—particularly the university-connection or university-resemblance of its professional education—may become increasingly important. This may be exactly the reason why seminary education—pulled between the demands of the churches and the status requirements of the professions — has become schizophrenic about its role and its goals.

There are several paradoxical aspects to this. While there is increasing uncertainty about the professional status of the ministry (which the clamor for more distinguished seminary degrees —especially a doctorate, such as Doctor of Religion or Doctor of Ministry—may reflect), theological education has never been on such a high academic level. As the Niebuhr report, *The Advancement of Theological Education,* indicates: "In general it appears that there were four times as many genuinely graduate schools of theology in the United States and Canada in 1955 as there were in 1923," and shows that whereas at the time of the Kelly report, *Theological Education in America,* in 1924 and the May-Brown report, *The Education of American Ministers,* in 1934 approximately 44 per cent and 50 per cent, respectively, of all theological students did not hold college degrees, in the mid-1950's it was estimated "that not less than 80 per cent of the estimated total enrollment of theological students" were college graduates.[11] The analogous figure from this Study's Seminarian Questionnaire based on 1962 enrollments is 88.9 per cent: of the

B.D. and S.T.B. candidates 76 per cent indicate they have B.A. degrees and 13 per cent B.S. degrees, and 2 per cent an M.A. (presupposing an undergraduate baccalaureate degree also). Thus both in regard to the academic status of theological institutions and the academic accomplishments of theological students a remarkable rise in standards has been seen within a relatively brief period. But, paradoxically, at this very time, as James Gustafson of Yale has put it: "The bulk of the Protestant clergy in the United States . . . suffer from acute *anomie*. . . . The Protestant minister's normlessness is not merely institutional; it exists for many ministers in the realm of belief as well. . . . This situation is felt to be a deep and agonizing crisis for many of the most sensitive and educated clergy."[12]

It would appear, therefore, that the rise in the academic level of theological education has accentuated rather than alleviated the schizophrenic feelings of the seminaries. For the better their students are and the more highly they train them, the more these students seem to be alienated from the churches. Gustafson quotes the quip of a Protestant theologian: "The task of the seminary is to unfit men for the ministry as the churches define it today." This might be taken to mean that with their theological understanding of the church and their greater sociological sensitivity to the cultural context for church service, such "unfit" men are actually the means through which the churches are to be changed and renewed. In so doing, the seminaries still serve the churches.

Another paradoxical aspect to this situation, however, is that the "unfitting" of men by the seminaries seems to happen in another and less positive way. That is, seminaries may be serving one of their chief functions as professional schools for their students in training them for other types of church service than the parish ministry. They may be not only "unfitting" them theologically, but also functionally, for professional work as ministers of local congregations. This may be explained in part by the fact that, like most other fields, the ministry is increasingly diversified in its specializations. The parish ministry is still the "standard" form of ministerial service, but it is a specialization among other specializations. As a student goes through seminary he is exposed to this variety of occupational possibilities in the ministry, partly through the fact that many seminary curricula make provisions for such specialized preparation; in some schools the student's choice is actually forced by the necessity of concentrating in a particular area of specialization during his studies, much as a college major field of study. In any case, the generalized choice of the ministry with which a student enters a seminary is likely to be focused on a specialized ministry by the time he leaves. As has been said, the parish ministry is one among these specialities, though it is often true that it appears to be the "leftover" on the specialization smörgåsbord, something one chooses if there is nothing else remaining.

In most seminaries, however, such tailored curricula for specializations do not exist. In view of this, one of the most astonishing facts which has come to light through this Study is the relatively small proportion of seminary students who see the parish ministry as their eventual occupational goal in the ministry. Only slightly more than one-third of all seminarians in the United States and Canada plan to serve in the parish ministry "eventually." About two-thirds of all seminarians expect to enter the parish ministry "immediately after seminary," however. The breakdown of results on Question 23 of the Seminarian Questionnaire: "Although there may be some degree of uncertainty in your mind, in which vocational areas will you probably serve immediately after seminary? eventually?" is as follows (A more detailed analysis is found in Part Two):

	Immediately after seminary	Eventually
Parish ministry	68%	33%
Educational ministry in local church	7	3
Campus ministry	3	5
College or seminary teaching	4	17
Full-time evangelism	1	2
Music ministry in local church	2	1
Denominational administration	—	3
Interdenominational administration	—	1
Military chaplaincy	3	3
Institutional chaplaincy	1	4
Missions	6	9
Other	4	4
No answer	4	19

Many problematical factors enter into the interpretation of these statistics. Why do so few seminarians see the parish ministry as the vocational area in which they are likely to serve in the long run? Obviously, their expectations at this stage in their career are neither binding on them, nor are they absolutely determinative of their ultimate vocational destination. Nevertheless, it is strikingly evident that among this generation of seminary students the parish ministry does not have a strong vocational appeal. This is underlined by the fact that such a large number expect to enter the parish ministry immediately after seminary, but expect to move out of it eventually. This would suggest that their immediate post-seminary plans are not based on a positive vocational decision but on a realistic appraisal of where they are likely to find a job when their training is finished. Furthermore, though it might be argued that the 19% who give no answer in respect to their eventual vocational expectations will probably go into the parish, even if they were to do so their present indecision would reflect a somewhat negative judgment on this probable prospect.

It might also be said that those who decide to enter the parish ministry after leaving seminary may be making a positive vocational choice and are not simply drifting into it, or being forced by practical factors such as finances or the gradual elimination of viable alternatives during the course of time. The responses to the Ministers Questionnaire would seem to substantiate this for a number of ministers.

The fact remains, however, that *during seminary* the vocational potentialities of the parish as an area of full-time ministerial service do not seem to strike the imagination of present-day ministerial candidates. It is no secret that the image of the parish pastor and/or the local congregation being projected today, especially among the intellectual "elite" in the academic worlds of the colleges and seminaries, is not an attractive one. These negative stereotypes of the church and the ministry circulating in such circles, and increasingly penetrating among the more critical and perceptive laity, may or may not be warranted by the actual practice of the pastors and the congregations. In some cases they are and in many others they are not. But such criticism, and even cynicism, about the traditional forms of ministry and congregational life is bound to infect seminarians and, at the least, make them hesitant and uncertain about their vocational plans for a traditional pattern of ministry, especially if it only guarantees personal "maceration" (Joseph Sittler), institutional "suburban captivity" (Gibson Winter), and the life-long "noise of solemn assemblies" (Peter Berger). Who would ask for that? Spiritual masochists—perhaps.

A contributing factor to the fostering of a generation of "uncertain servants" (Walter Wagoner), and perhaps a decisive one, is the character of the seminaries themselves. If, on one hand, the seminaries are exposing the weaknesses, the faults, and the failures of the classical forms of ministerial service and parish life (which is the right and responsibility of the seminaries as a part of their service to the churches), but, on the other hand, neither projecting viable alternatives nor giving their students the necessary practical training to actually function in—and thus to change—such forms, is there any mystery about why seminarians should be "uncertain" and why they are searching so diligently for vocational avenues of escape from the parish ministry?

The increasing variety of specializations in the ministry is a necessary and inevitable concomitant to the increasing complexity of social and ecclesiastical existence in our time. The "general practitioner" in both medicine and the ministry may be on the way out for that reason alone. This case is, however, far from proven, and the often assumed institutional bankruptcy of the classical one-minister congregation may be presumptuous and soliloquies over its demise premature. Certainly in the next generation or two, however much it is changed in the future, the "ordinary" congregation, with the form of ministry which it imposes, will remain as it has been—the organizational cornerstone of church life in North America.

What, then, are the seminaries doing? According to their catalogs and other written statements of purpose—especially publicity brochures—most seminaries claim their first and major purpose is to "train ministers" and particularly "parish ministers."

But is that in fact what they are doing? Or is it what they should
be doing?

One glaring disjunction between these common claims of seminaries and their actual performance is found in the fact that if,
as they say, their *primary* task is the preparation of parish ministers, and their curriculum is so structured, then they are providing an education which is appropriate to and oriented towards
the vocational intentions of only one-third of their students! It
may be argued that a great part of the seminary curriculum is
appropriate for *any* kind of ministry. This may be so, though
serious questions can be raised about the effectiveness of a
"broad, liberal theological education" in providing real professional competence in any particular vocational area of specialization. It may also be argued that a much larger proportion of seminarians will end up in the parish ministry eventually than intend
to do so during seminary. This is also true; but the fact remains
that those who have not yet decided in seminary to go into the
parish ministry, and those who have other vocational plans (which
together make up the large majority of seminarians), must inevitably feel a certain frustration in undergoing a course which
is, presumably at least, directed towards this particular vocational
area. The written comments on the Seminarian Questionnaire
and conversations with students and faculty members of seminaries give evidence of this loss of morale among many seminarians during their course of study, partly related to the apparent "irrelevance" of the seminary curriculum to their special
vocational interests and plans.

Ironically, the seminary course of study may not even be primarily relevant to its oft-declared purpose of preparing parish
ministers. As Paul Holmer writes in *The Making of Ministers:*
"As matters now stand, seminaries are becoming more and more
like universities . . . more and more like liberal arts colleges,
where the learning is best when it is least professional."[13] Engaged in a competitive race with other professions in which status
is determined partly through the approximation of the course of
professional study to university graduate-type education, and
increasingly sophisticated in the paraphernalia of "learned" schol-

arship research, the seminaries are as a whole more accurately described as graduate departments of theology (whether formally connected with a university or not) than professional schools for the ministry.

It may be welcomed by some and deplored by others, but if a seminary is considered to be engaged in both "graduate theological work" (Ramsey) and professional ministerial training, the present problems of seminary education are related not so much to its "graduate" character as to its "professional" character. More and more, seminaries display the marks of graduate education, university-style, and less and less the marks of ministerial training, professional-style. This "rise" in academic standards and the increasing university-style of the seminaries have been acclaimed by those who are concerned for the status and advancement of "theological scholarship" in America. The development has been hailed as the end of "trade-school" attitudes towards seminary training.

This may be so. But it should not be assumed that such academically-oriented and scholastically-styled education is not in itself "professional" training. It has a professional function and direction, but it is not primarily aimed at the parish. It is directed towards the academy itself. University-style theological education has a functional rationality: It is functionally related to the university and it is professionally oriented towards preparing men for teaching. Accidentally, as it were, and through the vestigial curricular remains of an educational pattern originally intended to prepare men for the parish ministry, this new academically oriented theological education is not totally irrelevant in the preparation of those going into other than the teaching ministry. However, it makes most sense and functionally is most effective in educating those whose professional intention is to become a teacher and/or research scholar.

This may be one clue why, according to the returns from the Seminarian Questionnaire, "college or seminary teaching" is by far the most popular alternative choice to the parish ministry as the anticipated eventual vocational field for theological students. For obvious reasons, only 4% of the seminarians expect to enter college or seminary teaching immediately after seminary, but 17% look forward to this possibility "eventually." This large percentage is even more impressive as a preferred choice when it is recognized that most of those who give this preference are likely to appreciate the scholastic ability and the advanced academic degrees required for this area of service; perhaps a significant number of the 19% who give "no answer" to their eventual vocational plans would also make college or seminary teaching their first preference, but have realistically ruled themselves out on these grounds.

One of the curiosities of the returns from the Seminarian Questionnaire is that though more than half of the seminarians have had experience as pastors and/or assistant pastors, only one-third intend to become parish ministers; thus a major function of the seminary is, and may be so anticipated by many students, to give parish ministers the training necessary to go into some other vocational field!

That a teaching career has such a strong attraction among the vocational "searchers" in seminaries, despite the limited openings available in the field and the considerable additional educational requirements demanded, is another indication that seminary education itself is functionally oriented towards academic professionalism. For those who are looking for an alternative to the parish ministry, the seminary course appears to be most self-validating educationally as a preparation for teaching. The "medieval" seminary curriculum in its standard form does not easily validate itself as a functional professional preparation for the parish ministry. The problem of functional "translation" is not so acute for teaching—even the most abstract "impractical" courses have relevance and utilitarian value for the future teacher, not only as general preparation but even as the raw materials and prototypes for similar courses to be given later by the student when he in turn becomes a teacher. The similarity in the titles and subject matter of college courses in religion to the seminary courses which the college teachers once took—and which makes some college departments of religion appear as "little seminaries"—is symptomatic of this.

It will be no easy task to introduce some order and rationality into this chaotic jungle of varied vocational intentions and educational preparations of students and institutional contradictions between stated purposes and functional operations of theological schools. Two major steps will be required to clear the ground before a systematic reconstruction can be undertaken.

In the first place, a functional criterion needs to be applied to a rational division of labor in theological education.

Both a theological seminary and a graduate school of religion are *functionally* professional institutions. In theory, at least, a seminary is primarily oriented towards the professional training of ministers, and particularly parish ministers. A graduate school is also engaged in professional training, but its functional orientation is towards the preparation of teachers and research scholars. Both types may be engaged in an educational task more diverse than this, but each has its own special professional *raison d'être*, and this determines its distinctive character and ethos.

In this sense, the two types of institutions, though comparable, need not be competitive. There may even be a considerable degree of similarity in their curricular structure and in the content of their courses, but the integrative factor is the functional aim of the whole professional training for each. For this reason the old dualism between *episteme* and *techne*, which has bedeviled theological educators in trying to develop well-balanced curricula, applies to both. Seminary training cannot be identified with *techne* and graduate school study with *episteme*. Both include the two elements, which must in both cases be maintained in dialectical equilibrium.

Nor should it be assumed that one type of education is "higher" than another. Functional effectiveness rather than scholastic sophistication is the valid criterion of judgment for professional education. As C. Umhau Wolf has put it:

Those who emphasize the so-called "graduate school" education and better (or more prestigious) degrees to indicate it as graduate education are not necessarily offering the ultimate panacea. . . . Those who emphasize the fact that the seminary must be a graduate school debate the issue as if there were only one alternative to good professional graduate training, namely a "mere" trade school. . . . A pastor . . . has the same right to expect academic excellence, theological integrity, and biblical understanding as the aspiring college teacher of religion.[14]

Unless theological institutions attain some degree of clarity about their functional aims as professional training schools, they are not only likely to be in an unrealistic competition with one another but their own educational integrity is bound to be compromised. A seminary, for example, which, unconsciously or deliberately, operates as a graduate school of theology while claiming to be engaged in training ministers probably will be a second-rate graduate school and at the same time will fail to prepare men effectively for the parish ministry. Or a graduate school of theology in a university may claim to be training men for the parish ministry, for example, and in the process neglect its own special scholastic tasks and jeopardize its status within the academic community.

This clarification of functional aims and purposes may be achieved in part through a realistic appraisal of the resources which are available to an institution, as well as its strategic position in the organizational structure of a church. A small denominational seminary, to take one illustration, is not likely to have the academic resources in faculty, student body, or library and research facilities to operate effectively as a graduate school of theology preparing men for teaching careers. On the other hand, its ecclesiastical position and its closeness to the life of the congregations make it peculiarly suitable for the professional training of parish ministers. If its total resources are so used and the whole educational process effectively rationalized for this professional purpose, there is no reason why its academic standards should not be at the highest level.

A large university divinity school, to take another example, may appear to have the resources to function effectively as a professional training school for a number of different kinds of ministry, including the parish ministry. But this does not always work out so happily in practice. The so-called "practical" departments, which are more directed towards congregational ministries, tend to be looked down upon by the students and teachers in more theoretical and academically more "respectable" fields as inferior. As a professor in a large interdenominational seminary in the East put it: "Our students couldn't be more detached from the church; they actually consider it 'humiliating' if they have to go into the parish ministry." The academic ethos of such institutions, basically scholastically-oriented, which may offer the free atmosphere for unbiased and untrammeled research and writing, at the same time often represents an isolation from the grass-roots life of the churches and may, as Reuel Howe points out, only produce a minister who "soon discovers that the biblical and theological language in which he was trained and on which he based his hopes is not understood by most of his people." When he has been "ejected from this womb of theological coziness" he finds that "the world does not operate on the same presuppositions or that it is not motivated by the same orientations."[15]

The point to all this is that each theological institution must decide what functionally it is best equipped to do in professional training and then set about doing it in the most effective way. This implies, of course, that there will be a wide variety of patterns of professional theological education, for not only is there a wide variety of types of theological institutions but also there is an increasing number of ministerial specializations for which men need to be trained. Some schools may provide professional training for a number of different specializations. Others may concentrate on only one. Together the whole community of theological educators may meet the functional needs of the churches for professional ministers, each institution making that contribution for which it is functionally best equipped "when each part is working properly."

A projection of what this kind of organic diversification might mean for one denomination's theological education system is made by Rolf Aaseng:

One seminary might have high entrance requirements and be frankly a high level graduate school in theology. Its students who want to enter the parish ministry would take a year of internship. Another school might concentrate on serving college graduates who do not have the prerequisites for a graduate course. A third seminary might specialize in serving older men who decide to study for the ministry. A fourth school might combine two approaches, with one program leading to a B.D. or S.T.M. degree after one year and a doctor's degree after four years, and another course for those with less academic qualifications.[16]

These are not the only permutations possible, of course, but this kind of rational reappraisal of the institutional resources and educational goals in theological education and imaginative attempt to project a new pattern which would have an organic and functional integrity is desperately needed for the whole enterprise of ministerial training in North America, and is a task for which the A.A.T.S. is peculiarly equipped and for which it has a special responsibility. The whole system of accreditation, for example, might be revised so that, without lowering the present standards, criteria based on these functional factors and the specialized purposes of different institutions would also be determinative.

In the second place, the ground may be cleared for later reconstruction by applying a functional criterion to prerequisites and entrance standards for theological schools.

It has been pointed out that a strong case can be made for changing recommendations (as in the A.A.T.S. Statement on Pre-Seminary Studies) for seminary preparatory work into formal requirements. Ernest C. Colwell has persuasively argued this in his essay in *The Making of Ministers*, presenting a tentative outline of what these requirements might be. This case is bolstered, though not necessarily Colwell's particular proposal, by a look at the major fields of study of seminarians while in college:

Religion, Theology, or Bible	15.4%
History	14.8
English	9.1
Philosophy	7.7
Sociology	7.2
Others	45.8

The A.A.T.S. Statement regards "as the most desirable" of the areas of concentration "English, philosophy, and history." One might cynically conclude from this that pre-seminarians (or those who counsel them) either don't know about the A.A.T.S. recommendations or don't care about them. In any case, it is requirements and not recommendations that are likely to be taken seriously by students—in any field. Perhaps only requirements are taken seriously by the seminaries themselves: their entrance practices would argue this. If the seminaries' educational work really does depend to an important degree on the kind of academic preparation a student has had in college—and the seminaries alone must decide this—the time may be approaching when the A.A.T.S. Statement on Pre-Seminary Studies needs to be translated into actual entrance requirements. This is one of the proposals of this Study. To do so might, incidentally, have the beneficial effect of separating vague, utopian hopes from concrete, actual necessities throughout the whole field of theological education.

The discussion of the change from recommendations to requirements—whatever the outcome might be—would itself make evident the fact that pre-seminary recommendations *or* requirements need to be *functionally relevant* to the vocational intentions of the students. That fact has been almost totally ignored in discussions of pre-seminary education up to this time. The diversity of professional goals of seminary students has definite implications for pre-seminary education. Is it really possible to recommend only *one* type of pre-seminary study for the different ministerial specializations? One recommendation (such as the A.A.T.S. Statement) may be appropriate if it is related to an institution preparing only one kind of minister—the parish minister, for example. But the data of this Study would seem to indicate that the seminaries are engaged in a much more complicated educational task than this—even when they themselves do not recognize it. What is good for the goose may be good for the gander. But if it is not, it is important to be able to distinguish between the two.

The limitations of a too simplistic approach to the problems of pre-seminary education are illustrated by the reports received by the Study from seminary faculty consultations considering the following questions posed by the Study directors:

a. From what colleges and universities do your best students come?

b. How well prepared do you want your students to be before entering seminary?

c. What are the major deficiencies of your entering students which might have been overcome by a more adequate pre-seminary education?

d. In what ways would you revise the present A.A.T.S. Statement on pre-seminary education?

In answer to Question a, the general consensus (of faculties enrolling a majority of the Protestant seminarians in the United States and Canada) was that, as one seminary president put it: "It is impossible to discern a pattern with respect to colleges and universities providing us with our 'best' students." Or as another seminary faculty says: "There appears to be little correlation between our best students and the institutions from which they come. Rather, the quality of students often represents their ability, maturity, and sense of calling rather than the kind of college or university in which they were trained." Some faculties felt that an institution which was too narrowly scientific or technological tended to produce graduates who found it difficult to comprehend abstract thought. On the other hand, another school reported: "One of our best was a graduate of the New York State College of Ceramics with a major in glass technology." And another faculty said that their two best students among recent graduates had both majored in architecture in college.

On the whole, the seminaries feel that their students are best prepared at good liberal arts colleges and humanities divisions of universities. On the question of the value of preparation in church-related institutions, there seemed to be little conviction one way or the other. Some doubts were expressed, however, on the sometimes assumed superiority of a church-related college preparation. One denominational seminary says: "Our Director of Admissions has evidence which indicates that our best students come from larger colleges and major, well-established universities, rather than from small, sectional and somewhat parochial schools." Most seminaries reported that they had not made a systematic study of the relation between colleges and universities and the performance of students from them in seminary. One which did, however, came up with the following results: "To our astonishment—using the criterion of honors announced at graduation for the past five years as one measure of a better student—approximately twice the proportion of our students who come from other than Lutheran Church-related colleges earned honors than did our students who came from Lutheran schools. (Fifteen of the 62 non-Lutheran college graduates, or 24.2%, earned honors, whereas only 24 of the 211 Lutheran-college graduates, or 11.3%, did so.) It would appear that the failure to have a Lutheran-college orientation to theology and to meet a specific corps of entrance requirements in advance of entering seminary were not only no disadvantage, but actually an advantage, if reference is made to these statistics alone."

It must be recognized that these statistics apply to graduates of only one denominational church-college system and not to all church-related institutions, but it might suggest similar analyses by other seminaries for the sake of comparison would prove valuable.

In answer to Question b, the general consensus is expressed in the words of one faculty: "It was generally felt that courses which concentrated in Bible, religion, and education were less desirable than a broader liberal arts major." Most seminaries favor a broad course in the humanities in college both as a means of providing a general cultural exposure and as a means of fostering critical and systematic habits of thought and expression. This advocacy of "a full-orbed liberal arts program" as the best preparation for seminary was not interpreted, however (with one or two exceptions in which it was argued that "students should not take courses in Religion or Bible" in college), as meaning the exclusion of religion courses. Indeed, there was concern expressed by several faculties over the "religious and biblical illiteracy" of their entering students. As one seminary sharply stated it: "Is it better that our students come as 'theological virgins' or that they shall have had some experience? . . . we would prefer that they came with a good mastery of biblical content and with some background in the philosophical and theological discipline on an admittedly introductory level but without the sophistication of a presumed synthesis."

In answer to Question c, "What are the major deficiencies of your entering students which might have been overcome by a more adequate pre-seminary education?" the responses varied from generalizations about lack of "a sense of responsibility and initiative," insensitivity "about social amenities," "low ability in self-expression," inadequate training in "proper study habits," and inability "to think logically and to organize their material," to specific curricular deficiencies. These were in order of frequency of mention: history (including historical perspective and knowledge of contemporary affairs), philosophy, modern languages, Greek, and Bible content. No concern was expressed over deficiencies in knowledge of doctrine, biblical criticism, or other more technical aspects of religion. The major deficiency, however, which almost every seminary faculty noted was the inability "to write and speak English clearly and correctly." Several seminaries, in commenting on the fact that "one of the most notable deficiencies of entering students is in English grammar and composition," traced this back to the precollege years and urged that the weight of the seminaries through the A.A.T.S. be thrown behind attempts being made in other quarters to give students "a more concentrated and solid academic background in the high school years."

In answer to Question d, the seminaries were near-unanimous in their approval of the general lines of the A.A.T.S. Statement on Pre-Seminary Studies, and of its basic educational philosophy. Considerable opposition was expressed to including a religion major as one of the preferred areas of concentration for undergraduate studies, particularly if this meant that students would be taking "in college courses what they will of necessity have to repeat in Seminary, even though on a different level." Some specific suggestions for revision of the Statement both in adding other recommended subjects such as Greek, music, mathematics, etc., and in minor verbal changes, will be passed on to the appropriate bodies of the A.A.T.S. for their consideration.

This general reaffirmation of the A.A.T.S. Statement by the

seminaries does, however, raise certain questions in light of the findings of this Study.

In the first place, the ineffectiveness of the Statement because of its advisory nature is underlined. One seminary reported that it had in the past used it in a legislative way: "In previous practice, we have interpreted a minimum adaptation of the A.A.T.S. suggestions as mandatory. Deficiencies therefore had to be met in addition to B.D. requirements, usually by additional college work." This practice is, however, the rare exception, and even in this case it is reported that the "tendency now is to permit entrance deficiencies to guide, wherever possible, the choice of seminary electives. Most deficiencies are therefore being made up within the seminary context."

If "recommended" prerequisites for seminary are not made mandatory, of what real use are they either in constructing the theological curriculum or in screening candidates for admittance? The seminaries seem to be in agreement over the general deficiency in English competence among entering students; as one faculty says: "Many students today do not know how to read, write, or spell." This, of course, is the experience in other professional schools as well; one of the significant problems graduate schools have with their doctrinal candidates is that they often lack the basic facility in English necessary to write their dissertations. But if this competency is necessary for seminary study, why not put teeth into the recommendations by making them requirements? It is, after all, the very first recommendation in the A.A.T.S. Statement, suggesting its prime importance. If existing instruments to test this competency—and others—are inadequate, the seminaries through the A.A.T.S. might well devise their own.

One seminary makes a "radical proposal." It is: "Give entrance tests in specific fields where we want mastery, enabling the student to demonstrate his mastery or lack of the same, and assigning make-up experience and training as the student actually needs it." Certainly it is clear that by hesitating to institute more stringent entrance requirements in regard to the "tools" of education, particularly graduate education, the seminaries are making their own task of theological education that much more difficult. And if they are seriously concerned about preparing competent ministers, for whom facility in the use of English is surely a *sine qua non,* one of the most constructive contributions they can make to the professional equipment of their students is to demand this competence of them when they enter.

Are the seminaries deterred from putting teeth into their entrance standards for this and other competencies by unconscious fears of reducing the numbers of students, particularly when the churches are anxious about the supply of ministers? Pope Pius XI in the Encyclical *Ad Catholici Sacerdotii* admonishes: "Bishops and religious superiors should not be deterred from . . . needful severity by fear of diminishing the number of priests for the diocese or institute." This papal warning of one who himself had been a theological educator, against being "wickedly kind"—*impie pios* —towards those who have "no aptitude for study and who will be unable to follow the prescribed courses with due satisfaction" might well be taken to heart by those who feel benign scruples about establishing high and stringent standards for entrance into seminary and for the whole enterprise of theological education.

But there may be another reason why seminaries have been hesitant to translate recommendations into entrance requirements. They have not yet fully accepted their role as graduate professional schools. As such the prerequisites which they demand would have to be related not only to their own academic work, but to the professional destination of their students. Entrance requirements would presumably be determined by their functional necessity to one or both of these ends. It is clear that in the case of English, for example, competency is required both for seminary study itself and in ministerial practice. It could be a requirement for all types of graduate theological institutions, whatever their special professional orientation, because every kind of ministry presumably requires this competency. Besides this, linguistic ability is often a key to other factors in determining the qualifications of candidates for the ministry. Alasdair MacIntyre, an English philosopher, commenting on some recent theological writings in the *Manchester Guardian,* says: "Defects of style are never merely defects of style," a point made with telling force by Richard Hoggart in his study of middle-class culture in England, *The Uses of Literacy*.[17]

By the use of this functional criterion an appropriate set of entrance requirements might be set up for every type of theological institution, a list which would probably be shorter than the present Statement of recommendations but more specific. If one examines the general philosophy behind the present A.A.T.S. Statement, even this may be more convincingly defended under this functional criterion. The Statement appears to presuppose only one kind of "seminary" and only one kind of professional intention among seminary students. As has been shown, this is a misleading oversimplification of the real situation that now exists. The variety and complexity of seminary types and student vocational plans mean that no one kind of pre-seminary education is going to be functionally appropriate to them all. Nevertheless, a broad liberal arts education and a catholic cultural exposure are functionally appropriate for them all. How functionally necessary this kind of education really is will determine to what extent the seminaries translate it into requirements. If they do not think it essential it will remain at the level of general recommendations and pious exhortations.

It is this lack of appreciation for the variety of professional plans of their students, for the need of each theological institution having well-defined professional goals, and for the functional relevance of pre-seminary education that makes thorough review of the present A.A.T.S. Statement necessary. It is not the specific recommendations which require such radical revision, nor the basic philosophy of humane studies which is articulated, but the presuppositions about the nature of professional training for the ministry which lie behind them which need re-examination.

This same kind of situation is to be found in other fields of professional education as well. Medical schools, like seminaries, have different admissions policies. However, the Association of American Medical Colleges and the Council on Medical Education and Hospitals of the American Medical Association recommend a minimum of two years of college work, including courses in English, physics, biology, and chemistry. Because of the intense competition for admission, many college students accept these recommendations as mandatory. Besides this, most medical schools require a stated number of hours of chemistry, biology, physics, English, mathematics, and a foreign language. As a result, though most schools recommend more courses in liberal arts for premedical students, the actual requirements and the admissions policy in which "college grades remain the major determining factor," mean that this is largely lip-service to the idea of humane education. As a recent study puts it: "More than half of the students questioned in the Survey stated that, by the time they had completed the courses required by the college and met the medical school requirements, little time remained for them to select subjects of interest to them as individuals."[18]

Dr. Herbert Ratner, of the Stritch School of Medicine at Loyola University, points out that the premedical curriculum for many future doctors is being shortened "to make the M.D. degree competitive in time with the Ph.D. degree." He feels that in so doing "we are streamlining the educational process in the wrong direction by stressing the technological at the expense of the humanities. . . . Most medical schools are confused about their basic purpose. We do not know any longer whether our goal is to turn out physicians or research men. . . . We should appeal to students as humanitarians, not as technologists; as makers of health in the suffering rather than pursuers of truth in the laboratory, which calls for a different bent of mind."[19] Both in the premedical curricula and in medical schools proper he finds that the courses are becoming increasingly narrower and more specialized. Eric Sevareid, the journalist, says that what is at stake is the "treatment of his patient as a complete human entity" and endorses Dr. Ratner's "eloquent plea against the rapid drift away from humanitarian individualism, in the highest sense of that phrase, within the practice of medicine."

The American Medical Association is itself disturbed by the trend, and the A.M.A. Council on Medical Education has put itself on record as holding: "Too much emphasis on research may turn United States medical schools into 'research institutes' and impair the quality of medical education." This is why, in recent days, medical educators are stressing "the importance of providing in the liberal arts college a broad cultural background . . . because of our firm conviction that the best preparation for any future job, including the job of being a good citizen, is a genuinely liberal education." However, they "admit to a certain feeling of concern that, although the cause of liberal education has seemingly received increasingly enthusiastic support during the past ten years, nevertheless, programs are appearing in some places designed to shorten the total educational span of the prospective physician by providing a greater concentration in the basic sciences and the elimination of time that could be devoted to the humanities, social sciences and programs of independent study in depth in any discipline of the student's choice."[20]

The point is the same as with the seminaries. Unless liberal arts education is accepted as functionally *essential* for professional study and practice, and so embodied in the admissions policies of the schools, the effects of general recommendations will be negligible on the actual educational structure and program.

It is interesting to note that among all professional and graduate institutions the business schools have seen the *functional* value of liberal education most clearly. This has not always been true, but today—notably in the case of Stanford's School of Business Administration—this has become a decisive criterion in their admissions policies; whereas at one time, for example, nearly one-fifth of Stanford's business administration students had majored in business or accounting in college, this has now been reduced to less than one-twentieth with preference being given applicants with undergraduate background in the humanities. The Harvard School of Business Administration is also pursuing this same policy, and the general trend is in this direction; as a recent study concludes: "a liberal arts undergraduate education is probably the best preparation for the kind of graduate business program outlined here. . . . In this connection, mention should be made again of the fact that students who have taken their undergraduate work in economics, engineering and liberal arts tend to score better in the Admission Test for Graduate Study in Business than those who have majored as undergraduates in accounting and business."[21]

It may be considered ironical, as Jacques Barzun suggests in an article in *The American Scholar*, that business schools—which might have been justification for being purely utilitarian in their approach—are showing the greatest appreciation for humane studies. Even more surprising is the fact that business itself has recognized this functional importance of liberal studies and has, in some cases, been ahead of the academic community in promoting it: "One of the most striking recent developments in the field of education for practicing executives has been the initiation of a number of programs that concentrate exclusively on the liberal arts and eschew all business subjects. Interestingly, business itself rather than the universities has taken the lead in promoting this type of program," notably the Bell System's experiment in liberal education for executives.[22] As this report goes on: "Liberal education for executives can serve two interrelated purposes. It may seek simply to develop the 'whole man' so that he can live a fuller and more fruitful life and be a more useful citizen. But a liberal education can also help, directly or indirectly, to improve managerial competence. It is this latter view that lies behind the Bell System's liberal arts program. . . . In general, the idea is that by helping them to be better men, liberal education helps executives also to be better businessmen."[23] The practical contributions of liberal education to managerial competence is spelled out impressively in the symposium *Toward the Liberally Educated Executive*, in which the question is raised: " . . . what kind of education or training is required to unlock those human qualities that are needed in guiding great modern businesses?"[24]

The educational philosophy which lies behind the present A.A.T.S. Statement on Pre-Seminary Studies would appear to reflect a similar positive appreciation of humane studies, but the unwillingness or inability to translate this into concrete admissions policies would seem to indicate that the seminaries are not yet as convinced of the functional significance of liberal arts education as is the business world. There can be little doubt, admittedly, that the seminaries are faced with an awesome educational problem in trying to give common training to men with such diverse undergraduate backgrounds, and with apparently equally diverse vocational plans. Nevertheless, that problem is magnified rather than resolved by unwillingness to translate general recommendations for pre-seminary study into firm entrance requirements.

Recognition of the complex of elements which go into the theological education of the "complete minister" may also have some benefits for the *persons* involved in the enterprise. For instance, the feeling among seminary and college theological teachers that they are in some sense competitors may be dissipated by mutual acknowledgment of this fact and of their functional differentiation as contributors to the whole process. At the Study-sponsored regional consultations already mentioned such remarks were heard: "How can we build a level educational floor when the preparatory ground is so uneven?" (seminary president); "The first year of the B.D. course may almost be looked upon as an attempt to cover what the student should have had in his college course" (seminary professor). And on the other side: "Students who have taken our religion courses in college are bored when they get to seminary: they even have the same textbooks" (college teacher).

This kind of misunderstanding can be seen as something more than personality clashes, or evidences of a status struggle. It may be common confusion in the face of a common unresolved dilemma, and particularly of a failure to see the different parts and stages as functionally differentiated elements necessary for the effective working of the whole process of education. Possibly when both college and seminary representatives appreciate the complexity of factors in theological training—such as the diverse academic backgrounds and different vocational aims of the students, the changing nature of the congregation and the role of the minister in it and in the church at large, and similar forces of change—and understand that to deal with these probably requires not just the minor correction and improvement of the present educational patterns of ministerial training but ultimately a radical restructing of the whole which will do justice to these complexities and yet be functionally integrated, they may also begin to see why and how the total theological resources of both college and seminary working fully in harmony are needed for the great common task of providing theological education for the whole church.

It is the conclusion of this Study that this kind of clarification of the issues and comprehensive rationalizing of the institutional patterns of theological education may best be accomplished by applying a functional criterion to the whole process. The college, in providing a broad, liberal arts program of studies for a student, is not simply producing a cultured gentleman and giving him the accessories for "gracious living" in a leisurely age; it is supplying him with the essential equipment necessary for him to function effectively as a student in a professional school and as a practitioner in a specialized occupation. Through the position of the undergraduate years in the educational progression, the particular educational resources at the disposal of the college and university, and the natural psychological sequence of vocational development for the individual student, "college days" are preeminently the time for this cultural integration.

In contrast, the skills and competencies necessary for professional practice are best provided, and most appropriately placed in the educational sequence, in seminary. This is the peculiar functional role of graduate theological training, whether it is directed toward the parish ministry or academic teaching. But since some of the ministerial specializations are so different— perhaps as different as law and business administration, to take two other professional fields of study—the time may be approaching when theological schools must make a choice and decide for which of these specializations it is training its students; or, if it has the means, provide specialized programs for a number of different specializations. Unless this is done, the ministry will not be considered a profession because it has not really been professionally trained. And until this specialized diversification takes place in and among theological institutions, there will be no real basis for determining a rational policy of prerequisites and formal entrance requirements.

To be included in discussion of critical analyses of the present forms of theological training as well as consideration of proposals for reform will have a therapeutic value for seminary students. When these deficiencies are not admitted—for example, the lack of logical and consistent patterns of educational progression from college to seminary courses of study and the functional disconnection between the theological curriculum and the various specialized ministries—the already confused student is apt to place the blame for his disoriented state purely on himself rather than on a malfunctioning system. The average seminarian has enough psychological burdens and conflicts without having to bear this gratuitous addition.

There is evidence that the tenuousness felt by students about their vocational plans, as well as about their own religious faith, may stem in part from the basic professional disfunctioning in ministerial education. Erik Erikson's fascinating psychoanalytic study, *Young Man Luther*, suggests how inner psychological and spiritual turmoil and conflict can eventually lead to maturity; but Erikson also suggests that these deep, personal struggles of faith are most likely to become creative rather than destructive when the educational system recognizes and actually utilizes them. And it is evident that only a well-integrated educational system is able to accomplish this delicate work.[25]

One must wonder whether the typical forms of theological training are not so fragmented and lacking in integration that they cannot pretend to offer this type of creative matrix for the development of their students, and may indeed only exaggerate their already accentuated insecurities. There is today a fateful confluence of two developments: an increasing confusion on the part of students not only about their vocational aims in the ministry but about their own personal religious beliefs and, at the same time, an increasingly confusing pattern of theological training. It may be of some comfort to students to know that their inner perplexities are to some extent reflections of a fragmented system of which they are a part.

This recognition may be a comfort, but simple acknowledgment of it alone offers no guarantee that the student is going to be given the kind of education that the minister needs to carry on the work to which he has been called, or the kind of training that nurtures sanctity, gives professional competence, yet preserves humanity. This is another reason why the seminary is the crux of the whole problem and the most effective institutional fulcrum for moving the whole world of theological education. Change must begin with the seminaries.

Pre-seminary education is one stage in the total training of a minister. In the North American setting, the institutional division between pre-seminary and seminary education may be taken *too* seriously. Ministers have been trained in other patterns in other generations and in other places. Theology has been taught in a variety of educational contexts. As Bishop F. R. Barry points out, such distinguished English theologians and churchmen as William Temple and Hensley Henson never attended theological college![26] Inhibited by a rigid institutional fundamentalism, attempts may be made to change or improve a particular system of theological training without realizing that questions could be raised both about the parts that make it up and the way in which they are put together. It may be possible to get a tolerable fabric of theological education for the ministry by a skillful patchwork on tattered remnants. But if a first-rate educational outfit could be provided by weaving something entirely new, should this not at least be seriously considered?

It may also be well to remember in these days of debate over the adequacy of the number of ministerial candidates that quality is still more important than quantity in the training of the church's ministry. The striving for excellence at both the college and seminary level will provide one firm base on which any plan of integration must rest, and without which the best plan will founder.[27]

The ancient organic principle in which each part fulfills its own peculiar function in order that the corporate whole will prosper applies to this field of professional education as well as to others. In that context, concentration on high standards at all levels may divest every functioning part of false expectations about institutional and curricular tinkering as a cure for all ills, but at the same time give the freedom to consider the widest and most catholic variety of curricular and institutional patterns—precisely because it is known that everything does not depend upon them in the last analysis.

FOOTNOTES

1. See H. Richard Niebuhr, Daniel Day Williams, and James H. Gustafson, *The Advancement of Theological Education* (Dayton, Ohio: The American Association of Theological Schools, 1957), and H. Richard Niebuhr, *The Purpose of the Church and Its Ministry* (New York: Harper and Brothers, 1956).

2. *A Report to the Board of Theological Education*, November 1963.

3. *Ibid.*, p. 7.

4. See Table 35 and cf. James O. Smith and Gideon Sjoberg, "Origins and Career Patterns of Leading Protestant Clergymen," *Social Forces*, 39, May 1961, pp. 290-6.

5. Quoted in Encyclical Letter *Ad Catholici Sacerdotii* of Pope Pius XI, 1935.

6. "The Status and the Advancement of Theological Scholarship in America," *The Christian Scholar*, 47, Spring 1964, pp. 7-23.

7. See Part Two, pages 212-213 for a comment on this anxiety over seminary enrollments.

8. Everett C. Hughes, "Professions," *Daedalus*, 92, Fall 1963, pp. 662 ff.

9. *Ibid.*

10. "Some Problems in the Sociology of Professions," *Daedalus*, 92, Fall 1963, p. 674.

11. Niebuhr et al., *op. cit.*, pp. 6 ff.

12. "The Clergy in the United States," *Daedalus*, 92, Fall 1963, pp. 735 ff.

13. *The Making of Ministers*, p. 27.

14. *Ibid.*, pp. 197 f.

15. *Ibid.*, p. 208.

16. *The Lutheran Standard*, 4, 1964, pp. 26 f.

17. Boston: Beacon Press, 1957.

18. J. E. Deitrick and R. C. Berson, *Medical Schools in the United States at Mid-Century* (New York: McGraw-Hill, 1953), p. 210. See also Charles H. Russell, *Liberal Education and Nursing* (New York: Teachers College, Columbia University, 1961) and other publications of the Institute of Higher Education: Earl J. McGrath and Charles H. Russell, *Are Liberal Arts Colleges Becoming Professional Schools?* Paul L. Dressel, Lewis B. Mayhew, and Earl J. McGrath, *The Liberal Arts as Viewed by Faculty Members in Professional Schools;* Earl J. McGrath, *Liberal Education in the Professions* and *The Graduate School and the Decline of Liberal Education.*

19. Interview published in pamphlet form by the Center for the Study of Democratic Institutions at Santa Barbara, Calif.

20. *Preparation for Medical Education: A Restudy.* The Report of the Committee on the Resurvey of Preprofessional Education in the Liberal Arts College, Association of American Medical Colleges (New York: McGraw Hill, 1961).

21. Frank C. Pierson and others, *The Education of American Businessmen: A Study of University-College Programs in Business Administration* (New York: McGraw Hill, 1959), p. 262.

22. R. A. Gordon and J. E. Howell, *Higher Education for Business* (New York: Columbia University Press, 1959), p. 302.

23. *Ibid.*

24. Robert A. Goldwin and C. A. Nelson, *op. cit.,* p. 84.

25. New York: Norton, 1958.

26. F. R. Barry, *Asking the Right Questions: Church and Ministry* (London: Hodder and Stoughton, 1960), p. 98.

27. Cf. *The Pursuit of Excellence: Education and the Future of America,* Special Studies Project Report V, Rockefeller Brothers Fund (Garden City, N.Y.: Doubleday, 1958).

CHAPTER FIVE

VOCATIONAL INTEGRATION

The "complete" minister must be cultivated, proficient, and mature. It has been suggested that these marks represent three types of integration—cultural, professional, vocational. The question has also been raised whether these forms of integration naturally follow a sequential pattern and whether the educational progression in ministerial education corresponds with them. In other words, do the integrative stages of personal development of the minister through which he becomes liberally cultured, professionally competent, and vocationally mature, fit in with the educational stages of the prevailing pattern of ministerial training in North America?

The sharp distinction between undergraduate and graduate, or pre-seminary and seminary, education may appear an artificial and parochial one imposed by the peculiar structure of the 20th century American educational system and may not seem to have any particular merit as a pattern for the education of the ministry. Since, however, it is the prevailing educational form, and will remain so for a considerable time, it has to be taken seriously. The question then remains (admitting that no one educational system is perfect), does this particular pattern—accidentally, if nothing else —have the potential for excellence in the training of ministers? Does the relatively sharp division between the undergraduate collegiate stage and the postgraduate seminary stage, for example, even if not deliberately planned in that way or not yet fully actualized, provide a convenient educational division of labor feasible in providing different elements for the essential equipment of ministers—i.e., the broad, liberal arts cultural background in the first stage and the professional technical training in the second? Or whatever the limitations of the present system in practice, is it possible so to adapt and adjust it that, without a major recasting, it might be seen to provide a viable educational form for that which *ought* to be done in the training of a relevant ministry for the modern world? Recasting of the form and experimentation in new patterns is not to be excluded, and indeed should be encouraged, but the standard pattern is a "given" which no theorizing can ignore and whose creative possibilities should not be underestimated. It is the conclusion of this Study that the present organizational pattern, and the educational progression it represents, does offer a rational correspondence with the natural stages of integration in ministerial development and that its failures lie not so much in its intrinsic structural limitations as in the inability to exploit efficiently the potentialities of each part in light of the specialized function it is best able to fulfill.

The former president of Harvard, James Conant, in his educational surveys, has drawn attention to the uniqueness of the American liberal arts colleges, which have no real counterpart in Europe where students move directly from high schools, lycees, and gymnasia to graduate or professional schools. In commenting on this, Reinhold Niebuhr points out that any study of American higher education "must begin with an initial distinction between professional and technical education and general education which prepares for both graduate training and for life, and which is, in America at least, the province of the 'liberal arts' colleges." From this he draws a functional distinction: "The professional schools transmit the skills and competencies of the various vocations and professions, and the technical schools transmit the sciences and crafts of the technicians and engineers which proliferate in an advanced technical society"; on the other side is "the general education of the colleges and universities, which is designated to broaden, to cultivate and to furnish the mind, to enrich the imagination and to redeem the student from the tyranny of time and place by giving him contact with cultures of other ages and civilizations."[1]

As has been seen, this logical division of educational labor has been vitiated in theological training by the fact that, on one hand, the undergraduate colleges, including the field of religion, have tended to become more and more professionally oriented, and, on the other hand, the seminaries have tended to become less so. In the latter case, this is partly due to the fact that seminaries continue to do what was once a necessity in times of lower educational standards — provide remedial "liberal arts" courses for poorly prepared students—and partly to the fact that the trend is in the direction of seminaries changing from professional "trade-schools" into graduate schools of theology. This change of educational roles, and ambivalence of functions, between colleges and seminaries today means that, for better or worse, the process of cultural integration and professional integration has become thoroughly mixed.

Evidence has been given that this confusion between the functional roles of undergraduate and seminary education may be a contributing factor to the obvious uncertainty of vocational aims of seminary students at this time. There is also evidence, however, gleaned from ministers themselves and from church officials responsible for supervising their work, that this vocational indecision is by no means resolved for all by graduation from seminary. In fact, the first years in ministerial practice is the time for many when this vocational uncertainty reaches a crisis. There are no comprehensive trend studies of ministerial "dropouts," but the suspicion is widespread that they are increasing. The general exposure of the disillusionment of ministers with their work through articles in popular journals on "Why I Left the Ministry" is new and may be symptomatic of this trend. One reason, incidentally, why an empirical study of such "dropouts" is difficult is that ministerial disillusionment may find a vocational out, not by leaving the ministry completely, but shifting into one of the less clerically-marked ecclesiastical occupations which the increasing specializations required by the churches have opened. As has been shown, seminary students already seem to be anticipating this eventuality—including, it should be noted, those who have had practical pastoral experience before and during seminary.

It can thus be seen that there is, beyond the cultural integration and professional integration necessary for the minister, an integration both deeper and more comprehensive: a vocational synthesis without which the other forms of integration may be negated and even be brought into war with one another. In this integration the whole person—his faith, his talents, his attributes—attains a new professional identity which permits his natural and spiritual endowments and his educational equipment to be so matched and harmoniously melded that he is able to function effectively in his occupational specialization without demoralizing conflict.

Presumably this integration is very gradually realized throughout the whole educational process, and is, furthermore, one which is so personal and individually different that each person must achieve it by and within himself. Nevertheless, an educational discipline can either facilitate it or militate against it. Erik H. Erikson, in *Young Man Luther,* draws an interesting parallel in this regard between the monastic training of the Middle Ages and the education of psychoanalysts today: "These are some of the psychological laws underlying the monastic system just described as well as newer systems of ideological conversion; all the systems are experiments in first aggravating and then curing the identity diffusion of youth."[2] What is being described is in part the process of growing up, of becoming mature. But this also involves becoming not only emotionally mature, for example, but also occupationally mature. And it is here that the educational system itself is so crucial. As Erikson continues: "Before he sees patients, however, the subjective phase of the training, the personal analysis, must overlap with years of practical and theoretical training in the new science. Often this means training in the particular awareness and habitual conceptualization cultivated by a particular training institute. . . . It is obvious, however, that no organizational rules can entirely obtain, nor any existing experience invariably predict, the destructive and crea-

tive spirits which will be freed by such a combination of the personal, the professional, and the organizational. Thus psycho-
analysis also has its monkhood, its monkishness, and its monk-
ery."[3]

If one pursues this parallel, it would appear that Protestant
ministerial training in comparison with psychoanalytic training
succeeds better in "aggravating" than in "curing" the identity diffusions of its students. Seen in this light, the vocational
uncertainty of seminarians may be neither exceptional nor to be
deplored; it may, indeed, be a sign that the educational process
is functioning properly. But if no adequate provisions are made
for curing these vocational "aggravations" then the training is
dangerously truncated.

American Protestant seminaries are not, as a rule, particularly
helpful at this point in offering a disciplined life of worship and
a cohesive communal ethos which would be spiritually integrative for the students, though steps have been taken to provide
more counseling facilities and psychological guidance. These
means, however, are likely to be superficial palliatives, which do
not get to the heart of the problem, unless the whole educational
program and common spiritual life are vocationally integrative
as well. Radical therapy will be of limited help to the individual in
facing this vocational crisis unless the academic structure itself is
supportive of the "curing" process. This is not surprising, for it is
increasingly realized in both psychiatric work and pastoral care
that the communal context cannot be ignored, and in fact must
be exploited, in dealing with individual cases. Health means
wholeness, in more than one way.

The chief limitation in the present pattern of ministerial training in this area, however, rests in the fact that educational and
pastoral supervision or direction of ministers largely ends when
they leave seminary. Therefore, precisely in those immediate five
or ten post-seminary years when the minister is getting his first
full occupational immersion and when the vocational crisis is
liable to be most "deathly" critical he is required to work out his
own vocational salvation, with fear and trembling, and to
achieve as best he can a tolerable spiritual equilibrium. The cas-

ualty rate, both as measured by those who leave the ministry entirely and those who shift into other occupational positions within the ecclesiastical body, is not insignificant. In short, not everyone survives this struggle. After every battle there is always painful reflection on whether the casualties were more than necessary and on whether more adequate training, more effective equipment, and more intelligent deployment of the forces could have prevented some of them. It is that question which faces the seminaries and the churches now.

In listening to the retrospective reflections of practicing ministers on their experience and in reviewing their total educational training in light of them, some answers begin to emerge. Those who received the College Teacher Questionnaire were asked to give the name of a minister whom they considered "an outstanding example of his profession." This group of "successful" practicing ministers received another questionnaire with the following statements, on which they were asked to indicate their agreement or disagreement:

	% in agreement
1. The best preparation for seminary is experience in a secular occupation	21.3
2. It should be possible to complete seminary work in less than three years	5.7
3. The minister's training should lead to a doctorate rather than a bachelor's degree	41.8
4. A religion major in college should be required for admission to seminary	13.3
5. Pre-seminarians should take less religion courses than do other students	24.3
6. My ministry has been influenced more by my college work than by seminary courses	11.3
7. Greek and Hebrew are necessary linguistic tools for the parish minister	33.1
8. Training in administration is the most important part in the minister's education	3.0
9. Seminaries should give first priority to training in communication skills	38.0
10. I have learned more theology in the parish than I did in seminary	42.5

The ministers were also asked the names of their college and seminary; year of graduation from each, whether they had additional advanced degrees, their denominational affiliation, and the number of years they had been in the parish. Finally, they were invited to make additional comments to express their opinions more fully.

It was these written observations, some several pages in length (and which the formulation of the statements was partly intended to provoke), which throw some new light on the question of vocational integration under consideration in this section. Statement 10, "I have learned more theology in the parish than I did in seminary," gained more assent than any other. From the fact that so little agreement was expressed for the suggestion in Statement 2, that the seminary course might be shortened, it may be assumed that the response to Statement 10 is not an indication of sharp criticism of the seminary course of study as such. Rather it suggests, as one minister put it, that whereas theology is "taught" in seminary, it is "learned" in the parish. Or to put it another way, occupational experience is required to "digest" the theological materials offered in seminary.

Furthermore, *this* theological "learning" or "digestion" requires maturity. As a Methodist minister, 17 years in the parish, writes: "Personally I feel my seminary training was adequate but that I had not matured enough to adequately digest it all. For example, to say that I have learned more theology in the parish than in seminary reflects more on my maturity than on seminary theology. There is no substitute for experience and I know of no way to include such in a seminary curriculum." A Congregational minister, with eight years practice, underlined this with a warning against pure "head knowledge" of the faith, and an Episcopalian, with seven years experience, expressed doubt that faith, in this sense, could be "taught" at all.

It is for this reason that several ministers express doubts about the wisdom of requiring a religion major in college for entrance into seminary (Statement 4). One, with 16 years experience in the parish and seven years post-seminary work as a student, felt that his own training had the "disadvantage of making me 'grow up too fast.' . . . I feel that a pre-theological course which becomes 'professional' will be a mistake. Ministers need to be human beings, and they need to share in many common experiences of their lay brethren. The professional theological degree, apart from the mainstream of the academic world, is bad enough."

A young professor of philosophy in a good private college, and himself an "amateur" theologian, made the same point in an interview for the Study: "I can conceive of an infant prodigy in mathematics, music, or science—but not in theology or philosophy. Not only do they deal with the substance of other disciplines, and thus presuppose them, but require for their mastery a considerable degree of personal maturity on the part of the students. It may be that neither philosophy nor theology can really be studied in the *proper* sense by undergraduates."

Jacques Maritain stresses this when he emphasizes the danger of cramming "adult knowledge into children"; in so doing "we run the risk of producing either an instructed-bewildered intellectual dwarf, or an ignorant intellectual dwarf playing at dolls with our science."[4] Erik Erikson also recognizes the problem when he writes of the peculiarities of the *homo religiosus* in whose development there is sometimes a "short-cut between the youthful crisis of identity and the mature one of integrity." The religious man, says Erikson, speaking from a psychological viewpoint, is "always older . . . and focuses in a precocious way on what it takes others a lifetime to gain a mere inkling of." But as a result "no wonder that he is something of an old man (a *philosophus,* and a sad one) when his age-mates are young, or that he remains something of a child when they age with finality."[5] In other words, "maturity" in religious things does not usually come early in life, nor is it usually bestowed precociously. Nevertheless, there is a mysterious element in religious development which does not lend itself to pure chronological categorization.

It is against this background that the high percentage of agreement with Statement 9, "Seminaries should give first priority to training in communication skills," is to be interpreted. Despite the strong form in which it was put, 38% of the respondees agreed. This might be taken to mean that practicing ministers feel that the "practical" fields ought to be strengthened and given a higher priority in the seminary course. But this does not seem to be the case. For example, though several argued the need for more training in administration—one, who had his M.A. in Business Administration, a Southern Baptist minister with 12 years in the parish, said, "This saved me"—nevertheless only 3% were willing to say, with Statement 8, that "Training in administration is the most important part in the minister's education." This again is strongly put, but the difference between the response to it and Statement 9 is striking. Those who added written comments on the point tended to be in agreement with a Methodist minister of 22 years service who said: "We do need courses on administration!" But he qualified this by adding: "Unless you have something to present to the parish, there isn't much need to administrate it."

In other words, these ministers are not inclined to believe that the acquiring of "communication skills" is to be accomplished purely by adding new subjects to the curriculum or in the sharpening of technical tools. They are deeply concerned about the problems of communication and they are frustrated by their difficulties in communicating effectively. As a young minister, three years in the parish, says: "Much of the church's influence is lost because it cannot communicate and relate." And another 15-year man writes that it is "imperative" and "direly needed" for the seminaries "to do a far more successful job in training in communication skills." Reuel Howe, at the Chicago Consultation of this Study, on the basis of his observation of men who come for post-seminary pastoral training courses—for refreshment and "retreading," said that over 90% of them express a "traumatic frustration" at their inability to communicate and are deeply distressed by this major defect, as they see it, in their ministry.

As has been said, the comments on the Ministers Questionnaire do not suggest that they expect the seminary course alone to correct this, particularly if this were solely thought to mean "beefing up" the offerings in the "practical" departments. One graduate of a "prestige" seminary has the "curious observation to make" that "the so-called practical courses have proved to be the least practical." And most of the comments express the same view: that is, that *all* subjects in the seminary curriculum are "practical" for the ministry and that if they are not, this may be sufficient grounds for excluding them. Several express the view that the seminary course does not give the appearance of having this integrated "practical" relevance and it is at this point that the chief reformation ought to take place. An Episcopal priest, with 10 years parish experience, projects what this might mean: "personal confrontation which seems to me always to be the critical leaven in any lump of learning . . . intimate association of students and faculty . . . a climate of free exchange . . . seminar work to be less binding to particular curriculum disciplines. Basic background in theology, Bible and history are, of course, needed, but maybe they can be truncated in such a way that the real meat which is too often choked down in the first years may be sought at the bone and chewed and digested in the enthusiasm of a student's working out his own concern. Maybe an early rather than a late assignment of tutors might be of some help. There also ought to be a real program of clinical training, plus 'on-the-job' experience, plus even an awareness of the opportunity to 'drop out' for a period to test what has been worked through intellectually in face-to-face communication with persons who have the sickness but don't believe in the cure . . . insistence that what is known must be owned in critically relevant terms rather than 'pasted on' on the top of one's understanding."

A group of senior students under the direction of Dr. Paul Morentz of Pacific Lutheran Theological Seminary in Berkeley outlined their idea of what an integrated and functionally relevant seminary curriculum might be, considered through the eyes of those just completing a traditional seminary course but approximating in some ways this minister's ideals:

FIRST YEAR
    1. Integration Seminar
       (Oriented towards the "theoretical" fields: church history, theology, biblical literature)
    2. Supervised teaching
    3. Small groups
    4. Tutorial study

SECOND YEAR
    1. Integration Seminar
       (Oriented towards the "practical" fields: pastoral care, education, evangelism, administration)

2. Supervised preaching
3. Small groups
4. Tutorial study

THIRD YEAR
Internship

FOURTH YEAR
Specialized Study
(Oriented towards both the "theoretical" and "practical" areas against the background of internship experience)

The United Theological Seminary of the Twin Cities began in the fall of 1964 a new curriculum "toward the end of the integration of the traditional polarities." It is organized "to help the student be confronted with contemporary social issues, a knowledge of the historic dimensions of the Christian faith, and opportunities to test his degree of integration through practical and theoretical experiences." As an illustration, a first-year student's weekly schedule in the first quarter will include:

Mondays: The Christian Faith and the Social Order
Tuesdays: The Christian Ministry, Worship and Preaching
Wednesdays: Study
Thursdays: Systematic Theology
Fridays: Integration (with "Key" Lecture, Integration Seminars,
     Field Education Seminars and Preaching Labs)

During all three years in this new curriculum each day will be similarly devoted to a single theological discipline. Senior courses are largely elective and are "intended to provide opportunity for depth study of problems confronting the church as it carries out its mission in the world." Field education is in three phases: (1) limited to six hours weekly with supervision and without remuneration during the first year, (2) limited to 15 supervised hours per week in the second year, and (3) an internship year, normally between the second and third years, or at least ten weeks full-time work under approved supervision during the summer following the second year.

This type of "radical reform" of the seminary curriculum is what many feel alone may get at the core of this "traumatic frustration" so many ministers face in trying to communicate. For communication, or the inability to achieve it, is basically connected with the problem of professional integration. It is in part, of course, the problem of translating—of "money-changing," as one minister put it— the theological words into secular ones. But as Richard Niebuhr warned, " . . . theology today is not simply an affair of translating ancient ideas into modern language, but of wrestling with ultimate problems as they arise in contemporary forms."[6] Put in this context, the problem of communication involves the task of integrating the seminary curriculum itself so that it is more functionally oriented, but also has educational ramifications extending out of both the pre-seminary and post-seminary periods of ministerial training and practice.

On the pre-seminary side, effective communication presupposes cultural integration. As a Presbyterian minister puts it in arguing for a "broad major" in college: "The Gospel is preached in the world and not in a vacuum tank. The minister must therefore know not only 'the Word' but the world in which the 'Word' is to be heard, understood and acted upon."

In Graham Greene's novel *The Living Room*, Father James cries: "I want to help you. I want to be of use. I want it if it were the last thing in life I could have. But when I talk, my tongue is heavy with the . . . Catechism." Commenting on this in terms of the whole problem of communication, the editor of the *Christian Advocate* writes: "If we are to speak God's redemptive Word to our world, we must do so from within the culture, and not from the comfortable isolation of a ministerial subculture."[7]

Thus, not only professional integration through a functionally integrative seminary course, but cultural integration through a secularly integrative college education are essential prerequisites for "breaking through" to the world with the Word and communicating with clarity and power.

An Episcopal priest, with eight years practice and now in the campus ministry, sums it up: " . . . a radical reformation of theological education *is* necessary. One wonders if it will even be possible to build on the present structure; perhaps a new structure must be erected, after the existing one has been torn down. There is an atmosphere of irrelevancy within most seminaries I have visited . . . there is a misunderstanding of the meaning of 'piety'; there is a dreadful gulf between faculty and students, and, indeed, between faculty members themselves; there is the beginning of a self-defeating 'role-playing' which often goes on to be perpetuated (as in a charade) in parish life, and, when this occurs, there also occurs a breakdown between clergy and laity, and there takes place a deadening process in a man's ministry. One sees this everywhere.

"The answer isn't for pragmatic 'gimmicks' to be packaged and handed out in seminaries; nor is the answer for 'a return to piety' in the sense of cutting oneself off from present-day communications methods. The answer is for a nonthreatened ministerial presence *in* the world (understanding the contemporary world, its feelings, its methods, its escapes, even its convenient pietistic poses when confronted by the church) which accepts and comprehends the tension of trying not to be wholly *of* the world (but, of course, one will somewhat and somehow err, and this is where grace comes in!). Instead of this, one frequently finds self-righteous, judgmental, selfish, 'pietistic' withdrawal *from* the world—coupled with an inability either to listen to the world *or* speak to it. Seminary could at least help a man to *listen to* the world; and to give up seeking false securities either behind clerical collars *or* packaged answers, but to be honest (openly) about trying to find—in dialogue—the right questions to consider *in communion* with other persons."

A "nonthreatened ministerial presence" may be another way of describing vocational integration. As this minister indicates, it cannot be realized through and in seminary alone. The vocational synthesis in the person *and* parson continues in service, in the world, and "in communion."

Thus, on the post-seminary side, the educational integration continues. Unfortunately, most churches and seminaries have been very slow in recognizing the cruciality of the immediate post-seminary years in the vocational integration of ministers. It has generally been assumed that this is a "do-it-yourself" job. As with many such, it is often botched. It should be noted that this is not a failing of theological education alone. Modern industry is much concerned with continuing education; in an article on

"Bringing Engineers Up to Date" in *Fortune* magazine G. A. W. Boehm writes: "How can he manage men with whom he can scarcely communicate? How can he judge the capabilities of men to be hired and advanced, when his own education is so hopelessly out of date? What, in fact, can be done with him?"[8] With accelerated technological and scientific change, the dilemma of educational anachronism is acute in engineering and related fields. It may be hardly less acute in the ministry. However, it would appear that the business and industrial world, with its pragmatic and functional spirit, has been quicker to recognize it and to take practical remedial steps to correct it than the churches.

Even beyond the remedial work of continuing education and supervision, the churches and seminaries have a permanent task of post-seminary responsibility for the ministry. Anachronistic or not, the first two stages of ministerial integration—cultural and professional—require completion with vocational integration, and this, as has been shown, though beginning in college and in seminary, reaches its most critical stage in the first years of pastoral practice. The crisis in communication, as has been indicated, is symptomatic of that fact.

It is encouraging that some pilot, experimental efforts are being made in this field. In the San Francisco Presbytery, to illustrate, a five-year post-seminary program for ministers has been instituted. On a regular basis—two hours, twice a month—a psychiatrist and a senior minister meet with the ministerial novice and discuss with him his work as well as his personal problems. The program is paid for by the congregations, or, if they are unable, by the Presbytery itself. The program is still in its initial stages, and so cannot be adequately evaluated, but the need for such experimentation is irrefutable. The San Francisco plan, just described, is only one form in which such continuing pastoral training and supervision may go on. The Institute for Advanced Pastoral Studies in Detroit is another type. The irreducible elements which would appear essential for the vocational integration to be facilitated in such programs are: church participation for pastoral oversight and seminary (or academic) participation for educational oversight. It is by nature a joint enterprise, and may, incidentally, be one more means of bridging the gulf between the academic world and the ecclesiastical world which is so unfortunate for both, the burden of which, in its disintegrative effects, falls so largely on the minister himself and through him on the people as a whole.

*   *   *   *   *

In considering the training of ministers in terms of three integrative stages—cultural, professional, vocational—and relating these to the normal sequence of educational stages—pre-seminary, seminary, and post-seminary—the impression may be given that the process itself is that simple and logically cut and dried. This is, of course, not true. Every normative pattern has its exceptions. Furthermore, the "stuff" of theological education is not just made up of inanimate institutions, curricula, catalogs, and programs which lend themselves to this kind of categorization. Persons are part of the "stuff" and they cannot ultimately be rationalized into systematic patterns, however satisfying such architectonic descriptions may logically appear.

This is particularly evident if one thinks of the dynamic content of each stage, and especially the last. Vocational integration, for example, like maturity (to which it is so closely connected), is never fully realized. Educationally it may be described as a terminal stage; but in the life of an individual it is open-ended. This is peculiarly true in the religious life. As Erik Erikson says: "This integrity crisis, last in the lives of ordinary men, is a life-long and chronic crisis in a *homo religiosus.*"[9]

Thus, running through the educational sequence and beneath the integrative stages of theological training there is a dynamic element which, while not necessarily contradicting this pattern, runs sufficiently counter to it and challenges it enough at other levels of human existence, so that this pattern cannot be absolutized. One way to describe this dynamic is in terms of the dialectic between "letter" and "spirit." This deep, underlying tension is a basic motif in the religious life. "Literacy" and "spirituality," "learning" and "piety," "knowledge" and "faith," "wisdom" and "foolishness," have played both contradictory and complementary roles in Christian history, individual and corporate. Paul's words to the Corinthians might be considered the text for this dynamic: " . . . the letter kills but the spirit gives life." The plaintive words of a seminarian on a questionnaire reflect this tension implicit in theological education: "I am unsure of myself spiritually and emotionally. . . . Now my spiritual life has weakened and my beliefs are unsure." There is an unresolvable dialectic between theological literacy and spiritual life which no "integration" can ultimately eliminate and which no educational systematization can structurally remove. Or to put it in another way, real integrity is both deeper and broader than integration— and more paradoxical.

Every Christian generation which has undertaken responsibility for educating its professional ministry has had to consider the implications for its task of the dominical injunctions against the "scribes," "pharisees," "elders": the religious literates. The demonic potentialities of literacy as exhibited by the most strident and consistent opponents to Christ's own ministry remain as a continual warning against educational sophistication in every age. Yet, at the same time, Christians are people of a Book. Their Lord could, after all, read, and did; he and the later witnesses to his life and resurrection appealed to Scriptures and acted upon the authority of the written word. Paul could dismiss all his education as "dung" and yet he remained a literate, learned man who powerfully employed both to spread the Gospel; he did not abandon his intelligence, nor did he betray his logical training, in asserting that "God made foolish the wisdom of the world"; he appeals to the intellects of his readers even in his argument that "since, in the wisdom of God, the world did not know God through wisdom, it pleased God through the folly of what we preach to save those who believe." He says that he does not use "lofty words" or depend on "plausible words of wisdom," yet he makes every effort to be plausible in presenting his literate witness to "a secret and hidden wisdom of God."

The man in whom this dialectic historically is most clearly and brilliantly epitomized is Augustine. "Inflamed with a passion for wisdom," as he confesses, a passion which at the same time led him away from the church as an agnostic and heretic and then eventually into it as a minister and theologian, this North African studied grammar and classical literature in Madaura, went on to Carthage for advanced studies in rhetoric, and as a brilliant student became an even more illustrious and successful teacher in Carthage, Rome, and finally Milan. Intellectually gifted, scientifically disciplined, philosophically trained, and, not least, fully immersed in the social and intellectual milieu of cosmopolitan Roman life, his epic journey of "faith seeking understanding" with its tempestuous moral struggles lived out in a "storm of mental hesitation" has become a classic example of the birth pangs of great Christian personality and of the fiery tempering of spiritual maturity.

Augustine's spectacular intellectual-spiritual pilgrimage into the Christian ministry cannot, of course, be matched by every ministerial student. Yet we see in his preparation, both formal and existential, essential elements in the making of a minister for every time and all places. One might say that his native ability alone insured the fact that he would achieve fame and lasting influence as a churchman once he had given himself to the clerical vocation. Yet would he have become so great in the ministry of the church if he had not, out of his human vitality and his intellectual passion, strayed so far from it in his relentless search for truth? What would he have become, despite his great gifts, if he had not learned to read and write? His own answer is plain: " . . . in this period of boyhood I did not enjoy my lessons, and I hated being forced to do them. However, I was forced to do them, and this was a good thing for me . . . the good that was done to me was from you, my God. . . . For by means of these rudiments I acquired and still retain the power to read what I find written and to write what I want to write myself."[10]

Nevertheless, despite his recognition that his cultural education has provided him with indispensable means for his ministry, Augustine is equally aware of the ambivalent character of literate learning for the spiritual life: " . . . what good did it do me that I, at a time when I was the vile slave of evil desires, read and understood for myself every book that I could lay my hands on which dealt with what are called the liberal arts? I enjoyed these books and did not know the source of whatever in them was true and certain. . . . I could understand quite easily and without the aid of an instructor every work on rhetoric or logic, geometry, music, and arithmetic." But, as he goes on, "What good to me then was that intelligence of mine, so quick and nimble in those arts and sciences? What good to me were all those knotty volumes which I unraveled without the aid of any human teacher, when all the time I was so disgracefully, so sacrilegiously, and so foully wrong in the doctrine of piety?"

In drawing this sharp contrast between literacy and piety, however, Augustine does not—as he might have and others have done —deny his native intellectual gifts or his cultural training. He only denounces their misuse: "This you know, my Lord God, since quickness of intelligence and precision in understanding are your gifts. But I did not use these gifts by making an offering of them to you. . . . For what good could my good abilities do me if I did not use them well?" True piety for Augustine, then, does not mean a renunciation of intelligence and culture. For natural abilities as well as human crafts are fruits of God's goodness in creation. Through the discipline of piety, good minds and good training are offered for ministry and service to the glory of their Creator: "For see, Lord, my King and my God, I would wish everything useful which I learned as a boy to be used in your service—speaking, reading, writing, arithmetic, all."

Ministry for Augustine is the re-establishment of the primal, created harmony of human existence and culture intended by God from the beginning when he "made heaven and earth." Because Augustine believes that God is Creator he can also affirm: "It was you who made for the craftsman his body, you who made the mind that directs his limbs, the material out of which he makes anything, the intelligence by which he grasps the principles of his art and sees inwardly what he is to make outwardly; you made his bodily sense by which he translates what he is doing from the mind to the material and then reports back again to the mind what has been done, so that the mind may within itself consult the truth done or not. All these things praise you, the Creator of all."

"The truth done or not." This criterion is as applicable to the minister as it is to the potter, the sculptor, the architect. They are all, in their own way, "craftsmen." If it may seem strange to apply the word to the Christian minister, it is no more strange than to call God the Creator of all human skills as Augustine does. Every human activity has the possibility within it of doing the truth—or not. The Christian minister is a "craftsman" in carrying the Word, in administering the Sacraments. Every craft has an end product. "People are trained and initiated to accept the authority of corporeal sacraments, but they would not get beyond this point unless their souls became spiritually alive on another level." Ministers, then, insofar as "we may speak of their labors," as Augustine puts it, "work out a *living soul* in it." This is indeed a "product," albeit a spiritual one, and the craftsmanship required is one in which cultural training in literacy is fused with spiritual passion and vitality.

It might be noted that the "killing" attributes of literacy—referring to Paul's "the letter kills"—is not all bad. Literacy "kills" illusions, superstitions, misconceptions; or to put it in current theological jargon, it helps to demythologize. This may seem remote from the problems of theological education. But is it? The ambivalent character of the Law—the "written code," the "letter"—as Paul describes it autobiographically, "the very commandment which promised life proved to be death to me"—is not this ambivalence mirrored in literacy itself, and particularly in theological literacy? That is, for the theological student the lethal power of literacy can be a liberation, breaking his mythological chains. But literacy, like the Law, while promising life, eventually may prove "to be death to me." Or to put it in another way, the letter indeed kills—but indiscriminately. In short, the very process of becoming culturally and professionally literate in college and seminary may spell spiritual death for the student. The agents of literacy—the teachers—are under the same threat. Kierkegaard has described this process very strikingly:

. . . this book, God's Word, is an exceedingly dangerous book for me, and it is a domineering book. . . . But there is a . . . way of defending oneself against God's Word. . . . For take the Holy Scriptures—shut thy door; but also ten dictionaries, twenty commentaries, and then thou canst read it just as tranquilly and unembarrassed as thou dost read a newspaper column. . . . All this interpretation and interpretation and science and newer science which is introduced with the solemn and serious claim that this is the way rightly to understand God's Word—look more closely and thou wilt perceive that this is with the intent of defending oneself against God's Word. . . . I insert layer upon layer, interpretation and science and more science (pretty much as a boy inserts a napkin, or several of them, under his pants when he is about to get a thrashing). . . I insert all this between the Word and myself, and then bestow upon this commentating and scientific method the name of seriousness and zeal for the truth, and then let this busy occupation swell to such proportions that I never come to the point of getting an impression of God's Word, never come to the point of beholding myself in the mirror.[11]

Or as P. T. Forsyth has put it: "We are not the fire, but we live where it burns. The matter we handle in our theological thought we can only handle with some due protection for our face. It is one of the dangerous industries."

Is it ever possible to bring literacy and spirituality together in this "dangerous industry" of theology and theological training? It is difficult, but it is not impossible. Presumably college graduates are culturally literate. Also, presumably, seminary graduates are theologically literate. But there is yet another kind of literacy which no man ever fully achieves. That is "spiritual literacy." And it is in this "literacy" that the gulf between literacy and spirituality is bridged.

This literacy, of course, is a very special kind. It is not taught in school, save in the school of life itself. It is found in no textbook, except the book of the human mind and spirit. It is nowhere written, except in the heart.

Paul speaks of it when he writes to the Corinthians: " . . . ye are manifestly declared to be the epistle of Christ ministered by us, written not with ink, but with the Spirit of the living God; not in tables of stone, but in fleshy tables of the heart." This is true "spiritual literacy": "Ye are our epistle written in our hearts, known and read of all men."

The "letter killeth." But there is a letter which lives: and that is the letter which the Spirit writes through lives—spiritual letters to be read by all men.

The struggle for mature, existential identity is a part of the struggle to become literate. But the struggle is resolved only when that literacy includes spiritual literacy. This may abound only with great pain, as was the case with Luther. His testimony may be a guide to the spiritual pilgrimage along the theological and ministerial path: "I did not learn my theology all at once, but I had to search deeper for it, where my temptations took me."

Or as he says elsewhere: Vivendo, immo moriendo et damnando fit theologus, non intelligendo, legendo, aut speculando: "A theologian is born by living, nay dying and being damned, not by thinking, reading, or speculating." That is why the theological graduation of ministerial students is perhaps of all the professions most appropriately called commencement, "that he which hath begun a good work in you will perform it until the day of Jesus Christ."

FOOTNOTES

1. Reinhold Niebuhr, *Pious and Secular America* (New York: Charles Scribner's Sons, 1958), p. 24.

2. Erik H. Erikson, *Young Man Luther* (New York: W. W. Norton and Company, 1958), pp. 130-40.

3. *Ibid.*, pp. 152 f.

4. Maritain, *op. cit.*, p. 9.

5. Erikson, *op. cit.*, pp. 261.

6. *The Purpose of the Church and Its Ministry*, p. 3.

7. *Christian Advocate*, 6, October 11, 1962, p. 2. (By permission of the Methodist Publishing House, Nashville.)

8. *Fortune*, 67, May 1963, pp. 120 ff.

9. Erikson, *op. cit.*, p. 261.

10. The quotations of Augustine are from the Rex Warner translation of the *Confessions* (New York: Mentor-Omega, 1963).

11. Søren Kierkegaard, *For Self-Examination* and *Judge for Yourselves* and *Three Discourses 1851*, translated by Walter Lowrie (Princeton, N.J.: Princeton University Press, 1944), pp. 56, 59f.

CHAPTER SIX

RECOMMENDATIONS

The discussion of the preceding pages has implied a number of specific recommendations which should be made more explicit. Certain issues have arisen out of the Study and are here selected as meriting the serious consideration of the two sponsoring organizations, the American Association of Theological Schools in the United States and Canada and the American Academy of Religion.

The following comments and recommendations are presented in relation to the data sources as these are listed and discussed in Part Two.

College and seminary visits. The widespread idea that seminaries are the last and most formidable stronghold of educational conservatism was not supported by the seminary visitations made by the directors. In every institution visited there is ample evidence of concern and interest regarding the problems of theological education. In many cases there is imaginative experimentation in curricular revision, in pedagogy, and in the creative integration of practical training and theoretical studies. More opportunities for continuing pastoral education are being provided, as are new approaches to the theological training of the laity.

There is, however, evidence that this new thinking and experi-

149

mentation is not being adequately shared between the seminaries for their mutual stimulation and benefit. Furthermore, there seems to be little communication with other professional schools, even in the same educational institutions. Thus the seminaries are not profiting from the experience of other educators in dealing with quite similar problems.

RECOMMENDATION: *That the A.A.T.S. encourage the exchange of information between seminaries on their discussions of the problems of theological education and ministerial training and of their curricular and pedagogical experiments, past, present, and projected.*

RECOMMENDATION: *That the A.A.T.S. explore the possibility of securing foundation support for: (A) Continuing consultations between theological educators (including Roman Catholic and Jewish) and representatives of other professional schools, and (B) A national conference on professional education.*

RECOMMENDATION: *That the A.A.R. be included in both the interseminary and ecumenical discussions of theological and professional education.*

College, university, and seminary catalogs. A study of course offerings reveals diversity in content in different colleges and universities for the "same" courses, a variety of academic standards, and variations in teaching methods—confirming the Niebuhr committee's suggestion that "the general tendency among the schools to accept 'an A.B. from an accredited college' as sufficient credential for entrance on the seminary course needs correction."

RECOMMENDATION: *That the A.A.T.S. survey its members on the advisability of constructing a standard seminary entrance examination in cooperation with the A.A.R. for the use of the seminaries in whatever way they may choose. Such an examination could be employed for screening applicants, for placing students in more advanced seminary courses after entrance, and for judging the need to provide remedial studies before or during seminary.*

Seminary faculty consultations. The seminaries are on the whole in agreement with the policy outlined in the A.A.T.S. Statement on Pre-Seminary Studies recommending a "liberal arts" program for prospective seminarians. However, a number of proposals were made for particular changes in the Statement, ranging from slight modifications to more radical revisions.

A major deficiency of the Statement is that it advocates a "liberal arts" pre-seminary academic program without an adequate explication of the reasons why such a program is advantageous—for the student himself, for the seminary, and for the pastor in his ministry. It also does not recognize the possibility of a religion major providing, in some cases, a satisfactory basis for such a "liberal arts" education.

The question as to the extent to which "recommendations" are really effective in determining pre-seminarians' courses of study needs to be investigated. It may be, as some have proposed, that the Statement should be shortened and made into *requirements* which would actually influence undergraduate curricula and pre-seminarians' academic programs.

On the other hand, the organic diversification of theological schools, the variety of undergraduate backgrounds and the different specializations required in the ministry suggest that a pluralistic approach should not be discouraged.

RECOMMENDATION: *That the A.A.T.S. set up a committee, including representatives of undergraduate education in the A.A.R. and from other undergraduate fields, for the revision of the Statement on Pre-Seminary Studies, taking into consideration the written proposals from the faculty consultations of this Study and studying the possibility of changing the Statement from one of recommendations to actual entrance requirements.*

RECOMMENDATION: *That the A.A.T.S. undertake a reappraisal of resources and goals in theological education, recognizing a variety of patterns, and encouraging institutional specialization for particular ministries, revising accrediting procedures as necessary.*

Regional consultations. Despite the existence of professional associations and the normal channels for contact in their churches, many college and seminary teachers—even within the same denominational family and educational system—had never met together until their involvement in the consultations of this Study.

RECOMMENDATION: *That the A.A.T.S. and the A.A.R. encourage the continuation of the regional consultations begun by this Study between seminary, college, and church representatives.*

College teachers. The College Teacher Questionnaire indicated that college departments of religion were generally held in high academic esteem and that doubts on this score of both religion teachers themselves and seminary faculties were for the most part groundless. There was also some indication that attempts to make undergraduate departments of religion essentially pre-professional would be damaging to their image in the academic community. The questionnaires also showed a sympathetic and lively concern of many faculty members in other fields not only for the contribution they might make in the education of pre-seminarians but also for ministerial recruitment—including among students majoring in their departments. The general consensus is that the role of a department of religion is to be seen chiefly in terms of its contribution to the academic "wholeness" of liberal education and in terms of its value in providing on a high intellectual level an introduction to religion for the whole student body, not just a technically oriented preparation for the future professionals.

Despite this consensus, there is a widespread impression that the A.A.R. has a hard "line" of policy which would urge upon all, or most, pre-seminarians a religion major as the best, or only appropriate, academic concentration at the undergraduate level. The directors frequently had the experience of being told that their Study, variously reported as contemplated or completed, had supported, or would support, such a policy.

RECOMMENDATION: *That the A.A.R. prepare a policy statement to clarify its official position on the place of religion in undergraduate education, indicating that the major function of religion departments is cooperation in the liberal education of all students.*

Ministers. Clergy respondents to the Ministers Questionnaire stressed the value of a broadly based undergraduate education not only for their later theological studies but in particular for their practice of the ministry. On the whole, they felt that they had "learned more theology" in the ministerial experience than through their formal theological studies, but they also recognized that their seminary training had prepared them to "digest" this experience theologically and that therefore an absolute separation between "theoretical" and "practical" learning was artificial.

RECOMMENDATION: *That the A.A.T.S. and/or the A.A.R. sponsor a study based on ministers' critical re-evaluation of their total educational experience as preparation for their actual ministerial service.*

RECOMMENDATION: *That the A.A.T.S. and the A.A.R. give assistance to experimental methods of teaching at the undergraduate level and in seminary, with special emphasis on life situation material and methods which relate parish research to more traditional materials.*

College presidents. Some college and university presidents are too little aware of the extent to which their institution is providing pre-seminary education, while others may be too much aware of it! In some cases, heads of institutions shown by the seminarian baccalaureate origins analysis to be "high producers" were either unaware of the fact, or did not know the actual number of pre-seminarians they had trained or were training. On the other hand, certain presidents emphasized their role in ministerial recruitment and pre-seminary education to a degree that seemed to imply that this was the basic *raison d'être* of their institution, possibly for public relations and financial reasons.

Some presidents of "secular" schools who are active churchmen and want their institutions to serve the churches feel unsupported by the churches and the seminaries, unaware that the latter are their allies in the struggle against the encroachment of professionalization into undergraduate education.

RECOMMENDATION: *That the A.A.T.S. and the A.A.R. communicate with college and university administrators, sharing with them the legitimate expectations of the churches regarding higher education in the perspective provided by this report.*

Baccalaureate origins studies. The church-related undergraduate schools still provide the bulk of seminarians, but the total numbers from other types is impressive. The seminary faculties suggest that many of their best students are coming from "secular" institutions at the present time. It may be that the difference between the pre-seminary education received in a large state institution and a small church-related college is sufficiently significant to require specialized educational programs for various "types" of students entering seminary, e.g., special sections in systematic theology divided according to the undergraduate academic background of the students.

RECOMMENDATION: *That the A.A.T.S. sponsor a trend study of the baccalaureate origins of seminarians and that the results of this study be shared with boards and committees of the churches responsible for ministerial recruitment.*

Seminarians. One previously reported finding from the Seminarian Questionnaire has caused considerable comment—the relatively small proportion of seminarians (33%) who anticipate the parish ministry as their ultimate vocational destination. This raises perplexing questions about motivation of seminary students, the popular image of the parish minister, and the educational purposes of a seminary.

The picture of the seminarian which emerges is of a person with a relatively narrow "religious" background both in regard to family origins and education—so pronounced that he might well be called "church-bound." The relation between undergraduate and seminary education may need to be seen in a new light: A dialectical connection between a healthy secularity and religious professional competency can be produced by college and seminary if each assumes its complementary role. This underlines one of the basic conclusions of the Study—that theological education is an enterprise in which family religious nurture, educational "secularization," professional training, and ministerial experience all have their unique and essential contributions to a final integral wholeness necessary for effective ministerial service.

It remains to be seen if theological education in North America still is—as H. Richard Niebuhr suggested—at the stage where "no clear-cut idea of the theological school or of theology as a whole is yet in prospect."

RECOMMENDATION: *That the A.A.T.S. carry out a census of seminarians at regular intervals and that the questionnaire used be prepared by a group representing all those who have research or other concerns in this area.*

RECOMMENDATION: *That the A.A.T.S. and the A.A.R., singly and in their joint enterprises, give attention to the totality of theological education—before, during, and after seminary—seeking appropriate means to employ the resources of each stage most effectively in the making of ministers.*

Part Two

Data Sources
and
Research Methods

1. KEY QUESTIONS
AND APPROACHES

The Advisory Board of the Lilly Endowment Study of Pre-Seminary Education met on December 7 and 8, 1961, to review the work of the directors, who had begun their two-year Study three months previously. The Board, which did not meet again until the conclusion of the Study, gave complete freedom to the directors, approving their perspectives and specific approaches, but not limiting their subsequent work thereby. The working papers for this meeting included a proposed "Research Design" and a check-list of "Main Issues." This part of the final Report is essentially a revision of those earlier documents after the completion of the recommended procedures. The leading features of the methods used are summarized in the list of "Sources of Data" at the end of this section and are elaborated in the remaining sections of the book in which some of the more significant findings are also presented. The questions which these procedures attempted to answer require a more systematic presentation here.

The "Main Issues" discussed by the Board in December, 1961, were considerations which had been raised during the first two months of interviews with 45 denominational officials of seven denominations and with personnel at 14 seminaries and 13 colleges and universities. They included 80 complex questions beginning with "What is the 'church'?" and ending with "Who does, and should, counsel pre-seminarians?" As the minutes of this meeting report, "In more than an hour of discussion confined largely to the questions on the first page (of six), a consensus developed that fundamental questions on the nature of the church and the ministry should be considered by the staff in a manner that can guide inquiry on the special problem of the Study—pre-seminary education." This tendency to view the problem of pre-seminary education in its wider dimensions had been previously indicated in Memorandum No. 4 by Dr J. Arthur Baird to the members of the N.A.B.I. Subcommittee on Pre-theological Education, in which the general statement of the project, "The Lilly Endowment Study of Pre-seminary Education in the colleges and universities of the United States and Canada," was broadened by two provisions: "(a) We would recommend that our study also be allowed to investigate the entire place of theological education on the undergraduate level. This would involve questions not directly related to the pre-seminary student, but certainly pertinent to the whole question. (b) The study would also be directed to the investigation of the undergraduate theological education of laymen and those going into church vocations other than the ministry. This, too, would be a secondary concern, and yet we felt that many of the concerns relating to pre-seminary education would also impinge upon this area."

Without listing here the 80 questions of the "Main Issues" check-list, their inclusiveness can be briefly demonstrated by the headings under which they were classified: Nature of theological education; Image of the ministry; Lay and professional ministry; Vocational choice; Career patterns; Graduate nature of seminaries; Curriculum revision, undergraduate—the religion major; Religion in higher education; Liberal arts; Departmental relations; Student religious culture; Testing instruments for seminary entrance; Training for ministerial specialization; Preprofessional training in other fields; Correlation between training and "success" in profession; Status of teachers of religion; Extracurricular theological training; Church guidance of preministerial students.

A brochure describing the purpose and concerns of the Study was prepared early in 1962 for inclusion in all mailings from the Minneapolis office. It summarized the many topics listed above in a simple declaration of purpose: "To determine how the total resources in theological education may best be used in the service of the church." Three concerns were noted: (1) The education of ministerial students prior to their entrance into the theological schools of the United States and Canada. (2) The theological education of the laity, especially in colleges and universities. (3) The relation between undergraduate religion courses and seminary curricula.

A preliminary report on the Study, published in the *Monthly Staff Report* of the A.A.T.S. in February and March, 1963, restated the intentions of the directors as follows: "In short, we are trying to see the education of a relevant and competent ministry as a *totality*, an integral process, in which both college and seminary training have their essential and distinctive functions. To seek ways in which the undergraduate education can be related to and integrated with seminary training *as it now is* fails to take seriously the possibility that Niebuhr and others are right when they find 'participation of the schools in the confusion of churches and ministers' about the ultimate purpose of the church and its ministry."

A shift in concern, or at least a widening of perspective, is described by the directors in their Introduction to the symposium on *The Making of Ministers* (p. xiii). "During the course of the Study it became increasingly apparent that the pre-seminary college preparation of ministerial students could not be arbitrarily marked off as a completely independent and self-contained stage in the process of theological education . . . . the education of ministers is a total process of learning, maturation, and vocational integration which has no sharp beginnings (college is certainly not the start of it!) and no end, other than death itself. A minister is being educated before he has reached a decision to become a minister and he continues to be educated all through his ministry, as long as it goes on, and he does."

An understanding of the continuity of the educational process

thus guided the formulation of the "special problem" of the Study
—its focus on the pre-seminary period. An interim report to the
A.A.T.S. in June, 1962, stated that: "The ultimate concern of
those responsible for the Study is not simply a coordination of undergraduate and seminary curricula (if that were possible) or
even the preparation of an 'ideal' pre-seminary training (which
would obviously be impossible). Rather it is to throw light (insofar as *that* is possible) on the *kind* of pre-seminary education
which not only helps to prepare men to be good seminary students, but far more importantly perhaps, helps to make them into
men, mature and well-equipped for the tasks of ministry to which
they have been called."

The detailed questions embraced in the above generalizations
are both directly expressed and implied in the research instruments discussed below. Nine key questions should be made explicit at this point, however, since they were included in the initial project statement of the N.A.B.I. under the heading, "Rationale for This Proposed Study." These questions were quoted
and paraphrased in the staff working paper on "Research Design."
Each of the following numbered paragraphs begins with an ex-
cerpt from the initial project statement and concludes with an
abbreviation from the "minimum check-list of substantive issues"
in the working paper.

1. This study is important because the nature of the present
college and university situation demands closer attention to this
area. One phenomenon often observed in American education
is the gulf between Christianity and the cultural mind-set of students and teachers. . . . To correct our religious illiteracy at the
college and university level . . . information is needed as to how
adequate our schools of education are to cope with the problem.
. . . *Issue:* Adequacy of higher education to deal with religious
illiteracy.

2. Another of the great needs for the undergirding of the religious life of America is . . . to deepen the theological understanding of the average Christian American who assumes that
religion is a major factor in his life, yet makes little provision for

it in his education. . . . The time when the average American has the best opportunity to deepen the academic understanding of his faith in any significant way is during the years at college. . . . This suggests the need for doing everything possible to insure the quality of the courses in religion. *Issue:* Improvement of undergraduate courses in religion.

3. Another facet of the current scene is the increasing strength of the work in theology and Bible being done in the colleges and universities. . . . One of America's greatest theological resources is not being sufficiently utilized. . . . How strong our college religion forces really are, and what factors, if any, are sabotaging their strength, it is the intention of this committee to discover. *Issue:* Strength of "college religion forces" and factors sabotaging them.

4. This study is important because the needs of ministerial training demand closer attention to the colleges and universities. . . . As the Niebuhr study pointed out, the traditional three-year program does not allow time to get in all the things that are essential to ministerial training. . . . "The general tendency among the schools to accept 'an A.B. from an accredited college' as sufficient credential for entrance on the seminary course needs correction." It is interesting that this committee (Niebuhr, et al.)[1] did not pursue such a provocative suggestion. *Issue:* Courses required, or at least recommended, for entrance into seminary.

5. The American Association of Theological Schools, in the statements it has issued from time to time for the counseling of preministerial students, has recommended that several semesters of religion be taken in college, but, for what have seemed to many as adequate reasons, has consistently omitted a major in religion as an option for such students. . . . There is a growing insistence that this whole matter be re-examined. As J. Allen Easley recently pointed out, " . . . the department of religion would be greatly strengthened by having the students interested

---

[1]H. Richard Niebuhr, Daniel Day Williams, and James M. Gustafson, *The Advancement of Theological Education* (Dayton, Ohio: The American Association of Theological Schools, 1957), p. 92.

in religion majoring in it. When the natural clientele of a department is drained away to other departments, the department in question must suffer. Seminaries have so oversold the idea that a pre-seminary student should not major in religion, that departments of religion tend to be weakened, and often have so little contact with pre-seminary students that they have difficulty answering inquiries which seminaries make about the students. . . ."[2] Majoring in . . . secular disciplines is more likely to channelize a student in an area outside his vocational concern than it is to give him desired breadth. . . . It is the feeling of the N.A.B.I. that there is sufficient confusion and conflict of opinion over this whole area of pre-seminary study to demand more objective empirical data. *Issue:* Religion major for pre-seminarians—relative breadth of religion and nonreligion majors.

6. This study is important because the needs of ministerial recruitment demand closer attention to the colleges and universities. . . . Exposure to a liberal education inevitably puts one's religious ideas "on trial." . . . It is a common observation of college counselors that when religious ideas are re-examined in the light of the so-called "secular" disciplines, at that time the "call" to the ministry is also re-examined by the theological student in this clear, cold light. . . . There is a conviction among many college teachers in religion that some of our finest men are lost to the ministry, or else sent to seminary with chips on their shoulders, because their adolescent concepts of religion were exposed to the searing effects of mature ideas, potentially anti-Christian and unsympathetically presented. (There is a need for) all students to be exposed to a presentation of the Bible and theology capable of relating itself adequately to other mature areas of thought. *Issue:* Counseling pre-seminarians to a presentation of relevant religion.

7. There is also the danger of losing our preministerial students in college by urging them to major in disciplines outside the area of religion. . . . There is a great need here for some clear facts

---

[2]J. Allen Easley, "The 'Statement on Pre-Theological Studies,'" *The Journal of Bible and Religion,* 25, July 1957, pp. 214 f.

as to just what is happening to our pre-college recruiting efforts during the college years. *Issue:* College and university effects on high school recruits to the ministry.

8. Another need has to do with the college as an area of initial recruitment. . . . To some the choice of courses or a major may not seem to be of great vocational significance. But to others who are on the scene and agonize with the college student over these choices, it is apparent that deciding on a major or a particular pattern of courses has great vocational determining power. . . . What is needed is some carefully gathered empirical data to determine the extent of the problem and the ways in which we can be most effective in our recruitment at the college and university level. *Issue:* College and university recruitment to the ministry.

9. This Study is important because the needs of the ministry are so complex and the problems involved so vast that the colleges, universities, and seminaries must join hands. Theological education is a total fabric involving not only church and denomination, but undergraduate and graduate schools. *Issue:* Communication and joint planning between seminary and undergraduate schools.

The above nine points of rationale, as phrased by one of the associations co-sponsoring the Study, stress concerns over the status of the college religion teacher, the attrition from the ranks of the pre-seminarians on the part of those who do not major in religion, and the lack of communication between seminary and college personnel as perceived from the college side. The directors were not supplied with the rationale of the Study from the perspective of the other co-sponsor, representing the theological schools, except as this was expressed in the A.A.T.S. Statement on Pre-Seminary Studies. Both sponsors shared in the selection of the directors and probably assumed that differences of opinion would either be reconciled in the factual data or made explicit and presented in some kind of creative tension.

Before describing the research procedures actually used, it should be explained why some possibilities were rejected. It had been suggested by the N.A.B.I. subcommittee that all colleges and universities offering courses in Religion, Bible, or Religious Education should be surveyed by a mailed questionnaire. "These questionnaires will presumably go to members of the Religion departments and certain other members of the faculty and administration in a position to give relevant information." However, it was decided by the Study directors that much of the information to be sought in this way could be obtained by inspection of college catalogs. Accordingly, catalogs were requested from over 700 colleges and universities in letters to their presidents, 500 of whom wrote letters in reply, a 70% response—probably higher than could have been expected from a questionnaire. The selection of a random sample of 70 colleges and universities, for which all catalogs were eventually received and from which the college teacher samples were drawn, provided a sound basis for limited quantitative generalizations. The rejected survey procedure was used independently by Allen R. Sharp in a Ph.D. dissertation, "A Study of Protestant Undergraduate Pre-Theological Education in the United States," completed in June, 1963, at Duke University. Dr. Sharp graciously made his data available to the Pre-Seminary Study and his findings are discussed in Part One above.

The difficulty of identifying all pre-seminary students until they actually arrive in the seminary weighed against attempting to locate them for mailed questionnaires. Although some pre-seminarians were interviewed individually and in groups, all quantitative generalizations regarding pre-seminarians are made retrospectively from the data of the Seminarian Questionnaire.

If it had been possible to do so, a research approach might have been planned to compare effective ministers with those considered less effective, determining significant differences in their educational preparation, especially at the pre-seminary level. With adequate instruments to sort ministers on the basis of their effectiveness, a simple research design would have yielded definitive answers to the key questions of the Study. However, the needed instruments are not available. In a review of the problems of choosing, defining, and measuring an effectiveness criterion, James E. Dittes concludes: "Serious and careful designation of personal characteristics and background, or of motivation, or of image of the clergy, or of particular recruiting or training procedures as predictive or productive of more effective clergymen must necessarily wait on better definitions of this criterion."[3] Perhaps the Seminarian Questionnaire data can sometime be linked to performance variables on the same subjects after appropriate instruments become available.

The research methods which were used in the Study were planned on a schedule which provided continual balancing of influences on the directors, who sought a comprehensive perspective, including and modifying the special views of the various types of informants. A deliberate effort was made to avoid the more narrow limitations which might have been imposed on the choice of methods and informants by the initial term of reference, "pre-seminary education." Resisting the temptation to assume that this term designated either a single ideal pattern or an encompassable reality, requiring only discovery and description, "pre-seminary education" was considered rather to point to (a) a *period* in the life of those who eventually arrive in seminary (whether or not they become ministers) and (b) a *function* actually or potentially articulated somewhere or somehow in higher education.

Definitions of basic terms in social science carry value loadings and commitments which make them political acts with social consequences as well as the means by which reproducible results, and thereby some measure of objectivity, can be achieved. Once the all-important definitions set limits to the research design, the "facts" tend to support the initial commitments implied by the definitions. Alternate definitions and value premises were retained by the Study directors as long as possible, although it should be apparent that a single, more or less coherent, point of view is expounded in relation to the empirical data throughout Part One. The reader is invited to attempt his own analysis of the data which follows, remembering that even this factual informa-

---

[3]James E. Dittes, "Research on Clergymen: Factors Influencing Decision for Religious Service and Effectiveness In the Vocation," Research Supplement to *Religious Education* (July-August, 1962), p. S-161.

tion was progressively limited by the narrowing and sharpening of the directors' conclusions.

The sections which follow explain in more detail (a) the college and university informants, and especially the college teacher questionnaire, (b) the consultations by seminary faculties and regional gatherings of college, university, and seminary personnel, (c) the baccalaureate origins studies and (d) the Seminarian Questionnaire. For convenience, all of the data sources are summarized here.

Lilly Endowment Study of Pre-Seminary Education— Sources of Data

1. *College and seminary visits.*

2. *College, university, and seminary catalogs.* All A.A.T.S. seminaries (125) and over 600 colleges and universities. Bulletins from a sample of 70 colleges and universities were analyzed more intensively.

3. *College presidents.* 500 responses (70%) from auto-typed letters to presidents of colleges and universities. Information on provisions and requirements for pre-seminary students, policies in other fields of pre-professional education, and attitudes toward pre-seminary education.

4. *College teachers.* 572 four-page questionnaires (55% response from 70 sample colleges and universities, including all religion teachers and 10% of the other teachers) identified by school, department, denomination, and own education. Opinions in: religion in the curriculum; images of the ministry and of the pre-seminarian; relative effectiveness, scholarship, and status of religion faculty members; recommendation of "outstanding clergyman."

5. *Seminary faculty consultations.* 60 written reports on faculty discussions of four questions on sources of best students, desired preparations, major deficiencies of students, and possible revisions of the present A.A.T.S. Statement on Pre-Seminary Studies.

6. *Regional consultations.* Tape-recorded discussions at Minneapolis, Chicago, Claremont, Atlanta, and Dallas, involving a total of 250 persons representing 50 seminaries and more than 100 colleges and universities.

7. *Ministers.* 265 responses (76%) from letters and one-page questionnaires to clergymen, each recommended as "outstanding example of his profession" by college teachers. Reflections on their own educational experiences.

8. *Baccalaureate origins studies.* (a) Tabulations on students enrolled in 122 theological schools in 1960-61 from catalogs and lists supplied by all A.A.T.S. member schools. Percentages from different types of colleges and universities. Rank order, number of graduates in seminary, and comparative indices for 298 schools in the United States with 20 or more graduates in seminary. (b) Comparable data for 1962-63 from Seminarian Questionnaire, including seminaries attended by 541 graduates of Canadian universities.

9. *Seminarians.* 17,565 twelve-page questionnaires (83% of the students enrolled in the fall of 1962 in 125 theological schools, all but two of the then current A.A.T.S. members in the United States and Canada, plus two nonmember schools). Identified by school, denomination, and seminary year, two IBM cards per respondent include data on social origins, age, marital status, motivations conceptions of the ministry, college majors and activities, present, degree programs, vocational intentions, and judgments on undergraduate and seminary teachers. All cooperating seminaries received carbon copies of printed summaries for their own students processed on the IBM 1401 by the Ministers Life and Casualty Union in August, 1963. Other tabulations for the Pre-Seminary Study include summaries for: eleven denominational groupings; each college and university type; students with different vocational plans, in different degree programs, and from different college major courses of study. Analysis of this questionnaire data is being continued by the associate director under a new two-year Lilly grant.

2. COLLEGE CATALOGS, PRESIDENTS, AND TEACHERS

On February 28, 1962, auto-typed letters signed by the Study directors were sent to 722 college and university presidents as follows:

Under a grant from the Lilly Endowment, Inc., we are engaged in a two-year study of pre-seminary education. In a preliminary survey of the baccalaureate origins of theological students now enrolled in accredited institutions, we have found that your school is one of those from which such students come to seminary. We would be grateful to you for your cooperation in this study in the following ways:

a. Request that your registrar send us catalogs listing the liberal arts faculty members and the courses they offer. (We are planning to send questionnaires to a random sample of college teachers in the next few months.)

b. Ask that the dean or department head most directly responsible for undergraduate courses in religion inform us of any policies and requirements that may not be fully explained in the catalog.

c. Inform us of special provisions you may have for pre-seminary students regarding their course of study, counseling, and financial support.

d. Report on new approaches in any field of pre-professional education being taken by the members of your faculty.

We intend to visit those campuses where developments in pre-professional training deserve our special attention. Meanwhile, your response to our four requests will help to make our survey adequately comprehensive and to enhance its general educational usefulness.

In the next few months, 526 catalogs were received. There were over 500 letters in reply from the presidents and additional responses from deans and department heads. There were 156 invitations to visit these schools. The catalogs and letters guided the selection of personnel for the regional consultations and influenced the itinerary of the directors. It is difficult to estimate the precise effect of each source of information, but the catalogs and presidents' letters certainly provided a necessary view of the wider context of higher education in which the pre-seminary problems appear. Some impressions and illustrations from this data source are detailed in Part One.

For more systematic analysis, a sample of 70 colleges and universities was selected. Intensive examination was made of the catalogs of all 70 schools and a sample of college teachers was subsequently drawn from them. According to conventional practice, two completely different sets of sample schools were drawn, and the set selected was the one which seemed subjectively to be more representative. The total population sampled was composed of 714 schools granting first baccalaureate degrees according to the *Education Directory, 1960-61* of the U.S. Office of Education. Roman Catholic and girls' schools had been excluded. The samples were drawn by use of a table of random numbers and from regional (accrediting association), control type (public, private, denominational), and size categories. The following colleges were included in the selected sample.

Adelphi College, Garden City, New York
Alcorn Agricultural and Mechanical College, Lorman, Mississippi
Arizona State University, Tempe
Asbury College, Wilmore, Kentucky
Baldwin-Wallace College, Berea, Ohio
Calvin College, Grand Rapids, Michigan
Carnegie Institute of Technology, Pittsburgh, Pennsylvania
Carson Newman College, Jefferson City, Tennessee
Clark University, Worcester, Massachusetts

Coe College, Cedar Rapids, Iowa
Colorado State University, Fort Collins
Concordia Teachers College, Seward, Nebraska
Dillard University, New Orleans, Louisiana
Eastern Oregon College, LaGrande
Emory and Henry College, Emory, Virginia
Furman University, Greenville, South Carolina
Harding College, Searcy, Arkansas
Henderson State Teachers College, Arkadelphia, Arkansas
University of Illinois, Urbana, Illinois
Kansas State College of Pittsburg
Kansas State Teachers College, Emporia
Kansas Wesleyan College, Salina
Kentucky Wesleyan College, Owensboro
Kutztown State College, Pennsylvania
Lenoir-Rhyne College, Hickory, North Carolina
Lincoln Memorial University, Harrogate, Tennessee
Linfield College, McMinnville, Oregon
Macalester College, St. Paul, Minnesota
University of Massachusetts, Amherst
Millikin University, Decatur, Illinois
University of Mississippi-Southern, Hattiesburg
Moorhead State College, Moorhead, Minnesota
Muhlenberg College, Allentown, Pennsylvania
National College of Education, Evanston, Illinois
New York State University College of Education at Albany
New York University, New York, New York
North Carolina College at Durham
North Central College, Naperville, Illinois
North Dakota State Teachers College, Minot
Northwestern State College, Alva, Oklahoma
Olivet Nazarene College, Kankakee, Illinois
Oregon College of Education, McMinnville
College of the Ozarks, Clarksville, Arkansas
Paterson State College, Wayne, New Jersey
Presbyterian College, Clinton, South Carolina
University of Puget Sound, Tacoma, Washington
Randolph-Macon College, Ashland, Virginia
Reed College, Portland, Oregon
St. Augustine's College, Raleigh, North Carolina
San Francisco State College, California
Shepherd College, Shepherdstown, West Virginia
Shippensburg State College, Pennsylvania
Southern University and Agricultural and Mechanical College,
     Baton Rouge, Louisiana
Southwest Texas State College, San Marcos
Temple University, Philadelphia, Pennsylvania
Texas Southern University, Houston
Thiel College, Greenville, Pennsylvania

Virginia Military Institute, Lexington
Washington University, St. Louis, Missouri
Wesleyan University, Middletown, Connecticut
West Texas State College, Canyon
Western Michigan University, Kalamazoo
Massachusetts State College at Westfield
Whitworth College, Spokane, Washington
University of Wichita, Kansas
Wilkes College, Wilkes-Barre, Pennsylvania
Wisconsin State College, Whitewater
College of Wooster, Wooster, Ohio
Yale University, New Haven, Connecticut
Yankton College, Yankton, South Dakota

All members of the Religion and Bible departments and all persons teaching courses in religion as indicated in 1961-62 catalogs of these schools are referred to as Sample A in the analyses of the College Teacher Questionnaire. There were 222 such persons in the 70 colleges and universities. Sample B is a 10% random sample of all other teaching staff members in these schools, 882 persons. In the universities included, Sample B was restricted to those in the Colleges of Arts and Sciences.

The 1104 teachers of Sample A and Sample B were sent a 4-page questionnaire and a covering auto-typed letter on November 15, 1962. The letter referred to the current issue of a magazine in which it was reported that: "The Lilly Endowment Study is another effort to assay the meanings of the crisis in religious vocation. It is surveying nearly 20,000 Protestant seminarians, along with college and university teachers." The letter said:

You are one of the teachers referred to on page 117 of the current issue of LOOK magazine (November 20, 1962). You have been selected in a representative sample of teachers in schools which regularly prepare students for graduate theological study.

Our survey of 20,000 seminarians reveals that the baccalaureate origins of these men is more varied than had been previously supposed. For example, over 7,700 attending theological schools in 1960-61 were graduates of state-supported and non-denominational colleges and universities, many of which have no specific pre-seminary curricula.

Accordingly, the enclosed questionnaire is being mailed to a carefully drawn sample of 1,104 teachers in all academic fields in all types of colleges. We would appreciate having your response at your earliest possible convenience.

The response to the college teacher questionnaire is indicated in Table 1.

Table I
RESPONSE TO COLLEGE TEACHER QUESTIONNAIRE

	Sample A (religion teachers)	Sample B (other teachers)	Total
Respondents	158 (71%)*	420 (52%)*	578 (56%)*
Non-respondents	56	391	447
Not delivered	7	41	48
Feel unqualified, or assume were included by mistake	1	30	31
First mailing	222	882	1,104

*Percentage of response from those to whom forms were delivered

The questionnaire "College Teacher Opinions on Pre-Professional Education of the Clergy" was developed with the assistance of Dr. Ruth E. Eckert of the University of Minnesota, a member of the Study's Board of Advisors. It bears some resemblance to the form used in her study of *Job Motivations and Satisfactions of College Teachers: A Study of Faculty Members in Minnesota Colleges* (with John E. Stecklein, published by the U. S. Department of Health, Education and Welfare, 1961). A multigraphed version was pretested at several Minnesota colleges. The final four-page version was printed. Most of the questions were answered by drawing a circle around one or more numbers in the right margins. Answers were punched on IBM cards and the tabulations were made by the associate director on a sorter at Mid-Continent Surveys, Inc., which donated the use of this equipment to the Study.

Sample A (the religion teachers) differed from Sample B (other teachers in the 70 schools) in several ways. There were more full professors among the religion teachers (41.8% to 34%) and more with doctorates (63.3% to 54.3%), but fewer with master's degrees (53.8% to 83.7%). Among the religion teachers, 53.1% had the first professional ministerial degree, the B.D. or S.T.B., as compared to 1.4% of the other teachers with the B.D. Differences on the more important questions of opinion are presented in the tables below.

Table 2

OPINIONS OF COLLEGE TEACHERS AND OTHERS ON THE COMPARATIVE DESIRABILITY OF DIFFERENT PROFESSIONS

Suppose a young man came to you and asked your opinion about taking up a profession. Assuming that he was qualified to enter any of these professions, which *one* would you first recommend to him?

	Pre-seminary Study results, college teachers, 1962:		*Gallup results:		
	Sample A (158 religion teachers)	Sample B (420 other teachers)	General Public		College trained
			1962	1953	1962
	(Percentage giving indicated response)				
Professor, teacher	27.8	39.5	12	5	18
Doctor	3.8	10.5	23	29	18
Government career	1.3	5.7	7	3	3
Engineer, builder	—	5.2	18	20	24
Clergyman	41.1	4.3	8	7	3
Lawyer	.6	2.1	6	6	8
Dentist	—	1.2	4	6	5
Business executive	—	1.0	5	7	7
Banker	—	—	2	2	—
Druggist	—	—	—	—	2
Other	2.5	3.6	4	7	4
None, don't know	—	—	11	8	8
No Response	1.3	2.6	—	—	—
+Criticism of assumptions	21.5	24.3	—	—	—

*As published by George Gallup, Director, American Institute of Public Opinion, August 14, 1962.

+The critical response to this question generally took the form of a statement of preference for a nondirective approach to counseling students.

NOTE: A breakdown of the responses to this question by college or university type is presented in Table 16 below.

Table 3

OPINIONS OF COLLEGE TEACHERS ON FIELDS OF STUDY PROVIDING A BROAD LIBERAL ARTS EDUCATION

In which fields of study at your school is a student most likely to obtain a broad liberal arts education?

FIELD OF STUDY	Sample A (158 religion teachers) (Percentage mentioning field as one of 3 choices)	Sample B (420 other teachers)
English	63.3	48.8
History	53.8	46.7
Philosophy	44.9	28.1
Education	9.5	17.9
Sociology	11.4	16.2
Religion, Theology, or Bible	39.2	5.0
Political science	10.8	14.8
Fine arts	7.6	9.0
Biological sciences	4.4	10.0
Modern languages	5.1	9.0
Psychology	1.9	6.4
Classics	.6	6.7
Others (including 11 fields listed in questionnaire)	22.6	32.9
No response	3.8	9.8

Table 4

OPINIONS OF COLLEGE TEACHERS ON FIELDS OF STUDY PROVIDING A NARROW CONCENTRATION

In which fields of study at your school would a student's concentration be most narrow?

FIELD OF STUDY	Sample A (158 religion teachers) (Percentage mentioning field as one of 3 choices)	Sample B (420 other teachers)
Business	34.8	37.1
Chemistry	47.5	33.3
Physics	31.6	24.3
Education	20.3	23.6
Music	22.8	17.9
Mathematics	21.5	18.1
Biological sciences	20.3	16.7
Premedicine	17.1	10.5
Speech and Drama	9.5	6.4
Religion, Theology, or Bible	2.5	8.8
Economics	7.6	5.5
Fine arts	5.1	6.2
Others (including 14 listed)	24.6	33.6
No response	6.3	11.0

Table 5

RECOMMENDATIONS OF COLLEGE TEACHERS
ON UNDERGRADUATE MAJOR FOR PRE-SEMINARIANS

Which undergraduate major would you recommend to a student who plans to go on to graduate theological study?

UNDERGRADUATE MAJOR	Sample A (158 religion teachers) (Percentage giving indicated response)	Sample B (420 other teachers)
Philosophy	24.7	27.6
Religion, Theology, or Bible	29.7	11.7
English	12.7	11.7
History	12.7	10.2
Sociology	6.3	11.4
Psychology	.6	6.0
Classics	3.8	2.6
Education	.6	2.1
Speech and Drama	—	1.2
Physics	—	1.0
Mathematics	—	.7
Political science	.6	.5
Others	—	2.8
No reply	8.2	10.5

Table 6

RECOMMENDATIONS OF COLLEGE TEACHERS
ON AMOUNT OF RELIGION COURSES FOR PRE-SEMINARIANS

Should persons studying for a professional religious career take more or fewer courses in religion and Bible than other students *while in college?*

ANSWER	Sample A (158 religion teachers) (Percentage giving indicated response)	Sample B (420 other teachers)
Should take considerably more	27.2	15.0
Should take some more	43.0	36.7
Should take about the same	20.3	32.9
Should take fewer courses in religion	7.0	12.4
No reply	2.5	3.1

Table 7

OPINIONS OF COLLEGE TEACHERS ON DIFFERENT
TYPES OF SCHOOLS FOR PRE-SEMINARIANS

In your opinion, which type of college-level training provides the best preparation for theological studies?

TYPE OF SCHOOL	Sample A (158 religion teachers) (Percentage giving indicated response)	Sample B (420 other teachers)
Denominational college	36.1	13.6
Private university	16.5	11.7
Denominational university	13.3	11.0
Private non-denominational college	7.0	11.2
State university	3.8	9.8
Bible college	.6	.7
Other public university or college	—	.7
All are good: it depends on the student	7.0	21.2
No opinion	8.2	13.1
No response	7.0	5.7

Which type provides the highest academic level of course work in religion?

TYPE OF SCHOOL		
Denominational university	27.2	26.2
Denominational college	24.0	10.5
Private university	15.2	13.6
Private non-denominational college	8.2	5.5
State university	1.3	2.1
Bible college	.6	2.6
State teachers college	—	.2
Other public university or college	—	—
All are good: it depends on the student	.6	6.0
No opinion	13.3	23.8
No response	9.5	9.5

Table 8

OPINIONS OF COLLEGE TEACHERS ON
RELIGION COURSES IN HIGHER EDUCATION

Do you believe that formal courses in religion belong in all schools offering a liberal arts baccalaureate degree?

ANSWER	Sample A (158 religion teachers)	Sample B (420 other teachers)
	'(Percentage giving indicated response)	
No	14.6	25.0
Yes	83.5	73.1
No response	1.9	1.9

If "No," why? Because the study of religion is:

Educationally inappropriate in some schools	5.7	12.1
Unconstitutional in state colleges and universities	5.1	8.3
Unscientific	.6	1.7
Divisive	—	1.2
Harmful to public relations and/or financial support	—	.5
Other	1.9	4.0
No response	88.0	76.9

If "Yes," why? Because the study of religion is:

Concerned with a central aspect of human culture	82.9	68.6
Supportive of character and morals	34.8	19.3
One of the classical scientific disciplines	32.9	14.5
A means of evangelism	8.2	2.4
Helpful to public relations and/or financial support	3.8	1.0
Other	4.4	3.6
No response	10.8	24.0

How would you characterize the provisions for the teaching of religion at the school where you are now teaching?

Formal provisions in the curriculum:

Inadequate	16.5	28.3
Adequate	44.9	43.3
Highly satisfactory	33.5	15.7
Excessive	1.9	2.4
No response	3.2	9.3

Informal and extracurricular provisions:

Inadequate	18.4	14.0
Adequate	55.1	52.6
Highly satisfactory	18.4	20.0
Excessive	3.8	3.6
No response	3.8	9.8

Table 9

COMPARISONS BY COLLEGE TEACHERS OF RELIGION FACULTY MEMBERS AND THE SUBJECT OF RELIGION WITH OTHER TEACHERS AND COURSES

Compare academic offerings in religion with those of other liberal arts courses . . .

	Sample A (158 religion teachers)	Sample B (420 other teachers)
	(Percentage checking linear scale above mid-point, religion relatively high or important)	
SCHOLARSHIP of faculty members	89.5	76.2
TEACHING SKILLS of faculty members	85.0	78.2
COUNSELING ABILITIES of faculty members	86.9	77.4
Importance of subject for:		
LIBERAL ARTS EDUCATION	88.9	67.9
UNDERSTANDING OF THE MODERN WORLD	88.8	75.4
PRE-PROFESSIONAL TRAINING OF THE CLERGY	87.3	75.4

NOTE: The linear scales were checked for each item by the respondents. Divided into ten numbered sections for analysis, the percentages of response in each section were plotted graphically. The distribution of responses was heavily on the high side for both groups of respondents as the table indicates. The response curves appear to be sufficiently regular to warrant this tabulation in terms of the distribution on the high side of the mid-points.

The table indicates, not unexpectedly, that religion teachers tend to rate themselves higher and their subject more important than they are rated by teachers of other subjects. The religion teachers differ most from other teachers in the importance they assign to religion for a liberal arts education. The smallest difference between the two groups of respondents is on the teaching skills of the faculty member in religion, the item about which the religion teacher himself is least confident, contrary to the favorable judgments by teachers in other fields.

This question offered the respondents an opportunity to make critical comparative judgments on the teachers of religion and upon the subject they teach. The image of college and university teachers of religion as revealed here is rather more favorable than may have been assumed by some of the initiators of the Study.

Table 10

OPINIONS OF COLLEGE TEACHERS ON
SELECTION CRITERIA FOR FACULTY MEMBERS IN RELIGION

In the appointment of faculty members to teach courses in religion, how would you personally rate these criteria of selection?

(Percentages of Sample A, 158 religion teachers, and Sample B, 420 other teachers, giving indicated response)

CRITERIA	Very important		Of some importance		Least Important	
	A	B	A	B	A	B
Academic qualifications	76.6	68.8	25.9	25.0	9.5	15.2
Moral and spiritual qualities ..	37.3	37.4	48.7	45.5	8.9	13.1
Religious affiliation	6.9	3.6	4.5	17.7	21.5	34.5
Ordination as a clergyman	1.3	2.4	4.4	6.4	57.6	37.6
No response	2.5	5.2	14.6	19.0	12	14.0

Table 11

KNOWLEDGE OF COLLEGE TEACHERS REGARDING
STUDENTS ENROLLED IN OR PLANNING TO
ENTER THEOLOGICAL SCHOOL

How many students do you know by name who ...

... are definitely planning to enter theological school?		Number of Students	*... are now enrolled in a theological school?*	
Sample A (158 religion teachers)	Sample B (420 other teachers)		Sample A (158 religion teachers)	Sample B (420 other teachers)
(Percentage giving indicated response)			(Percentage giving indicated response)	
1.3	41.9	None	3.2	35.0
19.0	38.1	1 - 4	23.4	39.5
14.6	8.3	5 - 8	10.8	7.9
60.8	8.3	9 or more	57.6	7.4
4.4	3.3	No response	5.1	10.2

Table 12

OPINIONS OF COLLEGE TEACHERS ON PRE-SEMINARIANS

If it is possible to generalize about your students whom you know to be preparing for full-time religious work, would you please attempt to do so with regard to the following?

	Sample A (158 religion teachers)	Sample B (420 other teachers)
SCHOLARSHIP	(Percentage giving indicated response)	
Above average for this school	25.9	21.4
Average	63.3	32.6
Below average of students here	3.2	4.0
No response	7.6	41.9
SELF-CONSCIOUSNESS AS PRE-MINISTERIAL STUDENTS		
They try to be distinctive	16.5	11.4
They try not to be recognizably different from other students	70.3	42.1
No response	13.3	46.4
ACCEPTANCE BY FELLOW STUDENTS		
Mostly well liked	41.1	31.4
Average acceptance	51.9	24.8
Have some difficulty in being accepted	1.3	1.4
No response	5.7	42.4
ORGANIZATION IN A PRE-MINISTERIAL GROUP WITH REGULAR MEETINGS		
All or most of them are	26.6	18.1
Some of them are	33.5	14.8
None are	25.9	13.8
No response	13.9	53.3

Table 13
COLLEGE TEACHERS' RECOMMENDATIONS OF RELIGION AS A VOCATIONAL FIELD

Have you recommended religion as a vocational field to any students?

ANSWER	Sample A (158 religion teachers) (Percentage giving indicated response)	Sample B (420 other teachers)
Yes	81.6	30.7
No	17.7	66.7
No response	.6	2.6

If "Yes," to how many students have you made this recommendation in the last five years?

None	.6	.5
1- 5	20.9	20.2
6-10	22.2	4.0
11-15	9.5	.5
16-20	3.8	.2
21-30	10.1	.7
31-50	3.8	.5
51-100	—	—
Over 100	3.2	.5
No response	25.9	72.9

If "No," why not?

I make no recommendations to students on their vocations	4.4	14.8
I do not recruit for religious vocations	3.8	8.1
The call to full-time religious service should come in other ways	6.3	16.9
I have not known students qualified or sufficiently interested	1.9	22.1
Other	2.5	7.9
No response	82.3	32.1

Table 14

OPINIONS OF COLLEGE TEACHERS ON FACTORS DETERMINING WHO WILL BECOME EFFECTIVE MINISTERS

How important do you consider each of the following in determining who will become effective ministers?

	Sample A (158 religion teachers)	Sample B (420 other teachers)
	(Percentage indicating either "very important" or "somewhat important")	
Having a broad academic background	85.4	83.8
Possessing public speaking ability	77.2	71.2
*Having a definite call to the ministry	75.3	73.1
Having a work experience before seminary	58.2	58.3
*Specializing in some academic discipline	62.6	52.6
Having father interested in the church	50.6	45.2
*Having mother interested in the church	50.6	45.2
Majoring in religion in college	40.5	36.4
*Attending a denominational college	33.1	36.0
Having a scientific background	30.3	31.9
*Being a minister's son	31.0	24.3
Other response or no response	24.7	22.4

*If ranked in terms of "very important" responses only, the five indicated items would be one or two places higher on the list. "Having a work experience before seminary" would be three places lower, this item being considered "somewhat important" by nearly 2½ times as many as considered it "very important."

Table 15

OPINIONS OF COLLEGE TEACHERS ON DEFICIENCIES OF CLERGYMEN

What seems to be the greatest deficiency of the clergymen you have known?

	Sample A 158 religion teachers)	Sample B (420 other teachers)
	(Percentage giving indicated response)	
Limited intellectual ability	22.2	31.2
Overconcern with organizational promotion and statistics	19.0	10.2
Inability to communicate	14.6	10.5
Lack of social and political awareness	8.9	13.6
Insensitivity in interpersonal relations	12.7	6.7
Tendency to be autocratic	5.7	11.2
Lack of a clear doctrinal position	9.5	6.9
Lack of courage before church officials or laymen	3.8	8.6
Ineptness in organizational matters	1.3	2.6
Other	9.5	11.0
No response	4.4	8.6

Table 16

OPINIONS OF COLLEGE TEACHERS ON THE DESIRABILITY
OF DIFFERENT PROFESSIONS:
DIFFERENCES BY TYPE OF COLLEGE OR UNIVERSITY*

Suppose a young man came to you and asked for your opinion about taking up a profession. Assuming that he was qualified to enter any of these professions, which *one* would you first recommend to him?

	Public college or university		Private college or university		Denominational college or university	
	(21 religion teachers)	(222 other teachers)	(40 religion teachers)	(85 other teachers)	(96 religion teachers	(88 other teachers)
	(Percentage giving indicated response)					
Professor, teacher ..	38.1	42.8	27.5	31.8	25.0	37.5
Doctor	4.8	11.7	2.5	8.2	4.2	5.7
Government career	—	6.3	5.0	8.2	—	3.4
Engineer, builder ..	—	5.9	—	3.5	—	4.5
Clergyman	33.3	1.4	22.5	3.5	51.0	13.6
Lawyer	—	2.3	2.5	2.4	—	1.1
Dentist	—	.9	—	1.2	—	1.1
Business executive .	—	1.4	—	—	—	—
Other	4.8	3.2	—	2.4	3.1	6.8
No response	—	3.6	—	3.5	2.1	2.3
Criticism of assumptions	19.0	20.7	40.0	35.3	14.6	22.7

*This table provides a breakdown by college or university type for the data presented in Table 2 above, omitting 26 responses from public teachers colleges.

3. CONSULTATIONS
AND OPINIONS

The letters from the Study directors to the presidents and deans of A.A.T.S. seminaries dated March 6, 1962, included reference to two types of consultations on pre-seminary education.

We believe that we would benefit greatly from your holding a faculty consultation on pre-seminary education. We would appreciate your sharing with us any consensus developed on the following questions, together with minority views resulting from one or more meetings during this calendar year.

    a. From what colleges and universities do your best students come? (Please try to provide a *qualitative* judgment. Quantitative data is available from other sources.)

    b. How well prepared do you want your students to be before entering seminary? (Please try to indicate specific courses you believe they should and should *not* take at the undergraduate level.)

    c. What are the major deficiencies of your entering students which might have been overcome by a more adequate pre-seminary education? (Please include extracurricular considerations and make specific recommendations.)

    d. In what ways would you revise the present A.A.T.S. statement on pre-seminary education?

In addition to these consultations at each seminary, we are planning a number of regional consultations to bring together theological school administrators and faculty members in one-day meetings with representatives from undergraduate education. We will let you know about the one in your region. . . .

A. Seminary faculty consultations

Replies from 103 of the 125 member seminaries specified dates for the requested faculty consultations. The Study directors attended several of these intramural meetings. Sixty others were reported in writing to the Study office. At some schools the discussion of the four suggested questions was conducted as a part of a larger program of curriculum revision. Highlights from these consultation reports are discussed in Part One and are briefly described below.

B. Regional consultations

1. *Minneapolis.* The first of the regional consultations brought together 50 seminary and college teachers and administrators from 10 colleges and 6 seminaries in Minnesota on February 22, 1962. Addresses by Dr. Paul L. Holmer of the Yale Divinity School and by Dr. Robert Michaelsen of the University of Iowa were later revised and published in the symposium on *The Making of Ministers.* The major emphasis at Minneapolis was on the nature of the ministry and some of the larger issues in theological education. Discussion by all of the invited consultants proved so helpful to the Study directors that plans were made immediately for the other four regional consultations.

2. *Claremont.* The California consultation was attended by 40 representatives of 15 colleges and 8 seminaries at the School of Theology at Claremont on April 6 and 7, 1962. These sessions were arranged by a host committee under Dr. Ernest C. Colwell, a member of the Board of Advisors to the Study. His remarks, later revised for inclusion in *The Making of Ministers,* were typical of these sessions, which focused on the undergraduate curriculum to be recommended or required for admission to seminary.

3. *Chicago.* On May 7, 1962, a Midwestern consultation was attended by 55 representatives of 18 colleges and 13 seminaries at the University of Chicago, with arrangements made by Dean Jerald C. Brauer of the Divinity School. Addresses or statements, later appearing in *The Making of Ministers*, were presented by: Dr. Reuel L. Howe, director of the Institute for Advanced Pastoral Studies, Bloomfield Hills, Michigan; Dr. Martin E. Marty, Associate Editor of *The Christian Century*; and Dr. C. Umhau Wolf, Pastor of St. Paul's Lutheran Church, Toledo, Ohio. Attention centered on problems of communication and relevance. The day at Chicago ended with a discussion of the A.A.T.S. Statement on Pre-Seminary Studies led by Dr. John L. Cheek of Albion College, a member of the Board of Advisors to the Study.

4. *Atlanta.* The Southeastern consultation on October 19 and 20, 1962, included 69 representatives from 28 colleges and 13 seminaries in nine states. Dean William R. Cannon of the Candler School of Theology and Professor Jack S. Boozer, Department of Religion, Emory University, served as hosts. Housing was provided at Emory, Columbia Theological Seminary, and the Inter-denominational Theological Center. As in the other regional consultations, there was a surprise, almost a chagrin, at the discovery that in many cases the college and seminary representatives had not—even as relatively close neighbors—made one another's acquaintance before. They found this to be true even when they had taught the same students and were members of the same denominational education system. The mutual interests and concerns expressed on this occasion also met the needs of the Study directors for a comprehensive review. The perspective provided by Dr. Arnold Nash of the University of North Carolina was later expanded to form the concluding essay in *The Making of Ministers.*

5. *Dallas.* The Council of Southwest Seminaries helped to plan the consultation which included representatives from their six schools and from 33 colleges, a total of 41 persons from five states, at the Perkins School of Theology, Southern Methodist University, on November 30 and December 1, 1962. Dean Joseph D. Quillian served as host and arranged for a typed transcript of

the discussions. He also invited the participants to send him outlines of the curricula they wanted considered. These he compared and related as a basis for a detailed agenda. The Study directors were provided with a valuable recapitulation of the entire range of topics in pre-seminary education, with a special emphasis on the problems of the region, including the demand on the colleges for undergraduate professional education of church workers who do not go on to seminary. Again, the general agreement was expressed that such gatherings ought to be held more frequently and perhaps on a regular basis. One of the major purposes of the Study was thus met prior to the publication of this Report. These regional consultations helped to bring a consensus that colleges and seminaries ought to be better informed about one another and that their programs ought to be more effectively integrated.

The suggested pretheological curricula discussed at Dallas and elsewhere included the following.

I.

Survey of Old and New Testaments, an introduction to modern biblical study
History of Religions
History of Philosophy, Philosophy of Religion, and Ethics
Greek (two years)
German (two years)
Broad education in liberal arts: English, History, Philosophy, Psychology, Sociology, and Speech

II.

Suggested major fields: English, History, and Sociology
Recommended courses in religion:

Introduction to Old Testament	1st year
Introduction to New Testament	2nd year
Christianity and Contemporary Issues	3rd year

Foreign language: Two years (either French or German)
Biblical language: Not required, but two courses in Greek are offered
Philosophy:
Introductory Philosophy
Problems in Philosophy

III.

Freshman Year:

English, Biology or Geology, German or Greek, Bible, Speech, Art, History of Christianity

Sophomore Year:

English, Physics or Chemistry, German or Greek, Philosophy (one semester), Sociology (one semester), Government (one semester), Psychology (one semester)

Junior Year:

Economics (one semester), English (Shakespeare), Philosophy (Ancient and Medieval), History of Civilization, Drama (one semester), Sociology

Senior Year:

Philosophy (Modern), Philosophy (Senior Seminary), Historical Geography (Bible), History (American Life and Thought), Sociology (Marriage and Family), Methodism (one semester), American Christianity (one semester), Essentials of Christian Faith (one semester)

IV.

General Education Requirements:

Communications (8 hrs.); Health and Physical Education (4 hrs.); Natural Sciences (12 hrs.); Social Sciences (12 hrs.); Humanities (12 hrs., including Introduction to Arts, Greek-Roman Culture and 3 hrs. of Greek); Biblical Literature (Old Testament History, 3 hrs.; Origin and Principles of Christianity, 3 hrs.).

Junior Year:

History of Christianity; Introduction or History of Modern Philosophy; Philosophy of Religion; World Religions; Christian Worship; World Civilization; History of Religion in America

Senior Year:

History and Principles of Christian Education; Protestant Doctrine and Ethic; New Testament Greek; English Literature

V.

Freshman Year:

Written Communication (6 hrs.); Art or Music (2 hrs.); Man and Civilization (6 hrs.); Elementary Foreign Language (6 hrs.); Introductory Science (8 hrs.); Health and Physical Education (4 hrs.)

Sophomore Year:

General Studies (3 hrs. of Psychology, Sociology, or Ethics); American Civilization and Institutions (5 hrs.); Intermediate Foreign Language (6 hrs.); English Literature (4-6 hrs.); Physical Education (2 hrs.); Electives (10-12 hrs.)

Junior Year:

Old Testament Literature and Life (2 hrs.); Life and Religion of Jesus or New Testament Literature and Life (2-3 hrs.); Religions of the World (3 hrs.); Other courses in Religion (15 hrs.); Nonmajor electives (7-8 hrs.)

Senior Year:

Religion (12 hrs.); nonmajor electives (18 hrs.)

C. Ministers

Some clergymen were invited to each of the regional consultations. Others were interviewed throughout the Study. There was also one systematic approach to ministers as a source of data on pre-seminary education.

Lacking an instrument to measure ministerial effectiveness or even an adequate criterion to measure, it was decided to choose a panel of ministers recommended for this purpose by the respondents to the College Teacher Questionnaire. The 572 teachers provided the names and addresses of 350 persons in response to this request:

We are seeking the names of clergymen who may be willing to share with us their reflections on their own educational experience. For this purpose, we would appreciate having the name and address of someone whom you regard as an outstanding example of this profession.

The clergymen recommended are not necessarily typical of their profession. Selected as outstanding by a representative sample of college teachers, they are more likely to be in college communities, and are probably more academically oriented than other ministers who might be regarded as equally "outstanding" by nonteachers. The ministers selected by the teachers proved to be good respondents. There were 265 replies (76%) to the following March 8, 1963, letter from the Study directors.

You have been named by one or more college teachers as a clergyman regarded to be an outstanding example of your profession. For this reason, we hope you may be willing to share with us your reflections on your own educational experience.

We hope that the enclosed check-list will suggest issues on which you will wish to comment, advising us on how the total resources of undergraduate and seminary education may be more effectively used in the preparation of competent ministers.

Your comments, signed or unsigned as you prefer, should be a significant addition to the data which has been provided to this study by 17,500 theological students, by five regional consultations of college and seminary faculty members, and by the college teacher sample from which came the recommendation of your name. A report volume and a separate symposium on pre-seminary education are to be published early in 1964.

As a practicing minister, your candid views on your own training are needed in the critical reappraisal of theological education which is taking place today. What parts of your education—college and seminary—have proved to be of greatest value in your ministry? In what ways did your training fail to prepare you adequately for your ministry? How do you think it could have been improved? Is a radical reformation of theological education necessary?

Your observations will be most helpful to us if received within the next month.

The Ministers Questionnaire on 5" x 8" paper was intended mainly to stimulate comment rather than to gather valid statistics. Its ten statements, with which the respondents were asked to agree or disagree, tended to be oversimplifications of complex topics. There were 27 letters in addition to detailed comments on the back of the form from more than half of the ministerial respondents. Their comments are discussed in Part One, as are the relatively less important agreements and disagreements with the statements in the questionnaire. (See pages 133-7.)

4. BACCALAUREATE ORIGINS OF SEMINARIANS

From the outset of the Study, the directors heard generalizations regarding shifting sources of ministerial students and differing estimates by college administrators on the numbers of their graduates attending seminaries. Two sources of data were used to gain a more accurate picture of the actual distribution of pre-seminarians in higher education in the United States and Canada.

The Seminarian Questionnaire was to yield data for fall, 1962. Meanwhile, published lists for 1960-61 were available for many seminaries in their 1960-61 catalogs. To these were added lists supplied directly to the Study office by those schools which had not published this information. The 1960-61 data was entered on a separate tally sheet for each of the 995 colleges and universities to provide a preliminary tabulation. Both sources of baccalaureate origins data—the 1960-61 lists and the Fall, 1962, Seminarian Questionnaires—provide more comprehensive and accurate descriptions than any previously available. It is possible to discuss trends in the type of undergraduate schools attended by pre-seminarians only in the broad outline suggested by the note to Table 17. Neither of these new data sources has sufficient accuracy to warrant a discussion of trends for the one-year interval involved. Therefore, only one source is used in the following table.

Table 17

TYPE OF COLLEGES AND UNIVERSITIES PREVIOUSLY ATTENDED BY 17,565 SEMINARIANS IN A.A.T.S. SCHOOLS, FALL, 1962

COLLEGE OR UNIVERSITY TYPE	Number	Per cent
Public (including multi-purpose teachers colleges)	3,541	20.2
Public teachers college ("d" in Education Directory)	151	.9
Private, regionally accredited	2,606	14.8
Denominational, regionally accredited	8,853	50.4
Bible college	114	.6
Women's college, public or private, accredited	55	.3
Catholic university or college, accredited	36	.2
Other U.S. colleges and universities including nonaccredited	440	2.5
Canadian, all colleges and universities	642	3.7
Foreign (Non-U.S. and non-Canadian)	422	2.4
Unknown	701	4.0
No response	4	–
	17,565	100.0

NOTE: Classification is according to *Education Directory, 1961-62, Part 3. Higher Education,* U.S. Office of Education. The Seminarian Questionnaire is further described in Section V below. The respondents represent 83% of those enrolled in A.A.T.S. member schools, fall, 1962. Comparative data for the early 1930's from "a selected list of 1,776 students" shows that 1,497 (84.3%) were college graduates. Of these: 230 (15.3%) were graduates of nonaccredited denominational colleges, 376 (25.1) were graduates of sectionally accredited denominational colleges, 40 (2.7%) were graduates of large independent universities, and 87 (5.8%) were graduates of state universities. This was said to be "an undesirable concentration in enrollment of students who are graduates of denominational institutions"—a total of 77%.[1]

It should be noted that all but four of the 17,565 respondents listed an undergraduate college or university whether or not they held a first baccalaureate degree. However, a trend toward the completion of undergraduate work leading to a B.A. or a B.S. by an increasing proportion of persons attending seminary is confirmed by this data. In 1924 it was estimated that 44% of seminary students had college degrees. Based on an analysis of 61 leading seminaries[2] in the United States for 1929-30, it was concluded

---

[1]Mark A. May, *The Education of American Ministers, Vol. III, The Institutions That Train Ministers* (New York: Institute of Social and Religious Research, 1934), p. 295.

[2]Robert L. Kelly, *Theological Education in America. A Study of 161 Theological Schools in the United States and Canada,* New York, 1924, p. 164.

"for the country as a whole it is safe to say that in 1930 about half (plus or minus five per cent) of all theological students did not hold college degrees."[3] By 1957, the Niebuhr, Williams, and Gustafson study concluded that the 134 reporting schools of 1955 had given evidence that "not less than 80 per cent of the estimated total enrollment of theological students in the United States and Canada consists of college graduates."[4] This trend continues. Among the fall, 1962, respondents to the Seminarian Questionnaire, 11.1% indicate no earned degree, only a certificate or diploma, or do not reply to the question. The other 88.9% claim a first baccalaureate degree or a higher degree which presupposes a B.A. or B.S.

Both sources of baccalaureate origins data guided the directors in other phases of the Study. Separate analyses by regions were prepared for the discussions at the regional consultations. Other regional analyses have been prepared for *ad hoc* committees studying the possibility of creating new centers of theological education in the Pacific Northwest and in the Detroit area.

Table 18 summarizes the 1960-61 baccalaureate origins data for 298 colleges and universities in the United States from which 20 or more "graduates" went on to A.A.T.S. member seminaries, according to the latter. The comparative rank of each undergraduate institution as a producer of seminarians is indicated in two ways: as a rank order in terms of numbers produced and as an index which takes into account the size of the college or university. The number of seminaries involved in each case is shown, and the number of Seminarian Questionnaire respondents is also included for comparison between the two data sources. The first 101 institutions from Table 18 are presented in order of the number of their former students in seminary in Table 19. Table 20 is a complete summary of the Seminarian Questionnaire data on seminaries attended by graduates of Canadian universities.

---

[3]Mark A. May, *op. cit.*, p. 325.
[4]Niebuhr, et al., *op. cit.*, p. 8.

Table 18

THE 298 AMERICAN INSTITUTIONS OF HIGHER EDUCATION
WITH 20 OR MORE GRADUATES ENROLLED
IN A.A.T.S. MEMBER SEMINARIES

Listed Alphabetically with: Rank; Number of Graduates in Seminaries, 1960-61;
Spring, 1961, Enrollments; Index; Number of Seminaries Attended by
Graduates; and Respondents to Seminarian Questionnaire

A. Rank in 298 schools with 20 or more graduates in seminaries, 1960-
61, from data in catalogs and lists supplied by seminaries

B. Number of graduates in seminaries 1960-61

C. Total students, Spring, 1961, according to *1962 World Almanac*

D. Index (B over C x 100)

E. Number of seminaries attended by graduates, 1960-61

F. Number of respondents to Pre-Seminary Study Seminarian Questionnaire, Fall, 1962

COLLEGE OR UNIVERSITY	A. Rank	B. Number	C. Students	D. Index	E. Seminaries	F. Respondents
Abilene Christian	232	26	2,293	1.13	13	12
Adrian	291	20	819	2.44	9	23
Alabama, U. of	108	45	12,235	.37	18	35
Albion	113	44	1,355	3.25	15	29
Albright	130	40	827	4.84	12	41
Alma	244	25	715	3.50	13	16
American U.	218	27	7,530	.36	16	32
Amherst	256	24	929	2.43	12	14
Anderson	30	101	1,008	10.02	13	47
Arizona, U. of	193	30	12,518	.24	17	25
Asbury	6	218	896	24.33	35	162
Atlantic Christian	188	31	1,069	2.90	8	25
Augsburg	58	68	1,079	6.30	10	81
Augustana (Ill.)	34	87	1,350	6.44	16	68
Augustana (S.D.)	88	52	1,351	3.85	11	51
Austin	126	41	890	4.61	8	42
Baldwin-Wallace	269	23	2,009	1.14	12	25
Ball State Teachers	232	26	6,806	.38	10	16
Barrington	178	32	445	7.19	10	43
Bates	244	25	843	2.97	11	21
Baylor U.	1	496	5,604	8.85	31	306
Belmont	163	34	395	8.61	5	20
Bethany (W.Va.)	152	36	721	4.99	15	33
Bethany Nazarene	170	33	822	4.01	7	26
Bethel (Ind.)	218	27	394	6.85	2	5

Table 18 (continued)

COLLEGE OR UNIVERSITY	A. Rank	B. Number	C. Students	D. Index	E. Seminaries	F. Respondents
Bethel (Minn.)	48	75	634	11.83	16	64
Bethel (Tenn.)	79	55	503	10.93	11	43
Birmingham-Southern	71	59	937	6.30	13	49
Bloomfield	232	26	416	6.25	14	17
Bluffton	256	24	390	6.15	14	14
Bob Jones U.	41	80	2,747	2.91	25	32
Boston U.	105	46	16,645	.28	19	50
Bridgewater	200	29	586	4.95	9	22
Brown U.	232	26	3,881	.67	16	27
Bucknell U.	218	27	2,260	1.19	15	10
Buffalo, U. of	291	20	11,178	.18	18	17
Butler U.	113	44	3,924	1.12	12	33
California Baptist	71	59	409*	14.43	4	34
California, U. of	7	192	47,539	.40	38	120
Calvin	30	101	2,150	4.70	9	102
Capital U.	14	160	1,281	12.49	12	141
Carleton	291	20	1,160	1.72	16	18
Carson-Newman	11	175	1,256	13.93	13	137
Carthage	99	48	581	8.26	13	36
Catawba	232	26	809	3.21	10	26
Centenary	178	32	1,401	2.28	11	34
Central (Iowa)	170	33	496	6.65	3	26
Central (Mo.)	232	26	736	3.53	11	32
Central Michigan U.	291	20	4,908	.41	9	14
Chicago, U. of	152	36	5,489	.66	18	13
Cincinnati, U. of	232	26	15,165	.17	18	32
Clemson	269	23	1,900	.61	5	12
Colgate U.	170	33	1,389	2.38	19	21
Colorado, U. of	145	37	9,600	.39	25	43
Columbia Union (Md.)	232	26	906	2.87	1	8
Columbia U.	232	26	22,195	.12	17	13
Concordia Senior (Ind.)	2	442	337	131.16	2	497
Concordia (Minn.)	27	102	1,621	6.29	13	78
Concordia Seminary (Mo.)	99	48	549	8.74	6	24
Cornell (Iowa)	269	23	746	3.08	8	13
Cornell U.	130	40	10,912	.37	20	33
Corpus Christi, U. of	40	81	560	14.46	5	49
Dartmouth	157	35	3,075	1.14	19	32
Davidson	25	105	952	11.03	22	68
Denison U.	244	25	1,453	1.72	13	21
Denver, U. of	244	25	4,505	.55	15	21
DePauw U.	59	67	2,181	3.07	20	51

Table 18 (continued)

COLLEGE OR UNIVERSITY	A. Rank	B. Number	C. Students	D. Index	E. Seminaries	F. Respondents
Dickinson	291	20	1,121	1.78	13	17
Drake U.	118	43	3,473	1.24	19	27
Drew U.	113	44	948	4.64	18	27
Dubuque, U. of	103	47	570	8.25	16	37
Duke U.	27	102	5,686	1.79	35	91
Earlham	207	28	870	3.22	14	33
East Tennessee State ...	218	27	3,734	.72	13	20
East Texas Baptist	47	76	432	17.59	6	58

*Fall, 1961 enrollment. Source: *Higher Education Directory, 1962-63.*

East Texas State	218	27	2,956	.91	4	14
Eastern Baptist	62	64	342	18.71	11	50
Eastern Nazarene	145	37	724	5.11	11	36
Eastern New Mexico U.	232	26	1,611	1.61	6	19
Elizabethtown	244	25	701	3.57	10	31
Elmhurst	25	105	850	12.35	19	91
Elon	218	27	1,256	2.15	9	25
Emmanuel Missionary ..	139	38	1,102	3.45	1	11
Emory and Henry	218	27	704	3.84	9	24
Emory U.	65	63	3,963	1.59	21	42
Erskine	135	39	619	6.30	7	33
Evansville	244	25	2,344	1.07	10	22
Florida Southern	163	34	1,886	1.80	19	36
Florida State U.	96	49	8,762	.56	17	39
Florida, U. of	77	56	11,938	.47	23	36
Franklin College of Indiana	244	25	600	4.17	14	11
Franklin and Marshall ..	79	55	1,341	4.10	16	43
Friends U.	207	28	645	4.34	15	19
Furman U.	8	189	1,505	12.56	14	114
George Washington U. .	291	20	9,405	21	17	20
Georgetown (Ky).	30	101	1,112	9.08	8	71
Georgia Institute of Technology	256	24	5,133	.47	8	35
Georgia, U. of	67	62	7,010	.88	20	53
Gettysburg	17	136	1,647	8.26	18	80
Gordon	65	63	431	14.62	16	49
Goshen	88	52	1,029	5.05	15	44
Grand Canyon	99	48	412	11.65	5	40
Greenville	96	49	542	9.04	18	31
Grove City	145	37	1,478	2.50	14	34
Gustavus Adolphus	45	77	1,116	6.90	16	72

Table 18 (continued)

COLLEGE OR UNIVERSITY	A. Rank	B. Number	C. Students	D. Index	E. Semi-naries	F. Respon-dents
Hamline U.	200	29	991	2.93	10	22
Hampden-Sydney	278	22	400	5.50	7	14
Hanover	269	23	803	2.86	9	21
Hardin-Simmons U.	12	171	1,535	11.14	7	106
Harvard U.	53	70	11,462	.61	21	69
Hastings	282	21	750	2.80	10	18
Heidelberg	130	40	900	4.44	14	36
Hendrix	200	29	561	5.17	10	26
High Point	92	51	978	5.21	12	47
Hobart	291	20	765	2.61	9	14
Hope	37	86	1,490	5.77	20	64
Houghton	37	86	794	10.83	32	47
Houston, U. of	188	31	10,610	.29	9	16
Howard (Ala.)	4	230	1,964	11.71	17	147
Howard Payne	18	128	1,088	11.76	8	92
Huntingdon	244	25	849	2.94	9	19
Illinois, U. of	53	70	26,010	.27	29	55
Illinois Wesleyan U.	188	31	1,165	2.66	13	22
Indiana Central	244	25	1,435	1.74	9	25
Indiana U.	113	44	24,963	.18	22	34
Iowa State U.	126	41	9,726	.42	25	36
Iowa, U. of	122	42	10,388	.40	15	25
Johnson Bible	170	33	191	17.28	6	18
Johnson C. Smith U.	232	26	806	3.23	6	16
Juniata	270	23	783	2.94	10	19
Kalamazoo	291	20	675	2.96	10	17
Kansas, U. of	218	27	8,719	.31	17	29
Kent State U.	278	22	9,269	.24	13	9
Kentucky, U. of	163	34	6,800	.50	10	22
Kentucky Wesleyan	157	35	638	5.49	10	33
King	200	29	253	11.46	6	21
Lafayette	256	24	1,463	1.64	14	17
LaGrange	269	23	403	5.71	6	26
Lakeland	269	23	385	5.97	6	27
Lambuth	193	30	560	5.36	9	22
La Sierra	256	24	979	2.45	24	12
Lebanon Valley	79	55	655	8.40	7	28
Lehigh U.	278	22	3,384	.65	11	16
Lenoir Rhyne	74	57	970	5.88	7	51
Linfield	256	24	913	2.74	7	27
Los Angeles State	188	31	14,642	.21	15	28
Louisiana	24	108	1,056	10.23	7	37
Louisiana Poly. Inst.	218	27	3,410	.79	8	18

Table 18 (continued)

COLLEGE OR UNIVERSITY	A. Rank	B. Number	C. Students	D. Index	E. Seminaries	F. Respondents
Louisiana St. U. & A. & M.	145	37	11,928	.31	16	27
Louisville, U. of	244	25	5,870	.42	14	21
Luther (Iowa)	32	100	1,193	8.38	5	80
Lycoming	178	32	952	3.36	14	33
Lynchburg	145	37	815	4.54	15	32
Macalester	139	38	1,586	2.40	20	37
Manchester	152	36	1,099	3.28	11	24
Marion	244	25	412	6.07	7	20
Marshall U.	200	29	3,731	.78	15	25
Maryland, U. of	152	36	20,882	.17	18	35
Maryville	62	64	706	9.07	18	60
Massachusetts, U. of	256	24	6,300	.38	10	11
McKendree	139	38	350	10.86	9	29
McMurry	79	55	1,119	4.92	9	30
Memphis State U.	200	29	4,989	.58	13	11
Mercer U.	9	186	1,342	13.86	12	95
Miami U. (Ohio)	135	39	6,518	.60	20	42
Miami, U. of (Fla.)	232	26	13,453	.19	16	25
Michigan State U.	61	65	20,545	.32	32	55
Michigan, U. of	56	69	24,229	.28	32	48
Midland	88	52	575	9.04	12	34
Milligan	282	21	440	4.77	9	18
Millikin U.	291	20	1,053	1.90	8	12
Millsaps	74	57	832	6.85	17	43
Minnesota, U. of	19	126	28,277	.44	41	127
Mississippi	5	226	1,720	13.14	10	105
Mississippi State U.	178	32	4,398	.73	15	26
Missouri, U. of	139	38	14,267	.27	20	47
Moravian	178	32	857	3.73	7	31
Morehouse	269	23	793	2.90	9	8
Morningside	256	24	963	2.49	13	19
Mount Union	200	29	893	3.25	13	17
Muhlenberg	41	80	1,036	7.72	9	64
Muskingum	118	43	1,167	3.68	14	37
Nebraska, U. of	163	34	8,465	.40	22	35
Nebraska Wesleyan U.	139	38	1,009	3.77	13	30
North Carolina, U. of	94	50	11,369	.44	20	45
North Central	84	53	862	6.15	13	29
North Texas State	99	48	6,932	.69	14	34
Northwest Christian	51	71	348	20.40	9	55
Northwest Nazarene	218	27	531	5.08	6	17
Northwestern U.	34	87	14,310	.61	28	41

Table 18 (continued)

COLLEGE OR UNIVERSITY	A. Rank	B. Number	C. Students	D. Index	E. Semi-naries	F. Respon-dents
Oakwood	291	20	339	5.90	4	6
Oberlin	130	40	2,327	1.72	15	39
Occidental	122	42	1,436	2.92	13	40
Ohio State U.	84	53	22,879	.23	25	54
Ohio U.	200	29	8,054	.36	17	29
Ohio Wesleyan U.	56	69	1,991	3.47	22	55
Oklahoma Baptist U.	3	235	1,258	18.68	10	139
Oklahoma City U.	92	51	2,554	2.00	16	40
Oklahoma State U.	152	36	10,074	.36	11	37
Oklahoma, U. of	71	59	10,571	.56	23	41
Olivet Nazarene	130	40	975	4.10	10	29
Ottawa U.	218	27	547	4.94	11	25
Otterbein	103	47	983	4.78	9	31
Ouachita Baptist	22	120	1,106	10.85	5	94
Pacific Lutheran U.	37	86	1,599	5.38	6	73
Pacific Union	256	24	1,129	2.13	1	13
Pacific, U. of the	200	29	1,707	1.70	10	16
Pasadena	130	40	1,002	3.99	14	28
Pennsylvania State U.	118	43	20,080	.21	23	36
Pennsylvania, U. of	188	31	16,393	.19	21	31
Pepperdine	291	20	1,236	1.61	9	13
Phillips U.	23	110	1,132	9.72	18	92
Pittsburgh, U. of	84	53	12,367	.43	18	48
Presbyterian	113	44	495	8.89	7	30
Princeton U.	94	50	3,828	1.31	25	40
Purdue U.	218	27	14,206	.19	19	31
Randolph-Macon	92	51	602	8.47	16	30
Redlands, U. of	122	42	1,555	2.70	16	50
Richmond, U. of	21	121	1,933	6.31	15	80
Roberts Wesleyan	282	21	422	4.98	8	18
Rutgers, State U. of	163	34	17,100	.20	19	33
St. Olaf	13	166	1,832	9.06	17	147
Sam Houston St. Teachers	291	20	4,192	.48	5	19
San Diego State	207	28	11,074	.25	18	18
San Francisco State	269	23	11,729	.20	12	31
San Jose State	291	20	14,288	.14	11	21
Seattle Pacific	139	38	1,156	3.29	20	43
Simpson	218	27	683	3.95	11	19
Sioux Falls	244	25	452	5.53	9	25
South, U. of the	178	32	720	4.44	10	24
South Carolina, U. of	170	33	5,557	5.93	11	26
Southeastern Louisiana	269	23	1,553	1.48	9	5

Table 18 (continued)

COLLEGE OR UNIVERSITY	A. Rank	B. Number	C. Students	D. Index	E. Seminaries	F. Respondents
Southern California, U. of	291	20	15,932	.12	12	27
Southern Illinois U.	74	57	12,171	.47	10	46
Southern Methodist U.	74	57	4,996	1.14	16	62
Southern Mississippi, U. of	178	32	4,349	.74	9	17
Southwest Missouri State	256	24	2,589	.93	11	20
Southwestern (Kan.)	163	34	621	5.48	16	27
Southwestern U. at Memphis	152	36	699	5.15	15	34
Southwestern U. (Texas)	105	46	685	6.72	11	36
Stanford U.	163	34	8,560	.40	19	32
Stephen F. Austin State	232	26	1,925	1.35	4	18
Stetson U.	43	78	1,334	5.85	15	52
Susquehanna U.	200	29	690	4.20	6	21
Syracuse U.	88	52	16,481	.31	22	47
Temple U.	84	53	19,296	.27	17	38
Taylor U.	65	63	783	8.05	18	54
Tennessee, U. of	122	42	10,918	.39	17	39
Tennessee Wesleyan	269	23	591	3.89	7	18
Texas, A. & M. Col. of	163	34	6,580	.52	11	26
Texas Christian U.	20	123	5,681	2.17	16	69
Texas Lutheran	103	47	571	8.23	6	49
Texas System, U. of	33	90	23,529	.38	30	76
Texas Technological	152	36	8,682	.41	11	31
Texas Wesleyan	50	73	1,269	5.75	8	51
Thiel	145	37	864	4.28	8	34
Transylvania U.	126	41	507	8.09	7	28
Trinity (Conn.)	113	44	1,335	3.30	17	35
Trinity U. (Texas)	218	27	1,642	1.64	12	26
Troy State	291	20	1,330	1.50	4	7
Tulsa, U. of	188	31	4,384	.71	17	29
Union (Ky).	178	32	662	4.83	18	29
Union (Nebr.)	218	27	868	3.11	3	7
Union U. (Tenn.)	49	74	645	11.47	8	56
Upsala	178	32	1,883	1.70	11	29
Ursinus	218	27	881	3.06	27	26
Valparaiso U.	269	23	2,543	.90	12	38
Vanderbilt U.	108	45	3,585	1.26	17	20
Virginia Poly. Inst.	207	28	6,129	.46	14	18
Virginia Union U.	178	32	994	3.22	11	18
Virginia, U. of	157	35	4,934	.71	16	29
Wagner	122	42	1,686	2.49	11	35

Table 18 (continued)

COLLEGE OR UNIVERSITY	A. Rank	B. Number	C. Students	D. Index	E. Semi-naries	F. Respon-dents
Wake Forest	15	151	2,455	6.15	19	90
Walla Walla	188	31	1,209	2.56	3	15
Wartburg	16	140	994	14.08	12	110
Washington and Lee U.	270	23	1,173	1.96	13	12
Washington U. (Mo.)	269	23	11,793	.19	18	26
Washington, U. of (Seattle)	113	44	24,160	.18	18	42
Wayland Baptist	51	71	528	13.45	5	53
Wayne State U.	178	32	20,919	.15	24	35
Waynesburg	193	30	865	3.47	11	21
Wesleyan U.	159	35	865	4.05	19	20
West Virginia U.	278	22	6,299	.35	14	21
West Virginia Wesleyan	56	69	1,093	6.31	14	55
Western Maryland	200	29	682	4.25	14	25
Westmar	135	39	621	6.28	10	35
Westminster (Pa.)	108	45	1,330	3.28	16	34
Westmont	178	32	456	7.02	10	29
Wheaton	10	184	1,791	10.27	36	150
Whittier	256	24	1,349	1.78	10	13
Whitworth	69	61	1,433	4.26	16	58
William Jewell	67	62	931	6.66	19	93
William and Mary	256	24	2,270	1.06	19	22
Wisconsin, U. of	60	66	27,386	.24	27	75
Wittenberg U.	43	78	2,342	3.33	10	94
Wofford	82	54	703	7.68	14	42
Wooster, College of	45	77	1,234	6.24	22	63
Yale U.	37	86	8,129	1.06	24	68

Table 19

101 AMERICAN INSTITUTIONS OF HIGHER EDUCATION IN ORDER OF NUMBER OF GRADUATES IN A.A.T.S. SEMINARIES, FALL, 1962

Rank	College or University	Number	Rank	College or University	Number
1.	Baylor U.	496	51.	Wayland Baptist	71
2.	Concordia Senior (Ind.)	442	53.	Harvard U.	70
3.	Oklahoma Baptist U.	235	53.	Illinois, U. of	70
4.	Howard (Ala.)	230	56.	Michigan, U. of	69
5.	Mississippi	226	56.	Ohio Wesleyan U.	69
6.	Asbury	218	56.	West Virginia Wesleyan	69
7.	California, U. of	192	58.	Augsburg College	68
8.	Furman U.	189	59.	DePauw U.	67
9.	Mercer U.	186	60.	Wisconsin, U. of	66
10.	Wheaton	184	61.	Michigan State U.	65
11.	Carson-Newman	175	62.	Eastern Baptist	64
12.	Hardin-Simmons U.	171	62.	Maryville	64
13.	St. Olaf	166	65.	Emory U.	63
14.	Capital U.	160	65.	Gordon	63
15.	Wake Forest	151	65.	Taylor U.	63
16.	Wartburg	140	67.	Georgia, U. of	62
17.	Gettysburg	136	67.	William Jewell	62
18.	Howard Payne	128	69.	Whitworth	61
19.	Minnesota, U. of	126	71.	California Baptist	59
20.	Texas Christian U.	123	71.	Oklahoma, U. of	59
21.	Richmond, U. of	121	71.	Birmingham-Southern	59
22.	Ouachita Baptist	120	74.	Lenoir Rhyne	57
23.	Phillips U.	110	74.	Millsaps	57
24.	Louisiana	108	74.	Southern Illinois U.	57
25.	Davidson	105	74.	Southern Methodist U.	57
25.	Elmhurst	105	77.	Florida, U. of	56
27.	Concordia (Minn.)	102	79.	Bethel (Tenn.)	55
27.	Duke U.	102	79.	Franklin and Marshall	55
30.	Anderson	101	79.	Lebanon Valley	55
30.	Calvin	101	79.	McMurry	55
30.	Georgetown	101	82.	Wofford	54
32.	Luther (Iowa)	100	84.	North Central	53
33.	Texas System, U. of	90	84.	Ohio State U.	53
34.	Augustana (Ill.)	87	84.	Pittsburgh, U. of	53
34.	Northwestern U.	87	84.	Temple U.	53
37.	Hope	86	88.	Augustana (S. Dak.)	52
37.	Houghton	86	88.	Goshen	52
37.	Pacific Lutheran U.	86	88.	Midland	52
37.	Yale U.	86	88.	Syracuse U.	52
40.	Corpus Christi, U. of	81	92.	High Point	51
41.	Bob Jones U.	80	92.	Oklahoma City U.	51
41.	Muhlenberg	80	92.	Randolph-Macon	51
43.	Stetson U.	78	94.	U. of North Carolina	50
43.	Wittenberg U.	78	94.	Princeton U.	50
45.	Gustavus Adolphus	77	96.	Greenville	49
45.	Wooster, College of	77	96.	Florida State U.	49
47.	East Texas Baptist	76	99.	Carthage	48
48.	Bethel (Minn.)	75	99.	Concordia Seminary	48
49.	Union U. (Tenn.)	74	99.	Grand Canyon	48
50.	Texas Wesleyan	73	99.	North Texas State	48
51.	Northwest Christian	71			

Key to Table 20: Canadian Universities with Graduates in A.A.T.S. Member Seminaries, Fall, 1962

NAME AND LOCATION OF UNIVERSITY	Number of graduates in seminary
1. Acadia University, Wolfville, Nova Scotia	23
2. Alberta, U. of, Edmonton and Calgary	35
3. Bishop's U., Lennoxville, Quebec	10
4. British Columbia, U. of, Vancouver	37
5. Carleton U., Ottawa, Ontario	8
6. Dalhousie U., Halifax, Nova Scotia	6
7. Manitoba, U. of, Winnipeg	24
8. McGill U., Montreal, Quebec	24
9. McMaster U., Hamilton, Ontario	53
10. Mount Allison, U., Sackville, New Brunswick	38
11. New Brunswick, U. of, Fredericton	1
12. Newfoundland, Memorial U. of, St. Johns	1
13. Ottawa, U. of, Ottawa, Ontario	2
14. Queen's U., Kingston, Ontario	32
15. Saskatchewan, U. of, Saskatoon	14
16. Sir George Williams U., Montreal, Quebec	37
17. Toronto, U. of, Toronto, Ontario	111
18. Waterloo U., Waterloo, Ontario	30
19. Waterloo Lutheran U., Waterloo, Ontario	11
20. Western Ontario, U. of, London, Ontario	44
	541

Key to Table 20: A.A.T.S. Member Seminaries Enrolling Graduates of Canadian Universities, Fall, 1962

DENOMINATION, NAME AND LOCATION OF SEMINARY	Students from Canadian Universities
CANADA	
Anglican:	
1. Huron College Faculty of Theology, London, (Ont.)	24
2. St. John's College Faculty of Theology, Winnipeg (Manitoba)	9
3. Trinity College Faculty of Divinity, Toronto (Ontario)	38
4. Wycliffe College, Toronto (Ontario)	25
Baptist:	
5. Acadia University School of Theology, Wolfville (N.S.)	17
6. McMaster Divinity College, Hamilton (Ont.)	28
Presbyterian:	
7. Knox College, Toronto (Ont.)	37
8. Presbyterian College, Montreal, (P.Q.)	16

206   Pre-Seminary Education

Key to Table 20 (continued)

DENOMINATION, NAME AND LOCATION OF SEMINARY	Students from Canadian Universities

United Church:
9. Emmanuel College of Victoria University,
    Toronto (Ont.) 94
10. Pine Hill Divinity Hall, Halifax (N.S.) 33
11. Queen's Theological College, Kingston (Ont.) 33
12. St. Stephen's College, Edmonton (Alberta) 17
13. Union College of British Columbia, Vancouver 18
Interdenominational:
14. McGill University Faculty of Divinity,
    Montreal (P.Q.) 62

UNITED STATES
Baptist:
    American Baptist Convention:
15. Andover Newton Theological School (Mass.) 6
    (also listed under United Church of Christ)
16. Berkeley Baptist Divinity School (Cal.) 2
17. Central Baptist Theological School (Kansas) 4
18. Eastern Baptist Theological School (Pa.) 1
    Baptist General Conference:
19. Bethel Theological Seminary (Minn.) 2
    Southern Baptist Convention:
20. Golden Gate Baptist (Cal.) 1
21. Southern Baptist Theological Seminary (Ky.) 4
22. Southwestern Baptist Theological Seminary,
    School of Theology (Texas) 2
Christian Churches (Disciples of Christ):
23. College of the Bible (Ky.) 1
Evangelical Covenant Church of America:
24. North Park Theological Seminary (Ill.) 1
Lutheran:
    The American Lutheran Church:
25. Luther Theological Seminary (Minn.) 2
26. Wartburg Theological Seminary (Iowa) 1
    Lutheran Church in America:
27. Lutheran Theological Seminary in Chicago,
    Maywood Campus (Ill.) 2
28. Lutheran Theological Seminary at Philadelphia (Pa.) 1
    The Lutheran Church—Missouri Synod:
29. Concordia Theological Seminary
    (Springfield, Ill.) 4
Mennonite:
    General Conference Mennonite Church:
30. Mennonite Biblical Seminary (Ind.) 9
    Mennonite Church:
31. Goshen College Biblical Seminary (Ind.) 3

Key to Table 20 (continued)

DENOMINATION, NAME AND LOCATION OF SEMINARY	Students from Canadian Universities
The Methodist Church:	
32. Boston University School of Theology (Mass.)	2
33. Drew University Theological School (N.J.)	2
34. Garrett Theological School (Ill.)	1
35. Interdenominational Theological Center (Ga.)	1
36. Perkins School of Theology of Southern Methodist University (Texas)	2
37. Wesley Theological Seminary (D.C.)	1
Presbyterian:	
Presbyterian Church in the U.S.:	
38. Union Theological Seminary in Virginia	3
United Presbyterian Church in the U.S.A.:	
39. Princeton Theological Seminary (N.J.)	5
Protestant Episcopal Church:	
40. General Theological Seminary (N.Y.)	4
Unitarian Universalist Association:	
41. St. Lawrence University Theological School (N.Y.)	1
Inter- or Nondenominational:	
42. Biblical Seminary in New York	3
43. Fuller Theological Seminary (Cal.)	7
44. Hartford Theological Seminary (Conn.)	1
45. Harvard Divinity School (Mass.)	3
46. Union Theological Seminary (N.Y.)	7
47. University of Chicago Divinity School (Ill.)	1

541

PRE-SEMINARY EDUCATION

Table 20
ENROLLMENT IN A.A.T.S. SEMINARIES BY 541 GRADUATES OF CANADIAN UNIVERSITIES, FALL, 1962

Source: Respondents to Seminarian Questionnaire

Canadian Universities

A.A.T.S. Seminaries	1	2	3	4	5	6	7	8	9	10	11	12	13	14	15	16	17	18	19	20
1. Huron	—	—	1	1	—	—	—	1	—	—	—	—	—	1	—	2	1	—	—	17
2. St. John's	—	2	—	—	—	—	7	—	—	—	—	—	—	—	—	—	—	—	—	—
3. Trinity	—	1	3	—	—	—	—	2	2	—	1	—	—	1	1	1	19	1	—	6
4. Wycliffe	—	—	—	—	—	—	—	3	—	—	—	—	—	2	1	1	18	—	—	—
5. Acadia	15	—	—	—	—	1	—	—	—	—	—	—	—	1	—	—	—	—	—	—
6. McMaster	1	2	—	—	—	—	—	1	16	1	—	—	—	—	2	1	1	1	1	1
7. Knox	—	—	1	2	—	—	2	—	5	—	—	—	—	2	1	—	7	9	6	2
8. Presbyterian	—	—	—	—	1	—	2	—	1	—	—	—	—	1	8	—	1	1	1	
9. Emmanuel	1	—	—	—	2	—	—	—	15	5	—	—	—	2	2	—	43	12	—	12
10. Pine Hill	—	—	—	1	—	5	—	1	—	24	—	—	—	—	—	—	1	—	—	—
11. Queen's	—	—	—	1	—	1	—	3	3	—	—	—	19	—	—	—	1	3	2	
12. St. Stephen's	—	17	—	—	—	—	—	—	—	—	—	—	—	—	—	—	—	—	—	—
13. Union College	—	—	—	14	—	—	1	—	—	—	—	—	—	2	—	—	1	—	—	—
14. McGill	1	1	4	4	3	—	2	10	4	3	—	1	—	—	2	22	3	—	—	2
15. Andover Newton	—	1	—	1	—	—	—	1	1	—	—	—	—	1	—	1	—	—	—	—
16. Berkeley Bapt.	—	1	—	—	—	—	—	1	—	—	—	—	—	—	—	—	—	—	—	—
17. Central	4	—	—	—	—	—	—	—	—	—	—	—	—	—	—	—	—	—	—	—
18. Eastern	—	—	—	—	—	—	—	—	—	—	—	—	—	—	—	—	—	—	—	—
19. Bethel	—	2	—	—	—	—	—	—	—	—	—	—	—	—	—	1	—	—	—	—
20. Golden Gate	—	—	—	1	—	—	—	—	—	—	—	—	—	—	—	—	—	—	—	—
21. Southern	—	2	—	1	—	—	1	—	—	—	—	—	—	—	—	—	—	—	—	—
22. Southwestern	—	1	—	1	—	—	—	—	—	—	—	—	—	—	—	—	—	—	—	—
23. College of Bible	—	—	—	—	—	—	1	—	—	—	—	—	—	—	—	—	—	—	—	—
24. North Park	—	—	—	—	—	—	1	—	—	—	—	—	—	—	—	—	—	—	—	—
25. Luther	—	—	—	—	—	1	—	—	—	—	—	—	—	—	—	—	1	—	—	—
26. Wartburg	—	1	—	—	—	—	—	—	—	—	—	—	—	—	—	—	—	—	—	—
27. Maywood	—	—	—	1	—	—	—	—	—	—	—	—	—	—	1	—	—	—	—	—
28. Phila. Luth.	—	—	—	—	—	—	—	—	—	—	—	—	—	—	1	—	—	—	—	—
29. Concordia (Spr.)	—	—	—	—	—	—	—	—	—	—	—	1	—	—	1	1	1	—	—	—
30. Mennonite	—	2	—	3	—	—	3	—	—	—	—	—	—	—	—	—	—	—	—	1
31. Goshen	—	—	—	2	—	—	—	—	—	—	—	—	—	—	—	—	1	—	—	—
32. Boston	—	—	—	1	—	—	—	—	—	—	—	—	—	—	—	1	—	—	—	—
33. Drew	—	—	—	—	—	—	—	—	—	—	—	1	1	—	—	1	—	—	—	—
34. Garrett	—	—	—	—	—	1	—	—	—	—	—	—	—	—	—	—	—	—	—	—
35. I. T. C.	—	—	—	—	—	—	—	—	—	—	—	—	—	—	—	1	—	—	—	—
36. Perkins	—	—	—	—	—	1	1	—	—	—	—	—	—	—	—	—	—	—	—	—
37. Wesley	—	—	—	—	—	—	—	—	—	—	—	—	—	—	—	1	—	—	—	—
38. Union (Va.)	—	—	—	—	—	—	—	1	—	—	—	—	—	—	—	2	—	—	—	—
39. Princeton	—	2	—	—	—	1	—	—	—	1	—	—	—	—	1	—	—	—	—	—
40. General	—	1	1	—	—	1	—	—	1	—	—	—	—	—	1	—	—	—	—	—
41. St. Lawrence	—	1	—	—	—	—	—	—	—	—	—	—	—	—	—	—	—	—	—	—
42. Biblical, N.Y.	—	—	—	1	—	—	2	—	—	—	—	—	—	—	—	—	—	—	—	—
43. Fuller	—	—	—	2	—	—	2	—	—	—	—	—	—	—	—	3	—	—	—	—
44. Hartford	—	—	—	—	—	—	1	—	—	—	—	—	—	—	—	—	—	—	—	—
45. Harvard	—	—	—	—	—	—	—	—	—	—	—	—	—	—	—	2	1	—	—	—
46. Union (N.Y.)	—	—	—	1	1	—	—	—	—	—	—	—	1	—	—	3	—	—	—	—
47. U. of Chicago	—	—	—	—	—	1	—	—	—	—	—	—	—	—	—	—	—	—	—	—
	1	2	3	4	5	6	7	8	9	10	11	12	13	14	15	16	17	18	19	20

5. SEMINARIAN QUESTIONNAIRE

The responses to a letter from the Study directors to the presidents and deans of A.A.T.S. member seminaries in October, 1961, included pledges of cooperation from 80%. Following approval by the Board of Advisors in December, 1961, the feasibility of administering a questionnaire to all Protestant seminarians was further checked in field trips of the next few months and in a second letter to the presidents and deans dated March 6, 1962, which said in part:

> With your assistance, all students enrolled in the fall of 1962 in each A.A.T.S. member seminary can be included in our survey. We plan to have the printed questionnaire booklet available to you in sufficient quantity by mid-August. It is recommended that one be given to each student as a part of his registration in September and returned to an office on your campus for forwarding to us.

All of the 125 member schools at that time returned a form saying, "We will deliver your questionnaire (to be received by us in mid-August) to all students enrolling in the fall of 1962. We expect our enrollment to total ———."

This pledge of 100% cooperation was reported to the biennial meeting of the A.A.T.S. in Toronto in June, 1962, and a memorandum from the Study directors was sent to all member schools on July 16, correcting enrollment estimates when necessary and suggesting procedures for administering the questionnaires. This was the third direct communication to all the schools and summarized the directors' hopes and intentions for this part of the Study as follows:

209

MEMORANDUM: REGARDING SEMINARIAN QUESTIONNAIRE
FROM: STUDY DIRECTORS

The seminarian questionnaire, which will provide one of the main sources of information for this Study, is now with the printer and will be ready for mailing soon.

As we explained in our report to the A.A.T.S. biennial meeting in Toronto in June, it is intended to have this questionnaire administered to all students in theological seminaries and colleges in the United States and Canada. It will thus provide not only an essential research instrument for this particular investigation, but also a base for related research in the future. It is, in fact, a kind of census of the theological student population of North America, the first of its type as far as we know.

We are grateful for the willingness of the seminaries related to the A.A.T.S. to cooperate in the administration of this questionnaire. In response to our March, 1962, letter, you have requested _____ copies. According to our records you enrolled _____ students in the academic year 1961-62. As has been pointed out before, we would like to have the questionnaire answered by *all* of your students, including those in graduate and special courses of study. Therefore, on August 15 we will mail you _____ copies. If you have an estimate of your fall enrollment which varies greatly from this figure, *we would appreciate your letting us know by return mail or collect phone call.*

It will take from 30 to 50 minutes for your students to respond to the pre-coded questions in the 12-page printed booklet. Some seminaries will plan to administer this questionnaire as a part of their orientation program. Others will use classes which include the entire student body. In some cases it will be more convenient to distribute it to the students individually for return to a registrar or dean after they have been completed. Whatever method of administration you decide upon, when you return them all we would appreciate your letting us know whether they have been answered in a group situation or alone at the student's leisure.

If you would like to have one or more file copies, we will be glad to send them on your request. However, the individual numbering of the questionnaires will provide us with a means of follow-up in cases of delay only if all booklets in our initial mailing are returned together —whether completed or not. They are to be folded and sealed upon completion, which—together with the serial numbering—should help you in administering them to insure full returns from all of your students.

Thank you again for your cooperation in this project. We hope that the results which come from these materials may be a contribution to the cause of theological education.

Meanwhile, various drafts of the Seminarian Questionnaire were revised, and one version was pretested in a group administration to 60 seminarians by the associate director. The following persons were among those making valuable suggestions, most of them in writing, on one or more items: Samuel W. Blizzard, Martin Bradley, Thurman Coss, James H. Davis, Harry DeWire, James E. Dittes, William Douglas, Ruth E. Eckert, Lois Erickson, Yoshio Fukayama, Edward Gross, Marvin H. Johnson, Quentin L. Hand, James L. Hawkins, Frederick R. Kling, W. Douglas Larson, Robert A. Lee, Murray H. Leiffer, Gerhard Lenski, Donald E. Miller, Peter H. Rossi, Ernest A. Rueter, Ross P. Scherer, Samuel Southard, Morris Taggart, Glen W. Trimble, Sam C. Webb, Lauris B. Whitman, John M. Vayhinger, and Jesse H. Ziegler.

The resulting Seminarian Questionnaire was printed on twelve pages, including a covering letter and a last page of name and address and the "name and address of someone who will know where you are or could forward a letter to you after you leave seminary." A gummed flap made it possible to fold and seal the completed questionnaire to maintain confidentiality. Almost 22,000 forms were mailed in August, 1962, to the 125 A.A.T.S. member schools and to two which have subsequently become members—the Methodist Theological School in Ohio and Concordia Theological Seminary, Springfield.

Upon inquiry from the seminaries, the Study directors informed all cooperating schools on November 20, 1962, that separate analyses of the responses of their students would be made available on request and at no expense to those seminaries which obtained a 95% response from their students. The generosity of the Ministers Life and Casualty Union, which donated computer time and programming assistance, eventually made it possible to make the summary print-outs available to all seminaries, regardless of the percentage of response.

All but two of the 125 member schools of the A.A.T.S. cooperated in delivering the Seminarian Questionnaire to all of their students. The 17,565 forms received from these 123 schools (and

from the two which have since become members as noted above)
represent an 83% response from their total 1962-63 enrollments of
21,213. More than half of the students responded in 120 schools.
The following 48 schools had a response rate of 94% or higher, and
those indicated with an asterisk returned forms for 99 to 100%.

*Acadia U.	*Div. School (Phila.)	Nazarene
Anderson College	Drake	New Church
Andover Newton	*Duke	Ohio (Methodist)
Asbury	*Episcopal (Cambridge)	Pacific Sch. Rel.
Austin	*Erskine	Perkins
*Bangor	Evan. Luth. (Capital)	*Phillips
*Bethany	Fuller	Pittsburgh
*Bexley Hall	Hamma	Princeton
Boston	I.T.C.	Prot. Epis., Virginia
Central Baptist	Johnson C. Smith	Southern California
Central Lutheran	Louisville Presb.	*St. John
*Church Div. Sch. Pac.	Luth. (Rock Island)	St. Paul (Methodist)
College of the Bible	McCormick	St. Stephen's
Columbia	McMaster	*St. Lawrence
Concordia (St. Louis)	*Midwestern Baptist	*Trinity (Toronto)
Cumberland	Nashotah House	United (Twin Cities)

The two nonrespondent member schools were the Evangelical
Seminary of Puerto Rico (57 students) and Berkeley Divinity
School (79 students). The dean of the latter explained that the
entire faculty considered administering the questionnaire, but
"our feeling was that a number of the questions ought not to
be asked or cannot be answered. For example, in a 'status conscious' age we did not like the idea of asking our students to
analyze the social standing of their parents."

In attempting to administer the Seminarian Questionnaire to all
students in the A.A.T.S. member schools, it was necessary to know
the number of students in each seminary. The annual release of
official statistics by Dr. Jesse H. Ziegler, Associate Director of
the A.A.T.S., for Fall, 1962, was used as reference. Although Dr.
Ziegler always warns against hasty interpretations of these figures,
articles appearing in November, 1962, in *Look* and *Saturday Eve-*

ning Post[1] elicited responses which were hasty and erroneous. Refutations in religious periodicals compounded the confusion. For example, editorials quoted an *ad hoc* committee to the effect that there had been that year "an increase in Protestant seminary enrollments," in refutation of reports to the contrary in the two secular magazines. As evidence, an increase was noted in enrollments in member schools of the A.A.T.S., which is almost but not quite the same thing. For the last few years A.A.T.S. schools have enrolled about 95% of the Protestant seminarians in North America, but membership changes and variations in methods of reporting cause fluctuations in enrollment totals greater than any actual increase or decrease of students.

Dr. Ziegler's official figures showed 20,729 students registered in the fall of 1962 in the member seminaries in the United States and Canada. The corresponding figure for 1961 was 20,466, an apparent increase of 263 students. However, as one of the Study directors pointed out, four new schools were counted for the first time in 1962, while one school was dropped from membership, leaving a net gain of 501 from the five schools which were not counted in both years. If we refer only to the 121 schools listed both in 1961 and 1962, there was a decrease of 238 enrollments (1.16%).[2]

The fact that there was less excitement attending the release of the 1963 enrollment figures may be due in part to the restraining reminders in preliminary reports of the Pre-Seminary Study that annual fluctuations should not be taken too seriously. Dr. Ziegler's description of seminary enrollments as having been on a "plateau" has the advantage of not attaching great significance to small changes. He has said, "There is no basis for complacency." Relative to population and other educational indices, "to maintain the same absolute numbers means relatively to move backward." Seminary enrollments lag behind the great increase

---

[1]Anonymous, "Why I Quit the Ministry," *Saturday Evening Post*, November 17, 1962, and Gereon Zimmerman, "Help Wanted: Ministers, Priests and Rabbis," *Look*, November 20, 1962, pp. 114-120.

[2]Dwight W. Culver, "So Nobody Knows! Refuting Conclusions on Seminary Enrollment," *Christian Century*, 80, January 23, 1963, pp. 111-12.

in the number of first baccalaureate degrees being granted each year. Nevertheless, Part One of this Report emphasizes the problem of quality rather than quantity in the supply of ministers.

The completed Seminarian Questionnaires were checked and coded for denomination and undergraduate school. All other items were precoded as circled by the 17,565 respondents. Two IBM cards for each student were punched at the University of Minnesota and by a commercial service. Technicians at the Ministers Life and Casualty Union reduced these to a single card for processing on their IBM 1401. A basic tabulation was programmed to provide a 14-page print-out of all responses except the respondent's denomination and college. The basic tabulation has been run for all seminarians; for all seminaries separately and in eleven denominational groupings; for each college and university type; and for students who differ in vocational plans, degree programs, and major courses of study. A separate program provided a summary by undergraduate school of respondent's denomination and seminary attended.

On August 23, 1963, all cooperating seminaries received carbon copies of the print-outs for their own students with directions for interpreting these sheets with reference to the original questionnaire. One year later they received print-outs for their male B.D. and S.T.B. students. Major denominational headquarters have been supplied with summaries by denomination of seminary and by respondent's denomination, together with additional breakdowns of the latter. These continuing analyses of the Seminarian Questionnaire data have been made possible on a part-time basis by a new two-year grant (1963-65) to the associate director for the "Research Project: The Protestant Seminarian."

The following tables present the totals for all seminarians and —when significantly different—for the students enrolled in B.D. or S.T.B. programs. The number of each question on the original form is indicated by "Q1," "Q2," etc., to facilitate comparisons with the print-outs supplied to seminaries, denominations, and other researchers.

Table 21

PRESENT AGE OF SEMINARIANS

(What is) your *present* age in years? (Q1)

Years	All seminarians (17,565)		All B.D. and S.T.B. students (12,329)	
	Number	Per cent	Number	Per cent
18	2	—	—	—
19	6	—	2	—
20	27	—	15	—
21	460	3	352	3
22	1,923	11	1,545	13
23	2,354	13	1,891	15
24	2,375	14	1,913	16
25	1,916	11	1,460	12
26	1,291	7	917	7
27	1,101	6	711	6
28	875	5	571	5
29	689	4	446	4
30	647	4	387	3
31	520	3	323	3
32	482	3	277	2
33	404	2	245	2
34	350	2	194	2
35	316	2	169	1
36	295	2	163	1
37	239	1	138	1
38	196	1	105	1
39	158	1	77	1
40-9	724	4	343	3
50-9	129	1	48	—
60-9	14	—	2	—
No response	72	—	35	—

Table 22

SEMINARIANS' AGE AT ENROLLMENT

(What was) your age in years at time of first enrollment in theological school? (Q2)

Years	All seminarians (17,565) Number	Per cent	All B.D. and S.T.B. students (12,329) Number	Per cent
15	9	—	3	—
16	16	—	11	—
17	33	—	20	—
18	101	1	57	—
19	77	—	30	—
20	285	2	121	1
21	2,203	13	1,553	13
22	4,671	27	3,585	29
23	2,160	12	1,544	13
24	1,363	8	946	8
25	1,072	6	741	6
26	869	5	619	5
27	730	4	499	4
28	563	3	396	3
29	468	3	336	3
30	415	2	291	2
31	282	2	192	2
32	293	2	204	2
33	234	1	160	1
34	241	1	155	1
35	203	1	127	1
36	168	1	111	1
37	136	1	88	1
38	113	1	71	1
39	117	1	63	1
40-9	415	2	228	2
50-9	62	—	29	—
60-9	10	—	2	—
No response	256	1	147	1

Table 23

MARITAL STATUS OF SEMINARIANS

What is your current marital status? (Q3)

ANSWER	All seminarians (17,565)	B.D. and S.T.B. (12,329)
	(Percentage giving indicated response)	
Single, no definite plans to be married at present	26	26
Single, have definite plans to be married before Sept. 1, 1963	5	5
Single, have definite plans to be married after September 1, 1963	2	3
Married for less than one year	9	10
Married for 1-2 years	16	18
Married for 3-5 years	16	16
Married for 6-10 years	12	11
Married for 11 or more years	12	10
Widowed	— (28 persons)	— (15 persons)
Divorced	— (73 persons)	— (45 persons)
Separated	— (10 persons)	— (10 persons)
No response	— (73 persons)	— (46 persons)

Table 24

SEX OF SEMINARIANS

What is your sex? (Q4)

ANSWER	All seminarians (17,565)	B.D. and S.T.B. (12,329)
	(Percentage giving indicated response)	
Male	93	98
Female	7	2
No response	— (30 persons)	— (15 persons)

Table 25

CITIZENSHIP OF SEMINARIANS

What is your citizenship? (Q5)

ANSWER	All seminarians (17,565)		B.D. and S.T.B. (12,329)	
	(Percentage giving indicated response)			
United States:				
Born in U.S.	91		93	
Naturalized U.S. citizen	I		I	
Canada:				
Born in Canada	4		3	
Naturalized Canadian citizen	—	(84 persons)	—	(50 persons)
Other, but I expect to stay in the U.S. or Canada	I		I	
Other, and I do NOT expect to stay in the U.S. or Canada	3		I	
No response	—	(60 persons)	—	(28 persons)

Table 26

RACE OF SEMINARIANS

What is your racial background? (Q6)

ANSWER	All (17,565)		B.D. and S.T.B. (12,329)	
	(Percentage giving indicated response)			
White	95		96	
Negro	2		2	
Oriental	2		I	
Other	—	(77 persons)	—	(44 persons)
No response	—	(36 persons)	—	(24 persons)

Table 27
SIBLINGS OF SEMINARIANS

How many brothers and sisters do you have? (Q7)

		All seminarians (17,565) (Percentage giving indicated response)
ANSWER		
Younger:	None	18
	1	31
	2	17
	3	8
	4	4
	5	2
	6 or more	2
	No response	19
Older:	None	22
	1	26
	2	12
	3	6
	4	4
	5	2
	6 or more	3
	No response	26

Table 28
LOSS OF FATHER BY SEMINARIANS

If you have lost your father, please indicate the circumstances. (Q8)

	All seminarians (17,565) (Percentage giving indicated response)
ANSWER	
I never knew my father	2
My parents were separated before I was ten years old	3
My parents were separated after I was ten years old	2
My father died before I was ten	3
My father died after I was ten	15
No response	77

Table 29
OCCUPATION OF HEAD OF HOUSEHOLD IN SEMINARIANS' PARENTAL FAMILY

Which of the following categories best describes the usual occupation of the head of the household in your parental family? (Q9)

OCCUPATIONAL CATEGORY	All seminarians (17,565) Number	Per cent
Professional—Doctor	203	1
Lawyer	146	1
Teacher or Professor	685	4
Clergyman	1,667	9
Engineer	638	4
Other professional	694	4
Elected or Appointed Public Official	226	1
Proprietor or Manager of Large Business	411	2
Proprietor or Manager of Small Business	1,866	11
Sales Manager or Administrator	736	4
Sales Worker in Finance, Insurance, or Real Estate	316	2
Sales Worker, Wholesale or Retail Store	422	2
Technician Related to Professional Service	253	1
Clerical	743	4
Skilled Worker	2,972	17
Door-to-Door Salesman	104	1
Service Worker	359	2
Unskilled Worker	1,168	7
Farmer or Farm Worker	2,057	12
Other	1,044	6
Head of the household is a WOMAN	819	5
Head of the household is RETIRED	1,438	8
No response	740	4

Table 30

FIELDS OF EMPLOYMENT, SEMINARIANS' MOTHERS, PATERNAL GRANDFATHERS, SPOUSES' FATHER, AND SPOUSES

If your mother was employed outside the home when you entered seminary . . . which field of employment best describes her job? (Q11A)
What field of employment best describes the usual occupation of your parental grandfather? (Q12)
What was your spouse's father's major occupation at the time of your marriage? (Q13A)
If working, what field of employment best describes your spouse's job? (Q13B2)

	Mother	Grand-father	Spouse's father	Spouse
		All seminarians (17,565):		
		(Percentage giving indicated response. If less than 1%, number of persons is indicated in parentheses.)		
FIELDS OF EMPLOYMENT				
Professional—Doctor, Lawyer, Teacher, or Professor	6	3	3	14
Clergyman	— (42)	4	4	1
Engineer	— (7)	1	2	— (29)
Other Professional	1	1	2	4
Public Official, Proprietor or Manager	2	10	8	— (23)
Sales: Manager, Administrator or Worker in Finance, Insurance, or Real Estate	1	2	4	— (40)
Sales Worker (Wholesale or Retail), Technician Related to Personal Service, Clerical or Skilled Worker	13	17	16	14
Door-to-Door Salesman, Service Worker, or Unskilled Worker	5	9	6	1
Farmer or Farm Worker	— (72)	35	9	— (10)
Other	2	2	2	1
No response	— (69)	15	45	65

Table 31

HOURS WORKED BY SEMINARIANS' MOTHERS

(What were the) approximate number of hours per week mother worked outside the home (when you entered the seminary)? (Q11B)

HOURS	All seminarians (17,565) (Percentage giving indicated response)
0-19	2
20-29	3
30-39	4
40	17
41 or more	4
No response	71

Table 32

SEMINARIAN SPOUSES' ACTIVITY OR EMPLOYMENT

What will your spouse be doing this fall? (Q13B1)

ANSWER	All seminarians (17,565) (Percentage giving indicated response)
Working full time	28
Working part time	7
Military service	— (4 persons)
Housewife	31
Going to school	7
Other	1
No response	35

Table 33

CHILDREN OF SEMINARIANS

How many children do you have now? (Count a current pregnancy as one child.) (Q13C)

NUMBER OF CHILDREN	All seminarians (17,565) (Percentage giving indicated response)	B.D. and S.T.B. (12,329)
None	23	25
1	15	15
2	14	13
3	8	7
4	4	3
5 or more	1	1
No response	35	36

Table 34

EDUCATION OF SEMINARIANS' SPOUSES AND PARENTS

Please indicate your spouse's highest educational attainment. (Q13D)
Please indicate your parents' highest educational attainment. (Q14)

	All seminarians (17,565)		
	Spouse	Father	Mother
EDUCATIONAL LEVEL	(Percentage giving indicated response)		
8th grade or less	— (67)	30	21
Some high school	2	13	15
High school graduate	9	18	26
Some college	17	11	13
College graduate	24	10	11
Nurse's training (not college)	4	— (35)	4
Secretarial, business, or other post-high school training	3	4	5
Graduate or professional degree beyond the bachelor's	5	11	2
Other	2	2	1
No response	34	2	2

Table 35

SEMINARIANS' COMPARISONS OF SOCIAL STANDING OF FATHERS' OCCUPATIONS WITH THE MINISTRY

How do you think the general social standing of your father's usual occupation compares with the prestige of being a minister? (Q15)

ANSWERS	All seminarians (17,565) (Percentage giving indicated response)
Father's occupation much lower socially	19
Father's occupation slightly lower socially	33
Father's occupation about the same socially	28
Father's occupation slightly higher socially	6
Father's occupation much higher socially	2
Father is (was) a minister	10
No response	3

Table 36

INCOME OF SEMINARIANS' FAMILIES OF ORIGIN

To the best of your knowledge, what was the approximate total income of all family members living at home at the time you graduated from high school? Consider annual income from all sources before taxes. (Q16)

INCOME	All seminarians (17,565) (Percentage giving indicated response)	B.D. and S.T.B. (12,329)
Under $3,000 annually	10	8
$3,000-$3,999 annually	11	11
$4,000-$4,999 annually	13	14
$5,000-$5,999 annually	14	15
$6,000-$6,999 annually	10	11
$7,000-$7,999 annually	8	9
$8,000-$8,999 annually	6	7
$9,000-$9,999 annually	5	5
$10,000-$14,999 annually	8	9
$15,000 or more annually	5	5
I have no idea	7	6
No response	2	1

Table 37

SIZE OF SEMINARIANS' HOME TOWNS

Which of the following best describes the community which you think of as your home town during high school days? (Q17)

ANSWERS	All seminarians (17,565) (Percentage giving indicated response)
Farm or open country	25
Suburb in a metropolitan area totaling—	
more than 2 million population	4
500,000 to 2 million	6
100,000 to 499,999	7
less than 100,000	8
Central city in a metropolitan area or city of—	
more than 2 million population	3
500,000 to 2 million	6
100,000 to 499,999	8
50,000 to 99,999	5
10,000 to 49,999	14
less than 10,000	13
No response	1

Table 38

SIZE OF SEMINARIANS' HOME CHURCHES

What was the approximate size of the church you attended during your last year in high school? (Number of adult members—high school and up—in the church you attended most frequently at that time.) (Q18)

	All seminarians (17,565) (Percentage giving indicated response)
ANSWERS	
Under 50 members	3
50 to 99	8
100 to 199	14
200 to 299	13
300 to 399	11
400 to 499	9
500 to 799	14
800 to 1,199	10
1,200 to 1,599	6
Over 1,600	7
Didn't attend then	4
No response	1

Table 39

RELIGIOUS INFLUENCES OF SEMINARIANS' PARENTAL HOMES

Please try to recall the religious influences in your parental home. (Q20)

	All seminarians (17,565) (Percentage giving indicated response)
INFLUENCES	
My parents regularly attended a church of the denomination indicated (as my own)	61
My parents regularly attended a church of a different denomination	12
My parents were church officials	42
I was encouraged to attend Sunday school	83
I was encouraged to attend church services	77
We regularly said a grace before meals	58
There were family prayers and/or readings from the Bible	31
There was at least one religious periodical regularly in my home	52
I can remember entertaining ministers and/or missionaries in our home	50
I would regard my parents as deeply religious persons	46
My parents were not interested in religion	9
My parents were not in agreement about religious matters	10
No response	1

Table 40

TIME OF SEMINARIANS' BAPTISM AND CONFIRMATION

When were you baptized and taken into full church membership or confirmed? (Q21)

	All seminarians (17,565)	
	Baptized	Full Membership
TIME	(Percentage giving indicated response)	
As an infant, in my first year	44	1
Between the ages of 1 and 5	5	— (41)
Between the ages of 6 and 10	13	13
Between the ages of 11 and 15	24	60
Between the ages of 16 and 20	9	15
When I was 21 years old or older	5	8
I do not know	— (82)	— (65)
I have not been	— (63)	— (33)
No response	1	2

Table 41

SEMINARIANS' DESCRIPTIONS OF RELATIONSHIPS TO GOD AND THE CHURCH

How would you describe your relationships to God and the church? (Q22)

ANSWERS	All seminarians (17,565) (Percentage giving indicated response)
I have never had a feeling of NOT belonging to the church	49
This feeling of belonging gradually developed before I was ten years old	22
I felt that I really belonged to the church when I became a member officially	29
I still do not feel a sense of belonging to the church	2
I had a conversion experience before joining the church	30
I had a conversion experience since becoming a church member . .	24
I have not had an experience which I would regard as conversion	22
My relation to God is through Christ, but not really through the organized church	29
My relation to God is immediate and direct, having little to do with my feeling of belonging to the church	21
I am more confident about my belonging to the church than about my relation to God	4
Other	13
No response	1

Table 42

SEMINARIANS' VOCATIONAL PLANS

Although there may be some degree of uncertainty in your mind, in which vocational areas will you probably serve? (Q23)

VOCATIONAL AREAS	Immediately After Seminary All (17,565)	Immediately After Seminary B.D. and S.T.B. (12,329)	Eventually All (17,565)	Eventually B.D. and S.T.B. (12,329)
	(Percentage giving indicated response)			
Parish ministry	68	76	33	38
Educational ministry in local church	7	4	3	2
Campus ministry	3	3	5	6
College or seminary teaching	4	3	17	16
Full-time evangelism	1	1	2	2
Music ministry in local church	2	— (37)	1	— (43)
Denominational administration	— (73)	— (36)	3	3
Interdenominational administration	— (18)	— (10)	1	1
Military chaplaincy	3	3	3	3
Institutional chaplaincy	1	1	4	4
Missions	6	5	9	8
Other	4	4	4	3
No response	4	3	19	16

Table 43

TIME OF SEMINARIANS' VOCATIONAL DECISIONS

If you are able to remember the time when you made the decision indicated (in Table 42), when was this? (Q24)

TIME	All seminarians (17,565) (Percentage giving indicated response)
Before I attended any school	1
During my first six grades in school	4
In the later years of elementary school, before I entered the 9th grade	5
During high school, in my early "teens"	18
In my first two years of college	13
In my last two years of college	17
While working full time after college graduation	10
In seminary	14
During military service	4
Other	10
No response	4

Table 44
PERSONS ENCOURAGING OR DISCOURAGING SEMINARIANS' VOCATIONAL DECISIONS

Indicate the extent to which different persons encouraged or discouraged your decision to enter a church vocation. (Q25)

PERSONS	Encouraged me most	Also encouraged me	Discouraged me
	All seminarians (17,565)		
Pastor(s)	34	41	2
Mother, or stepmother	12	46	8
Father, or stepfather	11	37	11
Other religious workers	8	31	1
College friends (students)	4	27	7
Teacher (high school, college)	3	21	5
Brother or sister	1	21	5
Girl friend	2	16	3
Wife	4	14	1
High school friends	1	14	7
Other relatives	2	8	3
Other	—	4	3
No response	18	12	64

Table 45
TIME AND PLACE OF SEMINARIANS' VOCATIONAL DECISIONS

In what kind of situation did you make your decision or commitment about some type of church-related vocation? (Not necessarily the public announcement of your decision.) (Q26)

ANSWER	All seminarians (17,565) (Percentage giving indicated response)
At no definite time or place I can remember, but over a long period of time	42
At a time and place when I was alone	25
In a summer camp, assembly meeting, or service	7
In a regular church worship service	6
In the presence of a minister or other church worker	4
In a church revival service	3
In the presence of one other person, not a minister or official church worker	2
In the presence of friends or relatives, but not during a formal service	2
In another type of revival service	1
Other	4
I have not made a definite decision or commitment to enter a church-related vocation	2
No response	2

Table 46
FACTORS INFLUENCING SEMINARIANS' VOCATIONAL CHOICES

What factors most strongly influenced your choice of a church vocation? (Q27a)

All seminarians (17,565)

(Percentage giving indicated response)

EXTERNAL FACTORS

Influence of other people	54
Religious activities in college	8
A book, article, or pamphlet I read	4
College courses in religion	4
A church vocations conference	2
Scholarship or assistantship	1
Appointment to church provided salary and/or parsonage	1
Loan from denomination	— (19 persons)
Other	21
No response	7

INTERNAL FACTORS

Interested in study and intellectual opportunities of the ministry	22
Dissatisfied with work experience in other areas	11
Desired to be like a certain minister	6
Wanted a chance to exercise leadership	3
Desired to be a part of a respected and secure profession	2
Liked working conditions (flexible schedule, independence, vacations)	1
Other	48
No response	7

Which of the following most influenced your decision to enter seminary? (Q27b)

An intellectual conviction which developed gradually	62
A vivid religious experience at a certain time and place	18
An interest in theology stimulated by college courses in religion	12
No response	8

Table 47

SEMINARIAN OPINIONS ON THE CALL TO THE MINISTRY

For each of the questions (a) through (e), indicate whether the first or second answer more nearly expresses your own experience or point of view. (Q28)

All seminarians
(17,565)

(a) In deciding whether to accept a candidate for the ministry, a seminary should be more concerned about:

His abilities and qualifications	43
Whether he has a genuine call of God	54
No response	3

(b) When I decided to enter seminary, I felt that the professional ordained ministry is:

In some way a superior form of Christian service	43
In no sense superior to other forms of work	55
No response	2

(c) It seems to me that a person who is ordained without a distinct certainty of being called by God to the ministry:

Commits a serious error—even a sin in some cases	47
Is simply being honest with himself and can still be a good minister	50
No response	3

(d) I think that a person should enter the ministry:

Only if he is certain it is God's will	43
If he is a sincere Christian, and thinks the ministry is where he can contribute	55
No response	2

(e) It is my belief that God's call to the ministry:

More or less implies that a person have the necessary intellectual qualifications	23
Quite often extends to persons of extremely modest ability through whom God can show his power	74
No response	3

Table 48

SEMINARIAN OPINIONS ON MINISTERIAL ACTIVITIES

Listed below are some activities of ministers. How would you rate each as describing (A) the adequacy of the minister of your home church—before you went to college, (B) the importance in the work of *any* minister, and (C) the enjoyment *you* would expect in doing them. (Q29)

All seminarians (17,565)
(Percentage giving indicated response)

ACTIVITIES	A In this activity my minister was . . . quite ade-quate	fairly inade-quate	B In the work of any minister this is . . . rela-tively impor-tant	rela-tively unimpor-tant	C I would expect to find this . . . prob-ably enjoy-able	prob-ably not enjoy-able
Private devotions, prayer, Bible study ..	74	13	93	2	89	4
Preaching the Word ...	74	22	96	1	90	5
Teaching	63	30	92	4	90	5
Officiating at worship ..	81	13	87	9	87	7
Studying and preparing sermons ..	72	23	96	1	86	9
Pastoral counseling	56	36	94	2	85	10
Visiting church members	60	34	92	4	83	12
Community leadership .	54	38	70	25	67	27
Administration, direction of program	67	26	76	19	50	44
Denominational and committee work	65	26	56	39	43	51
No response	4	27	2	49	3	30

Table 49

MINISTERIAL STATUS OF SEMINARIANS

What is your own ministerial status at present? (Q30)

	All seminarians (17,565)	B.D. and S.T.B. (12,329)
	(Percentage giving indicated response)	
MINISTERIAL STATUS		
Church member, but not licensed or ordained as a minister	39	41
Licensed, but not ordained	20	22
Ordained deacon (as in Methodist first ordination)	10	12
Ordained elder (as in Methodist second ordination)	2	1
Ordained clergyman	17	14
Under care of presbytery, synod, church committee, conference, etc.	16	19
Member "on trial" in conference, presbytery, synod or diocese	6	8
Full member of conference, presbytery, synod, or diocese	7	5
Student pastor	24	29
Other	13	11
No response	2	1

Table 50

SEMINARIANS' PASTORAL SERVICE IN A LOCAL CHURCH

If you have served as a pastor (or assistant pastor) in the local church (Q31):

All seminarians (17,565)
(Percentage giving indicated response)

(a) *Please indicate ...*

	Pastor	Assistant Pastor
(1) Total years of service (calendar years):		
None	9	10
1	8	11
2	6	6
3	4	3
4	4	1
5	3	1
6	3	—
7	2	—
9	1	—
9 or more	4	—
No response	57	68
(2) Years in your present position, if any:		
None		3
1		9
2		6
3		3
4		2
5		1
6		1
7		—
8		—
9 or more		1
No response		76

(b) *Please evaluate your experience.*

My pastoral work has been valuable, and I don't regret having begun it when I did	43
My pastoral work has helped to make my studies meaningful	41
I would recommend that pastoral work begin before seminary graduation	37
My pastoral work has interfered with my studies	14
I would recommend that pastoral work be started before entering seminary	14
I had to begin pastoral work when I did for financial reasons	11
Those who can afford it should defer pastoral work until seminary graduation	7
My pastoral work has raised serious doubts about my continuing in the ministry	4
My pastoral work has been valuable, but I began it too soon	4
It is difficult to see how my studies relate to pastoral work	2
Other	4
No response	45

Table 51

SEMINARIANS' EXPERIENCES AND ATTITUDES REGARDING FIELDS OF STUDY IN COLLEGE

Listed below are some fields of study in college. Please circle the number of any statements which describe your experiences or attitudes, (Q33)

STATEMENTS	All seminarians (17,565)				
	Social Sciences	Physical Sciences	English	Religion, Bible	Philosophy
	(Percentage giving indicated response)				
I took one or more courses in this field	94	89	96	81	80
I did NOT take any courses in this field	3	6	I	14	16
I found this subject very dull	7	15	9	5	10
I found this subject very interesting	65	42	50	63	51
Academic standards were highest in this field	27	28	31	26	25
Academic standards were lowest in this field	18	17	12	11	9
Teachers in this area urged me to continue	29	12	21	38	21
I admire many of the teachers in this area as persons, not just as professors	49	35	46	59	44
By and large, the teachers in this area are NOT the kind of person I'd like to be	11	15	11	5	12
No response	3	4	2	4	4

Table 52

SEMINARIANS' MAJOR AND MINOR AREAS OF
UNDERGRADUATE STUDY

During your college or college-level work, what were your major and minor areas of study? (Whether or not you were so registered, please circle the most important areas in your undergraduate program *as if* these had been organized into major and minor fields of study.) (Q34)

FIELD OF STUDY	All seminarians (17,565) (Percentage giving indicated response)	
	Major	Minor
Religion, Theology, or Bible	15.4	9.3
History	14.8	9.4
English	9.1	10.8
Philosophy	7.5	6.8
Sociology	7.2	5.8
Psychology	5.6	6.4
Languages	3.1	6.3
Education	2.8	3.0
Music	2.6	2.0
Business	2.5	1.0
Engineering	2.0	0.6
Speech and Drama	1.9	2.7
Physical sciences	1.5	2.6
Biological sciences	1.2	1.6
Mathematics	1.1	2.4
Economics	0.9	1.6
Premedicine	0.6	0.4
Home economics	0.2	0.1
Other	4.2	3.5
No response	15.0	23.5

Table 53

UNDERGRADUATE COURSES CONSIDERED BY SEMINARIANS AS MOST HELPFUL, SIGNIFICANT, AND DIFFICULT AND LEAST LIKED

Among your undergraduate courses, which was . . .

the most *difficult* for you? (Q35a)

the one you liked *least?* (Q35b)

the most *helpful* in preparing you for seminary? (Q35c)

the most *significant* course (not necessarily as preparation for seminary)? (Q35d)

| COURSES | All seminarians (17,565) | | | |
	Helpful	Significant	Difficult	Least liked
	(Percentage giving indicated response)			
Religion, Theology or Bible	29	14	1	3
Philosophy	18	15	10	6
English	12	12	10	9
History	9	12	6	7
Psychology	6	10	2	5
Sociology	5	8	1	6
Speech and Drama	2	3	1	2
Education	1	*	*	*
Music	1	*	*	*
*Others	8	16	63	53
No response	9	10	6	9

*NOTE: The coding system did not make it possible to count all responses for questions 35 a, b, and d. Mathematics, Languages, and Economics were combined in groups of courses which were considered "most difficult" (46%), "least liked" (42%) and "most significant" (13%).

Table 54

INFLUENCES AWAY FROM THE MINISTRY
REPORTED BY SEMINARIANS

If you did not major in religion (or Bible) in college, did you find in your departmental major any definite influences which could channel ministerial students away from the ministry? (Q36)

	All seminarians (17,565)
INFLUENCES	(Percentage giving indicated response)
Opportunities in other vocations	30
Intellectual excitement in other fields	26
Unfavorable attitudes of other students toward the church	21
Personal commitments and bias of instructors	21
Exposure of inadequacies of the institutional church	19
Graduate fellowships or assistantships in other fields	18
Emphasis on difficulties and irrelevance of the ministry	12
Textbooks and assigned reading	9
Other pressures	3
There were no pressures to abandon a church vocation	31
No response	23

Table 55
SEMINARIAN EXPERIENCE WITH RELIGION COURSES IN COLLEGE

If you took any courses in religion in college: How many different courses in Bible and/or Religion did you take? Include courses in religious literature, psychology of religion, etc., without regard to the department in which they were offered. (Q37a)

NUMBER	All seminarians (17,565) (Percentage giving indicated response)
None	7
1	7
2	10
3	9
4	11
5	8
6	7
7	4
8	5
9 or more	21
No response	11

If you had it to do over again, would you take the same number, more, or fewer courses in Bible and Religion? (Q37b)

Would take the same number	36
Would take more	31
Would take less	11
Not able to judge	11
No response	11

My college teachers of Bible and Religion were . . . (Q37c)

Superior in training and ability to teachers in other departments	14
Equal in training and ability to teachers in other departments	59
Inferior in training and ability to teachers in other departments	9
No response	18

Table 56
BREADTH OF SEMINARIANS' COLLEGE MAJORS IN RELIGION

If you majored in religion (or Bible) in college, did you receive . . . (Q38)

	All seminarians (17,565)
A broader general college background than would have been provided for other majors?	5
As broad a background as other majors?	15
A narrower background than other majors?	4
No response	76

Table 57

COLLEGE ACTIVITIES REPORTED BY SEMINARIANS

In which of the following activities did you participate in college?

All seminarians
(17,565)
(Percentage giving
indicated response)

(1) *Religious activities* (Q39a1)

Member of a denominational student group	41
Participated in religious "cell group" or small discussion group	35
Member of a preministerial club	33
Attended at least one state or national religious conference	32
Member or associate member of "college church" near the campus	31
Officer of one of the campus religious groups	29
Member or associate member of the campus church	19
Participated in campus interfaith committee or group	18
Member or SCM, or similar student Christian organization	15
Member of IVCF, or similar student Christian organization	11
Member of campus "Y"	9
Other	12
No response	14

(2) *Secular activities* (Q39a2)

Special interest group (e.g., Psychology Club, Outing Club)	34
Musical group	33
Fraternity, sorority (or equivalent)	32
Student government	27
Intercollegiate (varsity) athletics	18
Dramatic group	18
Campus group concerned with national or world issues	15
Editorial staff of a campus publication	13
Business staff of campus publication or other campus group	7
Other	12
No response	20

Please evaluate your extracurricular activities in terms of their value for you as preparation for seminary. Circle one of each pair of statements. (Q39b)

Religious activities were more important to me than secular activities	52
Secular activities were more important to me than religious activities	30
The activities circled above were more valuable to me than my academic work	15
My academic work was more valuable to me than the activities circled above	65
No response	13

Table 58

COLLEGE AWARDS AND HONORS RECEIVED BY SEMINARIANS

Listed below are a number of awards and honors. Which of these did you receive during college? (Q40)

	All seminarians (17,565)
AWARD OR HONOR	(Percentage giving indicated response)
Dean's List or Honor Roll	36
Prize or award for scholarship, research, or literary work	12
Phi Beta Kappa	3
Other honor society based on academic achievement	17
Graduation with honors (cum) (magna) (summa)	13
National Merit Scholarship holder, Finalist, or Semi-Finalist	1
Other scholarship awarded on basis of academic ability	15
Participation in "honors program" at this school	9
Took one or more graduate level courses as an undergraduate	12
No special honors	39
Other award or honor	9
No response	8

Table 59

COLLEGE GRADES EARNED BY SEMINARIANS

What was your over-all grade average in college-level study? (Q41)

	All seminarians (17,565)
GRADE	(Percentage giving indicated response)
A	2
A—	8
B+	17
B	19
B—	17
C+	23
C	10
C—	1
Below C	—
No response	3

Table 60

RELATIVE CLASS STANDINGS OF SEMINARIANS IN COLLEGE AND SEMINARY

What is your estimate of your class standing? . . . (Q42)

	All seminarians (17,565)		
	In senior year of college?	In first year of seminary? (if completed)	In later year of seminary? (if completed)
STANDING	(Percentage giving indicated response)		
Highest one-fifth	25	13	10
Above average	33	22	14
Average	33	28	14
Below average	3	5	1
Lower one-fifth	1	1	— (57)
No response	5	31	60

Table 61

ACADEMIC YEARS OF SEMINARY WORK COMPLETED BY SEMINARIANS

How many full academic years of seminary work have you completed? Include work in other seminaries and count part-time study toward total. (Q43)

	All seminarians (17,565)	
	Uncorrected	Corrected
ACADEMIC YEARS	(Percentage giving indicated response)	
None	17	25
1	20	31
2	18	25
3	10	12
4	8	4
5	5	2
6	6	1
7	4	—
8	4	—
9	3	—
No response	3	—

NOTE: The figures of the "uncorrected" column are obviously too high for the larger number of years and too low for one and two years completed. For example, some first-year seminarians indicated 5 academic years completed, apparently including their undergraduate work. The "corrected" figures are derived by substituting, when it is a lower figure, the difference between the respondent's present age and age at first enrollment in theological school. The "corrected" figures are still one year too high for those seminarians who (1) gave an incorrect response (number unknown) and (2) had birthdays between the beginning of the academic year and the date on which they responded to the questionnaire (an estimated 20% of all respondents).

Table 62
SEMINARIANS' STATUS ON ADMISSION TO SEMINARY

What was your status on admission to seminary? (Q44)

All seminarians
(17,565)

(Percentage giving
indicated response)

ANSWER	
Fully accepted for degree program	80
Accepted on probation	7
Accepted but required to make up some subjects	7
Accepted to nondegree program	4
Given advanced standing in some subjects	5
No response	2

Table 63
DEGREES HELD, ENROLLED FOR, AND EXPECTED EVENTUALLY BY SEMINARIANS

Please indicate the degrees you have already earned, those for which you are currently enrolled and the highest degree you expect to gain eventually. (Q45)

All seminarians (17,565)

DEGREES	Degrees you already hold Number	%	Degrees for which you are now enrolled Number	%	Highest degree you expect to gain some time Number	%
Undergraduate bachelor's						
B.A. (A.B.)	11,107	63	59	—	66	—
B.S.	2,143	12	14	—	21	—
Certificate or diploma in:						
Theology	240	1	677	4	260	1
Religious Education	96	1	113	1	52	—
Church Music	20	—	24	—	14	—
Professional bachelor's						
B.D.	1,067	6	11,739	67	3,362	19
S.T.B.	90	1	616	4	161	1
B.R.E.	18	—	34	—	14	—
B.C.M. (B.S.M)	30	—	86	—	11	—
Master's						
M.A. (A.M.)	531	3	482	3	1,720	10
S.T.M. (Th.M.)	135	1	742	4	2,028	12
M.R.E.	77	—	883	5	613	3
M.C.M. (M.S.M.)	15	—	147	1	147	1
Doctor's						
S.T.D. (Th.D.)	9	—	258	1	1,942	11
D.R.E.	—	—	17	—	217	1
D.C.M. (D.S.M.)	—	—	9	—	80	—
Ed. D.	—	—	7	—	148	1
Ph.D.	19	—	314	2	3,285	19
Other	352	2	92	1	255	1
None	238	1	170	1	383	2
No response	1,378	8	1,082	6	2,786	16

Table 64
SEMINARIANS IN NONDEGREE PROGRAMS

If you are not registered this year in a seminary degree program (or diploma or certificate program), please explain your program of study. (Q46)

ANSWER	Respondents to question (4.5% of 17,565 seminarians)	
	Number	% of those responding
Entering as special student, NOT YET classified or registered for degree program	160	20
Entering as special student, full course load	224	28
Registering as special student, part-time	192	24
Other	221	28

Table 65
SEMINARIANS' TRAINING IN LANGUAGES

What is your training in languages? (Q47)

ANSWER	All seminarians (17,565) (Percentage giving indicated response)
Modern languages (equivalent of TWO years of coursework completed):	
French	24
German	30
Spanish	19
Other	4
Classical languages (equivalent of ONE year of coursework completed):	
Latin	33
Greek	57
Hebrew	23
Other	1
In order to meet seminary entrance requirements, it was necessary for me to take a language course AFTER I received my college degree	8
I am STILL required to take at least one language course to make up a deficiency in seminary entrance requirements	5
No response	11

Table 66

SEMINARIAN VIEWS ON DUPLICATION OF COURSES IN COLLEGE AND SEMINARY

If you have taken courses in seminary which were, in some sense, a duplication of college courses, in what subjects was this either wasteful of your time and effort or helpful to you? (Q48A)

	All seminarians (17,565)	
	Wasteful Duplication	Helpful Duplication
COURSE	(Percentage giving indicated response)	
Old Testament	3	30
New Testament	3	29
Church History	2	17
Theology	1	12
Philosophy	3	18
Other	3	3
No duplication	17	11
No response	73	46

Table 67

SEMINARIAN COMPARISON OF SEMINARY AND COLLEGE COURSES

How have your seminary courses compared to your college courses? (Q48B)

	All seminarians (17,565)
ANSWER	(Percentage giving indicated response)
Standards of Work	
Higher standards in college	8
Higher standards in seminary	45
No difference	14
Level of Difficulty	
Higher level in college	9
Higher level in seminary	43
No difference	15
Competence of Teachers	
Teachers in college better	5
Teachers in seminary better	42
No difference	20
Methods of Teaching	
Relatively more lecture in college, less discussion	25
Relatively more lecture in seminary, less discussion	20
No difference	22
Size of Classes	
Larger classes in college	30
Larger classes in seminary	21
No difference	16
Relation to Professors	
More individual contact with professors in college	16
More individual contact with professors in seminary	37
No difference	15
No response	33

Table 68

SEMINARIAN OPINION ON FACTORS DETERMINING WHO WILL BECOME EFFECTIVE MINISTERS

How important do you consider each of the following in determining who will become effective ministers? (Q49)

FACTOR	Very Important	Somewhat Important	Relatively Unimportant
	(Percentage giving indicated response)		
Having a definite call to the ministry	66	23	10
Having a broad academic background	61	28	7
Possessing public speaking ability ...	46	43	5
Having a work experience before seminary	27	45	22
Specializing in some academic discipline	24	44	22
Having father interested in the church	24	42	27
Having mother interested in the church	23	43	28
Attending a denominational college..	12	36	45
Majoring in religion in college	6	31	55
Having a scientific background	3	28	51
Being a minister's son	4	25	65
Other	5	—	—
No response	5	5	7

All seminarians (17,565)

Table 69

SEMINARIANS' READINESS FOR COURSES IN THEOLOGY

Do you think you were ready for courses in theology before you were permitted to take them? (Q50)

All seminarians (17,565)

ANSWER	(Percentage giving indicated response)
Yes, and I would have benefited by taking courses in theology earlier	27
Yes, but there would have been no advantage in taking such courses earlier	28
No, I needed preparation in other fields before taking theology courses	31
No, I still feel unready for courses in theology	2
I have not yet taken any courses in theology, and do not know if I am ready	9
No response	3

Table 70

SEMINARIAN OPINION ON GRADUATE STATUS OF SEMINARIES

Do you consider it essential that seminary study for the parish ministry assume a preparation in a four-year undergraduate college program? (Q51)

	All seminarians (17,565)
ANSWER	(Percentage giving indicated response)
Yes, four years of college work should be required for admission to seminary	57
Yes, but exceptions should be made for persons who decide late	37
No, seminary work should begin earlier	4
No response	2

Table 71

SEMINARIAN OPINION ON THEOLOGICAL DEGREE ALTERNATIVES

Assuming that seminaries require a bachelor's degree for admission to the professional course of ministerial training, do you think that a Master's or Doctor's degree should be granted for the completion of the three-year seminary course? (Q52)

	All seminarians (17,565)
ANSWER	(Percentage giving indicated response)
Yes, a Master's degree should be granted	49
Yes, a Doctor's degree should be granted	6
No, the B.D. (or S.T.B.) is an appropriate professional degree	42
No response	3

Table 72

SEMINARIAN ATTITUDES TOWARD TERMS DESCRIBING PROFESSIONAL RELIGIOUS LEADERS

Listed below are different terms used to describe the same profession. Please indicate which term you hear others use most frequently to describe the full-time, professional, religious leader, which term you would most like to have used for yourself when you are (or if you are, or if you were to be) qualified, and which term you most dislike to have applied to yourself. (Q53)

TERM	All seminarians (17,565)		
	Most frequently hear used	Preferred for self	Most disliked
	(Percentage giving indicated response)		
Pastor	17	41	1
Minister	25	21	— (74)
Reverend	19	5	18
Brother	12	8	12
Teacher	—	3	1
Priest	2	4	14
Clergyman	2	2	3
Preacher	11	2	9
Pastoral director	— (18)	1	5
Parson	— (51)	1	9
Prophet	— (21)	— (40)	14
Other	— (0)	— (7)	— (1)
No response	10	13	14

Table 73

SEMINARIAN OPINION ON MINISTERS' DEFICIENCIES

What seems to be the greatest deficiency of the ministers you have known? (Q54a)

All seminarians
17,565)

(Percentage giving
indicated response)

DEFICIENCY	
Overconcern with denominational promotion and statistics	18
Inability to communicate	15
Tendency to be autocratic	13
Insensitivity in interpersonal relations	12
Lack of social and political awareness	9
Limited intellectual ability	9
Lack of a clear doctrinal position	7
Lack of courage before church officials or laymen	6
Ineptness in organizational matters	4
Other	7
No response	4

The deficiency can best be overcome in the future by: (Q54C)

Emphasis in seminary on devotional and spiritual life	21
Individual study	20
Internship training under direct guidance of a competent minister	18
Counseling and/or psychotherapy	13
Reformulation of the seminary curriculum	10
More rigorous selection of ministerial candidates	10
Courses at the pre-seminary level	9
Emphasis in seminary on organizational problems of the church	7
Post-seminary training	7
Other	11
No response	7

Table 74

SEMINARIANS' REASONS FOR HESITATING

If you have seriously hesitated about going to seminary, what was the chief reason? (Q55)

	All seminarians (17,565)
REASON	(Percentage giving indicated response)
Feeling of personal inadequacy or lack of talent for the ministry ..	16
Financial expense of seminary	14
Interest in another profession or field of study	12
Lack of a clear conception of the ministry	4
Feeling of the irrelevance of the ministry for contemporary problems	4
Unwillingness to identify with the institutional church	4
New appreciation for the role of laymen in the church	3
Loss of some religious convictions	3
Parental dissuasion	1
Social disapproval of other students	— (67)
Advice of professors	— (38)
Other	25
No response	18

Table 75

SEMINARIAN THEOLOGICAL POSITIONS ON ENTERING COLLEGE AND IN SEMINARY, FALL, 1962

How would you describe your theological position? (Q56)

	All seminarians (17,565)	
	On entering college	At this time
POSITION	(Percentage giving (indicated response)	
Conservative	45	37
Fundamental	20	5
Liberal	16	16
Neo-orthodox	5	18
Ecumenical	3	10
Modernist	1	2
Other	6	7
No response	4	5

Table 76

SEMINARIAN MALES IN B.D. (OR S.T.B.) PROGRAMS BY DENOMINATION OF RESPONDENT WITH NUMBER AND PERCENTAGE OF UNDERGRADUATE MAJORS IN RELIGION

DENOMINATION	B.D. (or S.T.B.) males	Religion majors: Number	Religion majors: Percentage	Percentage of all religion majors
Southern Baptist Convention	1,668	474	28.4	25.2
American Baptist Convention	344	51	14.8	2.7
The Methodist Church	2,370	280	11.8	14.9
Presbyterian Church in the U.S.	347	30	8.6	1.6
United Presbyterian Church in the U.S.A.	993	72	7.2	3.8
The American Lutheran Church	661	11	1.7	0.6
Lutheran Church in America	556	19	3.4	1.0
Missouri Synod	538	159	29.6	8.5
Christian Churches (Disciples of Christ)	440	208	47.3	11.1
Evangelical United Brethren Church	215	18	8.4	1.0
United Church of Christ	607	56	9.2	3.0
Protestant Episcopal	774	24	3.1	1.3
United Church of Canada	157	3	1.9	0.2
Others	2,421	474	19.6	25.2
	12,091	1,879	15.5	100.1

NOTE: The way in which the total responses to the Seminarian Questionnaire may be skewed by the larger denominations is shown in Table 76. Although seminarians who majored in religion in college differ to some extent in their responses to other items from those who majored in other fields, the differences are in part a function of the denomination of the respondents.

For example, regarding marital status of B.D. (and S.T.B.) males, 34% of those responding were single, but only 24% of the religion majors among them were single. The corresponding figures for Southern Baptists were 19% and 11%; for United Presbyterian, U.S.A., 38% and 26%, respectively.

For Southern Baptists, the seminarian who majored in religion is slightly more likely to plan on being in the parish ministry eventually and slightly less likely to plan on being a college or seminary teacher. However, for the United Presbyterians, U.S.A., B.D. males who majored in religion are less likely than their counterparts who majored in other fields to plan on the parish ministry eventually (38% to 45% of those responding to the question) and more likely to plan on teaching (33% to 23%).

These illustrations should be sufficient to indicate the necessity for continuing analyses of the Seminarian Questionnaire data on a denominational basis and for the separate seminaries. They should also warn against placing too much emphasis on the combined totals for different variables. For this reason, the conclusions in Part I are not directly based on the data in this note.

For their thus limited usefulness, the responses to other items show the seminarian who majored in religion, as compared to other seminarians, to have: (1) a median age one-half year older, (2) produced more children, (3) wives less likely to have graduated from college, (4) parents with less education, (5) a father with a lower occupation and income, (6) a background in a smaller church, (7) been baptized later—Southern Baptist weighting being influential here, (8) made an earlier decision regarding his vocation, (9) been more influenced by his parents in making this decision, (10) been more engaged in a premature practice of his profession, (11) won fewer honors in college, (12) received lower grades in college and seminary, (13) been on probation AND/OR received advanced standing, (14) had both more wasteful and more helpful duplication of college courses in seminary, (15) more liking for the term "brother" applied to the clergy, and (16) been more conservative, both in college and seminary.

Index